Street by Street

C000229799

WIG...

ASHTON-IN-MAKERFIELD, LEIGH, SKELMERSDALE

Abram, Aspull, Atherton, Billinge, Golborne, Hindley, Ince-in-Makerfield, Orrell, Rainford, Shevington, Standish, Tyldesley, Westhoughton

3rd edition June 2008
© Automobile Association Developments Limited 2008

Original edition printed May 2002

This product includes map data licensed from Ordnance Survey® with the permission of the Controller of Her Majesty's Stationery Office. © Crown copyright 2008. All rights reserved. Licence number 100021153.

The copyright in all PAF is owned by Royal Mail Group plc.

Published by AA Publishing (a trading name of Automobile Association Developments Limited, whose registered office is Fanum House, Basing View, Basingstoke, Hampshire RG21 4EA. Registered number 1878835).

Produced by the Mapping Services Department of The Automobile Association. (A03711)

A CIP Catalogue record for this book is available from the British Library.

Printed by Oriental Press in Dubai

Ref: ML201y

Key to map pages	ii-iii
Key to map symbols	iv-1
Enlarged map pages	2-3
Main map pages	4-73
Index – towns & villages	74
Index – streets	75-87
Index – featured places	87-89
Acknowledgements	89

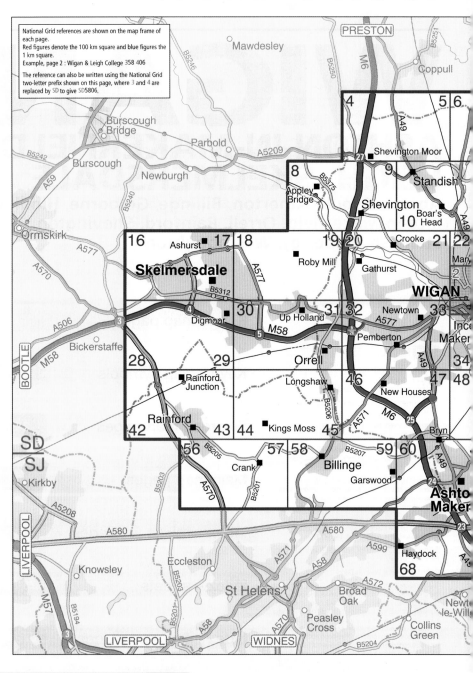

ii

National Grid references are shown on the map frame of each page.
Red figures denote the 100 km square and blue figures the 1 km square.
Example, page 2 : Wigan & Leigh College 358 406

The reference can also be written using the National Grid two-letter prefix shown on this page, where 3 and 4 are replaced by SD to give SD5806.

PRESTON

Mawdesley

Coppull

Burscough Bridge

Parbold

Burscough

Newburgh

Ormskirk

Shevington Moor

Standish

Appley Bridge

Shevington

Boar's Head

Crooke

16 Ashurst 17 18

Skelmersdale

Roby Mill

Gathurst

WIGAN

19 20 21 22

Digmoor

Up Holland

M58

Newtown 33

Pemberton

Maker

28 29 Orrell

34

Rainford Junction

Longshaw

New Houses

46 47 48

Bickerstaffe

BOOTLE

M58

Kirkby

Rainford

42 43 44 Kings Moss 45

SD / SJ

56 Crank 57 58 Billinge 59 60

Garswood

Ashto Maker

Knowsley

Eccleston

Haydock

68

St Helens

Broad Oak

Newt le-Will

Peasley Cross

Collins Green

LIVERPOOL

WIDNES

Enlarged scale pages   1:10,000   6.3 inches to 1 mile

0   1/4   miles   1/2

0   1/4   1/2   kilometres   3/4   1

ESTON

Rivington

M61

dlington

Grimeford
Village

7

Bolton
West

S

Horwich

A673

rod

13 14

15

Scot Lane
End

6

Lostock

Aspull

23 24

25 26

27

B5239

A6

Wingates

ew
brings

Pennington
Green

Hunger
Hill

5

Westhoughton

Water's
Nook

Deane

36

37 38

39 40

41

A58

Hart
Common

Daisy Hill

Greenheys

M61

Hindley

A577

Hindley
Green

Hag Fold

Little Hulton

A6

35

Atherton

49 50

51

Shakerley

54

55

B5237

Abram

Howe
Bridge

Tyldesley

Ellenbrook

Bickershaw

A578

Westleigh

Higher
Folds

Astley

Boothstown

52

53

63

Leigh

66

67

Crankwood

A573

A579

A572

Blackmoor

Astley
Green

Pennington

A580

64

65

Golborne

71 72

73

A580

Glazebury

Lane
Head

A572

Culcheth

Croft

A574

B5212

KNUTSFORD

WARRINGTON

BLACKBURN

Egerton

A666

A675

Eagley

A676

B6213

Astley
Bridge

B6226

A58

B6196

Halliwell

A58

Bolton

Breightmet

BURY

A673

A676

A579

B6209

A665

A6053

Little
Lever

B6199

Farnworth

A667

4

3

Walkden

Kearsley

A666

ROCHDALE

2

A6

15

14

A580

MANCHESTER

Worsley

A572

13

SD

SJ

M60

12

M602

Patricroft

11

10

M62

A57

Urmston

STOCKPORT

Irlam

B5158

B5213

Flixton

B6320

WARRINGTON

4.2 inches to 1 mile **Scale of main map pages 1:15,000**

0   1/4   miles   1/2   3/4   1

0   1/4   1/2   kilometres 3/4   1   1 1/2

Junction 9	Motorway & junction	*LC*	Level crossing
	Motorway service area (Services)	●—●—●—●	Tramway
	Primary road single/dual carriageway	- - - - - - -	Ferry route
(Services)	Primary road service area	....	Airport runway
	A road single/dual carriageway	— · — · — · —	County, administrative boundary
	B road single/dual carriageway	▾▾▾▾▾▾▾▾▾	Mounds
	Other road single/dual carriageway	**17**	Page continuation 1:15,000
	Minor/private road, access may be restricted	**3**	Page continuation to enlarged scale 1:10,000
← ←	One-way street		River/canal, lake, pier
	Pedestrian area		Aqueduct, lock, weir
- - - - - -	Track or footpath	465 ▲ Winter Hill	Peak (with height in metres)
■■■■■■■ ■■■■■■■	Road under construction		Beach
[- - - -]	Road tunnel		Woodland
P	Parking		Park
P+🚌	Park & Ride	† † † † †	Cemetery
🚌	Bus/coach station		Built-up area
⇌	Railway & main railway station		Industrial/business building
⇌	Railway & minor railway station		Leisure building
⊖	Underground station		Retail building
⊖	Light railway & station		Other building
+++++++	Preserved private railway		

⊓⊔⊓⊔⊓⊔⊓	City wall		♜	Castle
A&E	Hospital with 24-hour A&E department		🏛	Historic house or building
PO	Post Office		Wakehurst Place (NT)	National Trust property
📖	Public library		Ⓜ	Museum or art gallery
ℹ	Tourist Information Centre		🏃	Roman antiquity
ℹ	Seasonal Tourist Information Centre		⚊	Ancient site, battlefield or monument
⛽ ⛽	Petrol station, 24 hour Major suppliers only		🏭	Industrial interest
†	Church/chapel		✽	Garden
🚻	Public toilets		◉	Garden Centre Garden Centre Association Member
♿	Toilet with disabled facilities		🌷	Garden Centre Wyevale Garden Centre
PH	Public house AA recommended		🌲	Arboretum
◑	Restaurant AA inspected		🛒	Farm or animal centre
Madeira Hotel	Hotel AA inspected		🦌	Zoological or wildlife collection
🎭	Theatre or performing arts centre		🦉	Bird collection
🎥	Cinema		🐦	Nature reserve
⚑	Golf course		🐟	Aquarium
▲	Camping AA inspected		V	Visitor or heritage centre
🚐	Caravan site AA inspected		⛄	Country park
▲🚐	Camping & caravan site AA inspected		⌒	Cave
🎢	Theme park		🌾	Windmill
🏛	Abbey, cathedral or priory		🛢	Distillery, brewery or vineyard

I grid square represents 250 metres

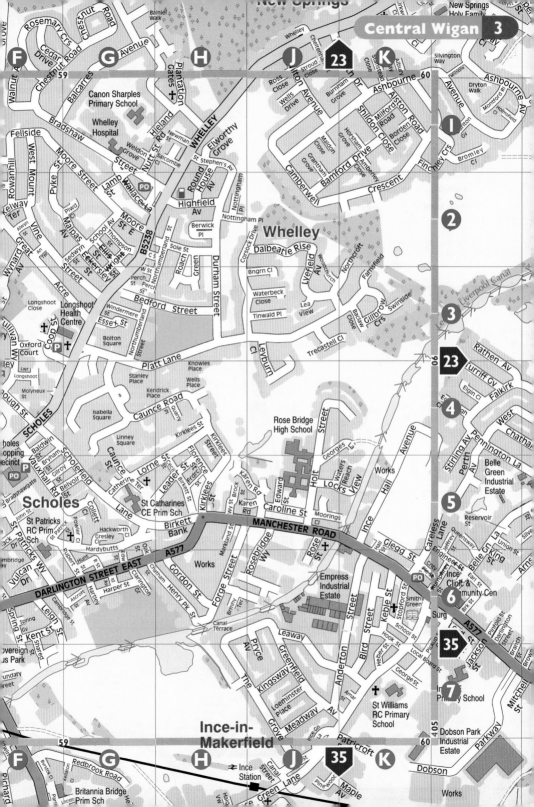

4

A · B · C · D

354 · 55

1
Chisnall Lane
MOSSY LEA ROAD · Broadhurst Lane
Mossy Lea
Ainscough Business Park
PO
Wrightington Mossy Lea Primary School
Hind's Head Av
Chisnall Hall
Chisnall Av
Chisnall Lane
Manse Avenue
B5250
✝

2
...y Lane
12
Langtree Old Hall
M6

3
Tunley Moss
Moss House Farm

MOSSY LEA ROAD
St Josephs Catholic Primary School

4
Pepper Lane
Hunger Hill
Muss Lane
411
Mossy Lea Fold
Wrightington Hotel & Country Club
✝
Boundary Lane
M6
Pepper Lane
Hyatt Crs
Robin Hill Drive
Robin Hill Lane
Rchrd Rd
Harris Rd
Chisholm
Douglas Rd
Ribble Rd
Pepper Lane

Shevington Moor
Standish Community High Se...

5
Dobson Cl
CROW ORCHARD RD
Cripple Ga Lane
Parkway
Fr Dr
Hsktn Dr
Whiteacre
Oaklea
Chrtn Gv
Broadacre
Old Road
Brookfield Road
Brbr Cl
Marple
Shevington Moor
Cresseli
Ashurst Rd
Beacon
Fairacre
Almond Brook Road
✝
Works
Premier Inn

A · B · C · D
354 · 55
9 Junction 27
CROW ORCH...
SHEVI... N LANE
ROAD
ALMOND BR...

1 grid square represents 500 metres

E F G H

56 57

13

St Johns
ntary Aided

Rd

Coppull
Moor

on

Coppull Moor Lane

Crane St

Bogburn La

Hic

Bibi Lane

Bogburn La

Lancashire County
Wigan

Talbot
House

12

Gorse
Hall

6

Platt

Bradley Lane

Hutton Street

4

411

rhurst Av

Langtree Lane

Langtree
Hall

Bradley Hall
Trading
Estate

5

Marwick
Cl

Sheldon Avenue

Langley

Edale Dr

Littleton

Rudyard Av

Bradley Lane

Bentham Pl

Belfry
Crs

Copeland Drive

Canon
Close

Ingleby
Cl

imrose
La

A49

Hywd
Gv

Nrthw'y

Sterndale
Av

St Maries
RC Primary
School

Woodland

Dovegate Dr

Moores La

Greenwood Road

Avondale Street

Churchlands Cl

Sprat

Brw

James Sq

Adelphi St

James
Pl

Broomfield Rd

Ormsby
Cl

Be

Road

Oakengates

Fontwell Cl

56 57

E F 10 G STANDISH H LANE

dshaw Works

Simfield
Cl

angham
Rd

Wheatsheaf Wk

Langton Av

Smalley St

Collingwood

RECTORY

B5239

St Wilfrids
CE Primary
School

Standish Court
Golf Club

Brooksi

PO

MARKET

Wilfrid's Pl

Mrkt Pl

Hea
St

Woodhurst

Inglby
Dr

Primrose
La

dstar

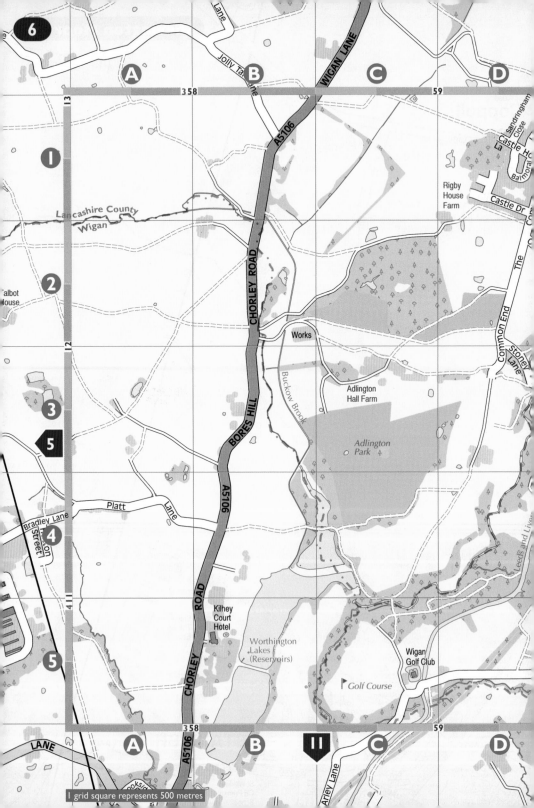

6

A   358   B   WIGAN LANE   C   59   D

1

Lancashire County
Wigan

Talbot House

2

12

3

5

Platt Lane

Bradley Lane

4

11

5

A5106

CHORLEY ROAD

BORES HILL

A5106

CHORLEY ROAD

Jolly Tar Lane

Buckow Brook

Works

Adlington
Hall Farm

Adlington
Park

Rigby House
Farm

Sandringham
Close

Castle HO

Balmoral

Castle La

Castle Dr

The

Common End

Stoney Lane

Leeds and Liver

Kilhey
Court
Hotel

Worthington
Lakes
(Reservoirs)

Golf Course

Wigan
Golf Club

LANE

A   358   A5106   B   II   C   59   D

Arley Lane

1 grid square represents 500 metres

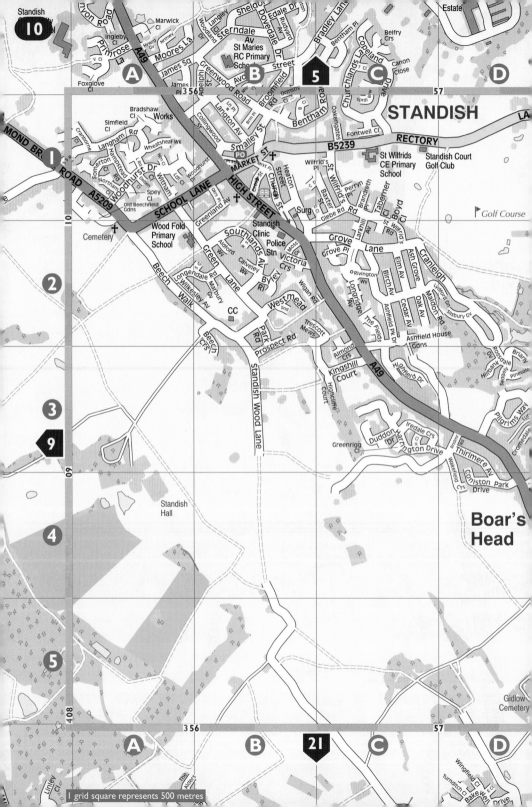

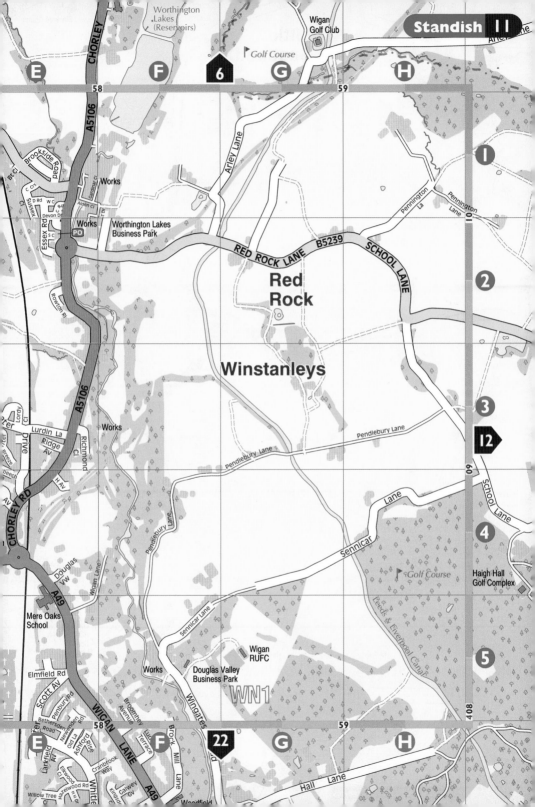

Worthington Lakes (Reservoirs)

Wigan Golf Club

Golf Course

E **F** 58 **6** **G** 59 **H** Arley Lane

CHORLEY

A5106

Brookside Road

Br Cl
C Cr
D Rd
W Cl
Devon Dr
Alden Cl
Genoa Cl

Sussex

Essex Rd

PO

Works

Works

Works

Worthington Lakes Business Park

Arley Lane

Pennington La

Pennington Lane

I

RED ROCK LANE   B5239   SCHOOL LANE

Red Rock

2

Rowton Rd

Winstanleys

SCHOOL LANE

3

12

Lordy

Lurdin La

Ridge Av

Richmond Cl

Works

Pendlebury Lane

Pendlebury Lane

Pendlebury Lane

60

School Lane

Drive

AV

H Av

beech

breeze

Jays

4

Sennicar   Lane

Golf Course

Haigh Hall Golf Complex

CHORLEY RD

Douglas Vw

A49

Wigan Lane

Sennicar Lane

Leeds & Liverpool Canal

5

Mere Oaks School

408

Elmfield Rd

Works

Wigan RUFC

Douglas Valley Business Park

WN1

Scott Av

Panbury Rd

Bethersden Road

Newbolden

Old La

Astford

WICAN LANE

WHITE

Broomhey Avenue

Brock Mill Lane

Wingates

Terrace

E Larkfield Av   **F** 58 **22** **G** 59 **H**

Cranbrook Way

Ellwood Rd

Hazelwood Rd

H Dr

Kingsor

Galway Gv

Willow Tree

Woodfield

Hall   Lane

A49

12

Arley Lane

Little Scotland

A 360 **B** **7** **C** 61 **D**

Blackrod Church School

Sibberings Farm

Bolton
Wigan

Copperas Lane

Little Scotland

Tucker's Hill Brow

Tucker's Hill Farm

I

Pennington La

Pennington Lane

Freezela

2

Willoughbys

Meadow Pit Lane

MEADOW PIT LANE

B5239

Meadow Pit Lane

Toddington Lane

Stamley

3

II

RILEY LANE

St Davids CE Prim Sch

Haigh

Gorse Farm

Lane

School Lane

Copperas

Lane

Copperas

Church St

Victoria Ct

B5239

Stancliffe Grove

Gorses Dr

4

Golf Course

Haigh Hall Golf Complex

Haigh Hall Country Park

Henley Street

HAIGH

Ratcliffe Road

Copesthorne Ct

Parklands D

Ashfield Drive

Crescent

Our Lady RC Prim Sch

Aspull Clinic

St Mary's Rd

St John's Rd

St Elizabeth's Rd

5

New Road

Cncl Bldg

Holly Rd

ROAD

Brayford

Crawford Avenue

Manor Gv

Balcarres Road

St David's Crescent

Lindsay Ter

408 360

A **B** **23** **C** 61 **D**

Higher

Road

Crawford

Woods Road

1 grid square represents 500 metres

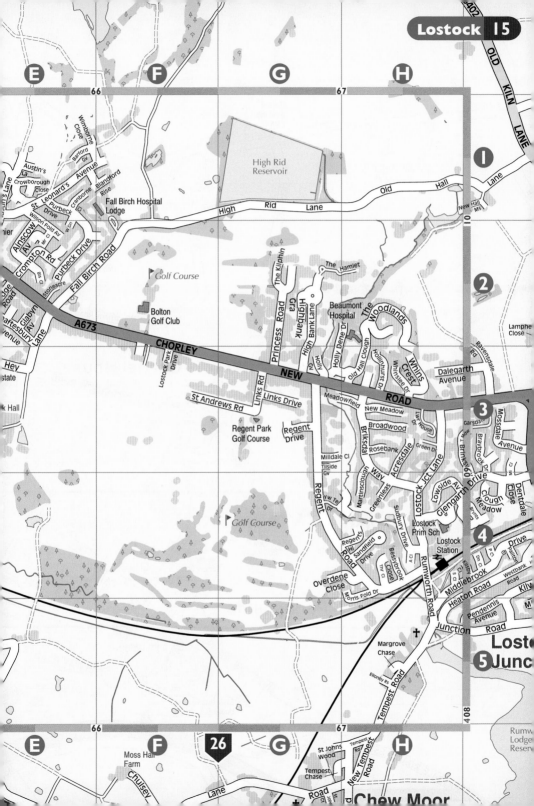

Holland
Lees

Forest Fold
Farm

Golf Course

E

F

52

8

Road

G

53

H

08

I

Ba...
Brow

Bank Top

Roby Mill

Leeds & Liverpool Canal

Ayrefield Road

2

Gat

M6

07

Gabriel Cl

Cemetery

Roby Mill
CE Primary
School

Whitley

Road

School Lane

oby
ill

Stoney Brow

Lafford Lane

Dean
Woods

3

20

Whitley Road

4

Whitley Rd

St Teresas
Catholic
Primary School

Lafford Lane

Dean
Wood
Av

Cathurst Road

CATHURST

406

Spring Road

W

College Road

Golf Course

Eton Way

Coniston Rd

Derwent Road

5

Oxford

Dean Wood
Golf Club

Grove Road

Dingle Av

Hillbean Cl

Woodside Av

Grs Av

Windermere Rd

Thrimte Rd

Rydal

Ulliswater Av

Thames Dr

Millers
Nook

Hall Bridge Gardens

Grasmere Av

Parliament Street

Dean Cl

Rivington Dr

Douglas Dr

St Pet...
Catho...
Scho...

E

52

F

31

G

53

H

St Thomas
The Martyr CE
Prim Sch

Surgery

Priory
Brooklands

Mill House Vw
Priory Nook

Spencer's Lane

Highgate Road

Con Vw Dr

PO

Bridgehall Dr

Abbey Cl

Alma Hill

Hall Green

The D...

B.S.L.

Works

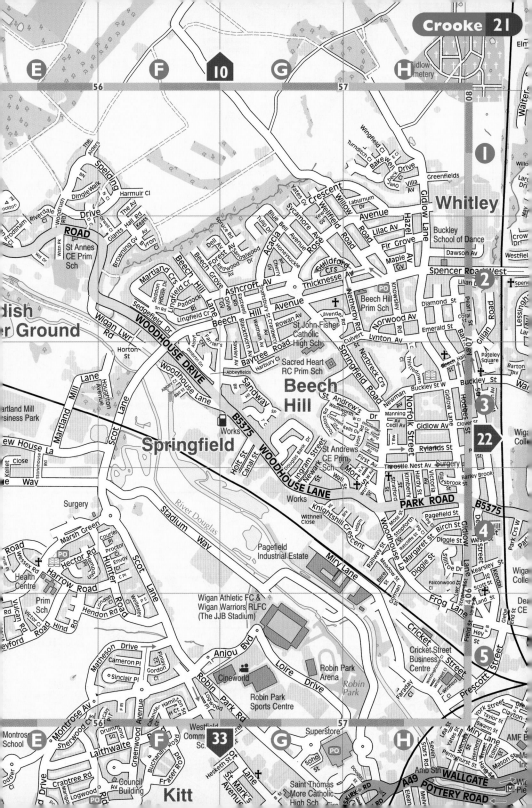

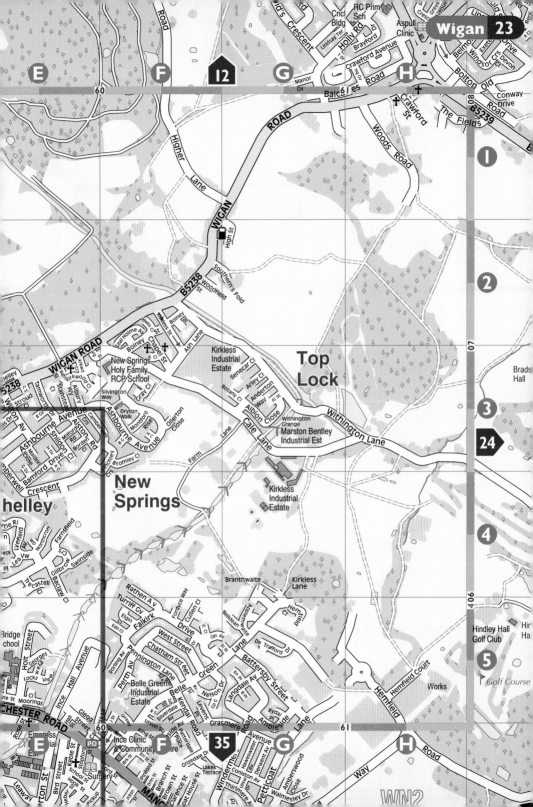

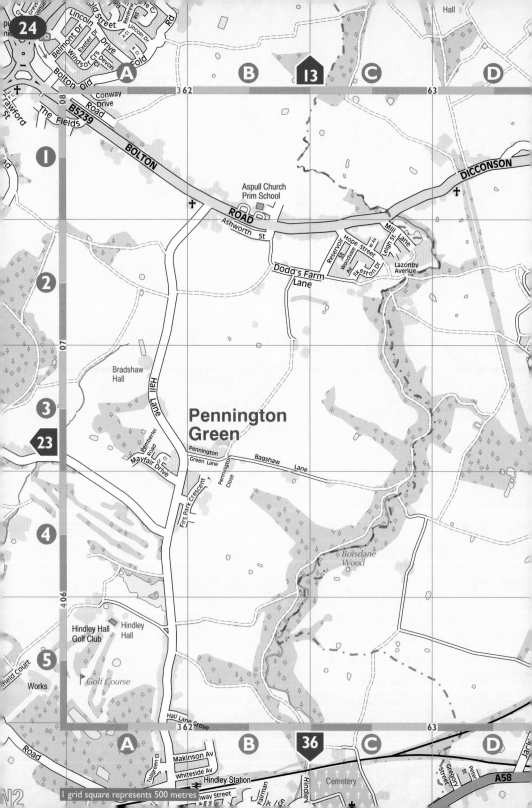

E · F · 14 · G · M61 · H

I

Four Gates

Dodd Lane
Industrial
Estate

CHORLEY ROAD

Wingates

Wingates
Industrial
Estate

Carlies

Lancaster Way

Long Lane

Golf Course

Westhoughton
Golf Club

WESTHOUGHTON

The Fairways

Rarochial
CE Primary
School

The Grange

Westhoughton
CC

WIGAN ROAD

A58

Hewlett
Street

ROAD

Cooper
urning
B5239

Code Lane

Wimberry Hill Rd
Elland
Close

Barrs Fold Cl

Barrs Fold Road

Great Bank Road

Old Fold Road

Old Lane

Meadows
Green

Gorsey

Coverdale Rd

Chorley
Road
Barnabys Road
RVC Dr
Wingates Gv
Bamber
Crt
Holden Lea
Hardy
Cl
Lever St
Greensmith Way
Anderby Wk
Wellington
Street
Westhoughton
Industrial Estate
Herbert
Street
Wesley Street
Peel Street
Beatty Dr
Kerans Dr
Collingwood Way
Durrington
Place
Breaktemper
Leigh Street

STREET

Fawcetts
Fold
Ploughfields
Wingates
Sq
Dixon St
Albion St
Part St
Seddon
Street
CHURCH
Central
Glebe
Lord St
Grndy St
Sch St
Cemy
Clinic

Westhghtn
Station

Comtech
Bus Park
Works
The Gates
Prim Sch
Aspen
Cl
26
Cherwe
Arundale
Windrush
Dr
Sacred Heart
RC Prim Sch
Westhoug
Prim Sch
Kings street
DRIVE
Dams Head
Fold
Town
Hall
George
Street
CRICKETERS WAY
Sunny Garth
Poplar
Grove
Broad Walk
Oxlea Gv
The Crescent
Southfield Drive
Rosebery
S
Rielands
Clough Ave
Grn
Elm
Rd
Hollin
Acre
Hawthorn
Rd
Washacre
Prim Sch
Washac

Market Street
Police
Station
A58

Bristle Hall
Way

2
3
4
5

Sacred Heart

B5236

G · 37 · G · H

Hart St
Cmmn St
B H St
Bk Cn St
ROAD
Cunningham Road
Oakhurst

Sandyway
Bardwell
Fairstead
Templet
Walkr Dr

Saluway
Old
Lane

Chelsea

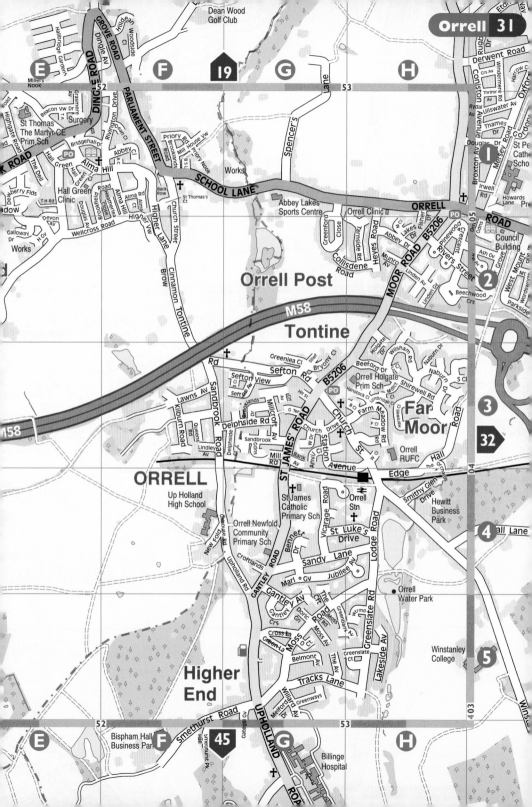

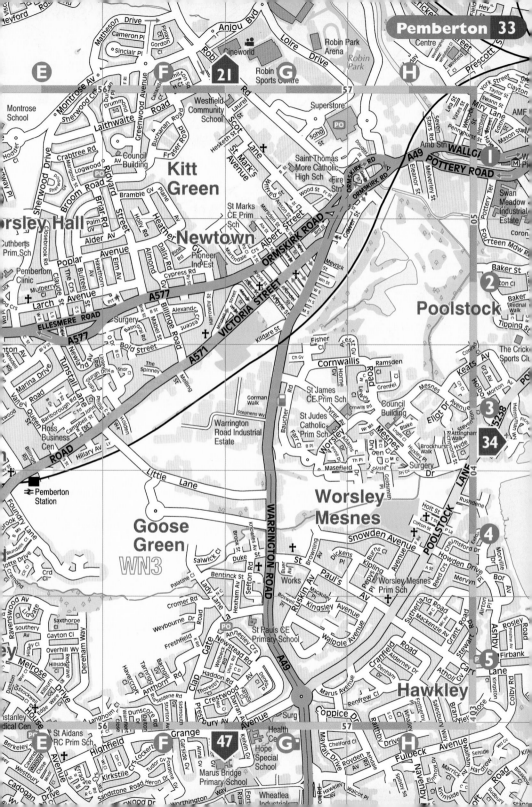

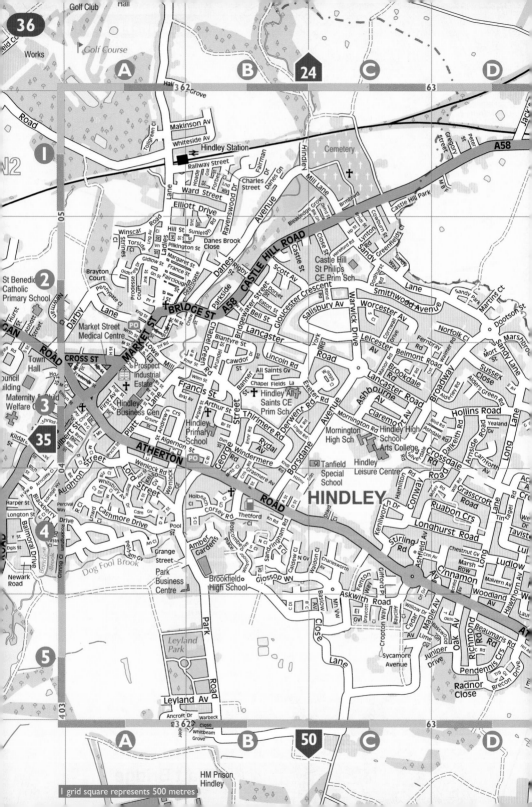

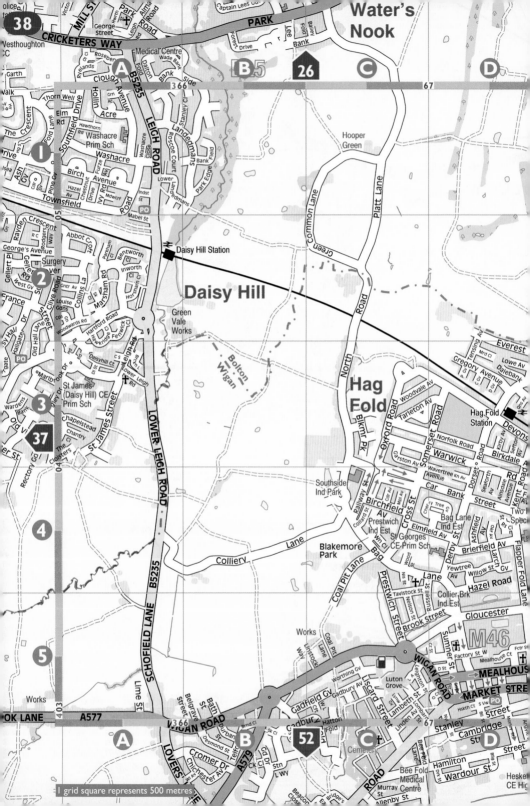

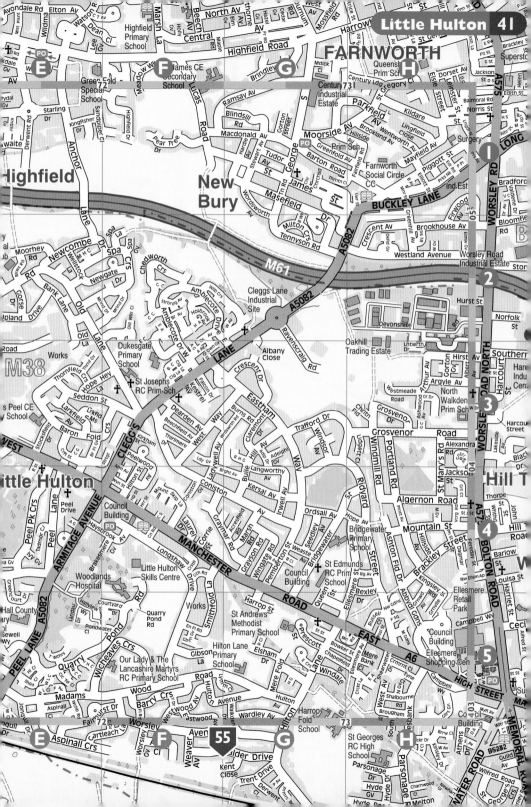

E   F   29   G   H

48   49   03

**Rainford
Junction**

Crawford

News Lane Drive

Cromer Drive

Crosby Crs

andal

PO

Rainford Station

Rail Close

Crawford

+

I

News Lane

Maggots
Nook Road

Nook Road

Maggots

Henderson Drive

Brow

2

Langwood Lane

02

Reeds

3

Hyde's Brow

44

Graysons Road

Brook Lodge Primary School

Rainford High Technology College

Holiday Moss

Helen Bank Dr

Harrison Drive

Lane

Rufford Road

Scarisbrick

Witton Way

Duxbury Close

Avenue

Old Parklands

Lathom Drive

Higher Lane

Standish Drive

Garswood Road

Rav'l

4

Corpus Christi Catholic Prim Sch

Victoria St

All St

Arnian Road

Croxteth Drive

The Spinney

RAINFORD

Muncaster

Drive

Old Hall Gdns

+

B5203

Arnian Way

Heyes Avenue

Heyes Grove

Sandon Grove

N G

5

Gardens

ASH

The Avenue

BIG

Wh'I Av

CROSS PIT LANE

CHURCH ROAD

Leyland Road

Pilkington Street

Rainford CE Prim Sch

Rainford Health Centre

Lakeside Gdns

Knw'l

Messam

Lakeside court

B5205

+

Council Building

Medical Centre

Southern's

Eagle Crescent

Rookery

HIGHER

Fire Clay Farm

E   F   56   G   H

48   49

BOROUGH ROAD B5203

Holly Crs

All Saints

Church

Road

Thickwood Moss Lane

Festival Road

Walmesley Drive

Carter Avenue

Green

Herd Gv

LANE

44

A · 3 50 · B **30** C · 51 · D

Long Lane

Crawford Village
Primary School

Manor House Dr

Works

1 Crawford

† Crawford Road

Oakleigh
Holland Court

†

Lancashire County
St. Helens

2

Langwood Lane

Maddocks

Robin's Lane

3

◄ **43**

Pimbo Road

*Holiday
Moss*

4

Kings Moss

King's Moss La
Fir Tree Cl
Brook La
Pimbo Rd
Crank Road

5

Fire Clay
Farm

A · 3 50 · B **57** C ◄ Red Cat Lane · Gores Lane · ...CK LANE · 51 · D

GORE'S LANE

5205

1 grid square represents 500 metres

MOSS

Belmont

The Av

Greenways

Tracks Lane

Greenslate Ct

Lakeside Av

Higher En...

31

E   **F**   **G**   **H**

52   53   03

Smethurst Road

Gategill Gv

UPHOLLAND

Smethurst Pk...
Hall

Bispham Hall
Business Park

Billinge
Hospital

I

Park R...

Crank Road

Coppice Dr

Banbu
Rd

Cheltenham D

Bspm
Ct

Winchester
Rd

Coleridge Rd

Burns
Close

Longshaw

Keats
Av

Tennyson Drive

Milton
Gv

Wordsworth

Cob Mr Av

Cb Mr
Ct

B5206

Old
Rd

Longshaw
Rd

Park

2

Brownlow
La

Trevelyan Dr

Dalecrest

Wellbrook Av

PO

Longshaw
Rd

Av

Park Av

Norfolk Rd

Cl

Longshaw
Avenue

Rd

Brownlow

Longshaw
Common

Hunter's Cha

Paignton
Cl

Longshaw Tr Dr

Longshaw
Common

3

46

Houghwood
Golf Club

4

▶ *Golf Course*

Houghwood

Red

Oakley
Beacon

Road

A571

Coultshead
Av

St Aidan's
Cl

5

Barn

E   **F**   **58**   **G**

52   53

Crookhurst
Av   Ash
Gv   Crs

Norbury
Av

Wells

Cl

Stuart
Cl

Ross

STREET

Loxham Flds

Belmont Rd

Council
Building

Conway
Crs

Royden
Av

Greenhill
Av

Greenhill
Rd

Conway Dr

Andrew

Windsor Road

H

Maple Cl

Larch Close

Elm
Drive

Well W.

Roby W

Roby W

Den Fold Dr

Gorsey Brow

Sev Brow

School Brow

School Dr

MAIN

Pin...

St Aidans
CE Prim
Sch

Health
Cen

Blackleyhurst

NEWTON

...NFORD   ROAD

BILL

48

Hawkley

PO

Firbank Rd

Colby Rd

A

Concord Av

Darley Rd

Thurston Av

Hawkley Hall High School

B

34

C

D

3 58

59

Avenue

Navenby Road

Marrick Av

Whitecroft Road

Killington Cl

Selside

Hartbrow

Breahow

Sunbury

Stanedge Gv

1

Easton

Torver Cl

Hassnes

Sandwith Cl

02

2

Park House Farm

Leeds & Liverpool Ca

Brinkside Av

3

Wasdale Rd

Park Av

47

Road

ate Lane

Bryn Gates Lane

Ba

401

4

Three Sisters Racing Circuit

Three Sisters Road

Three Sisters Rd

South Lancashire Industrial Estate

5

Beech St

Kingfisher Ct

Lockett Rd

Antler Ct

Redgate Rd

Lockett Road

Kestrel Dr

Beaver Ct

Ashton Grange Industrial Estate

Nicol Mere

Beeches

Highwoods Cl

Roman Rd

Wolsey Rd

Surg

Nicol Mere School

BRYN

A

Benjamin Fold

3 58

59

B

61

Stubshaw Cross

C

BOLTON

ROAD

Bolton Rd

Severn Road

Avon Rd

Welland Road

D

Luke St

Conway Rd

Hope St

Willow Grove School

Lockett Business Park

1 grid square represents 500 metres

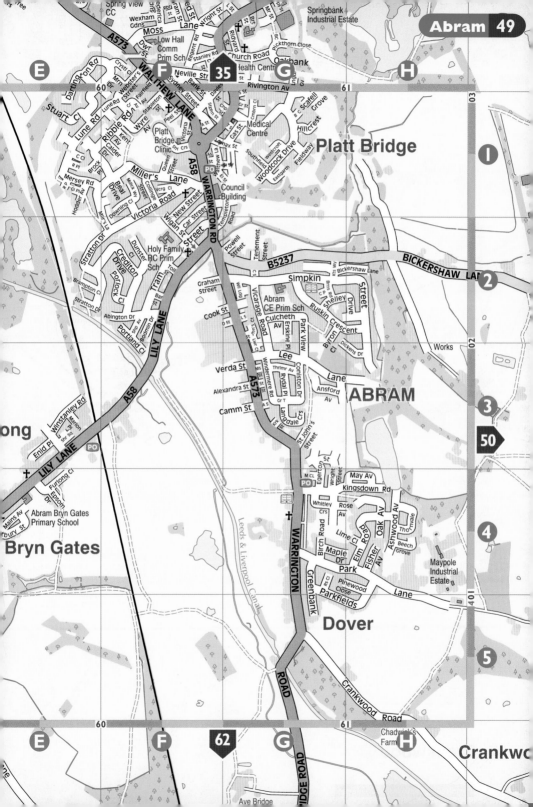

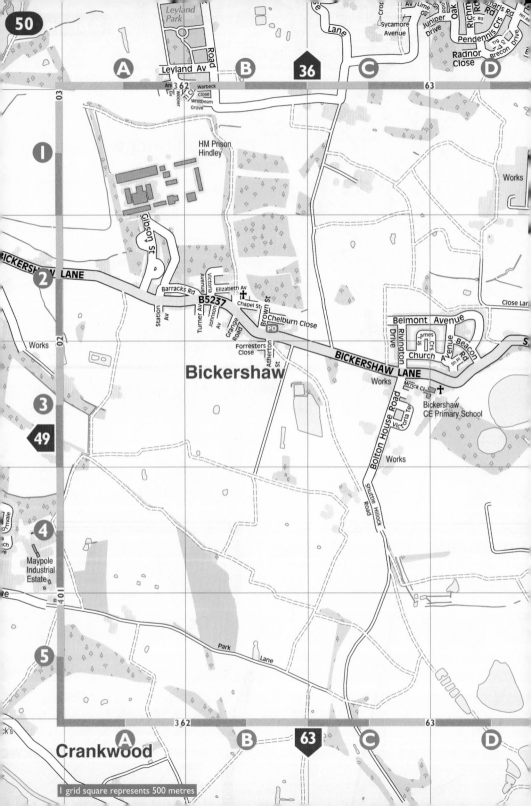

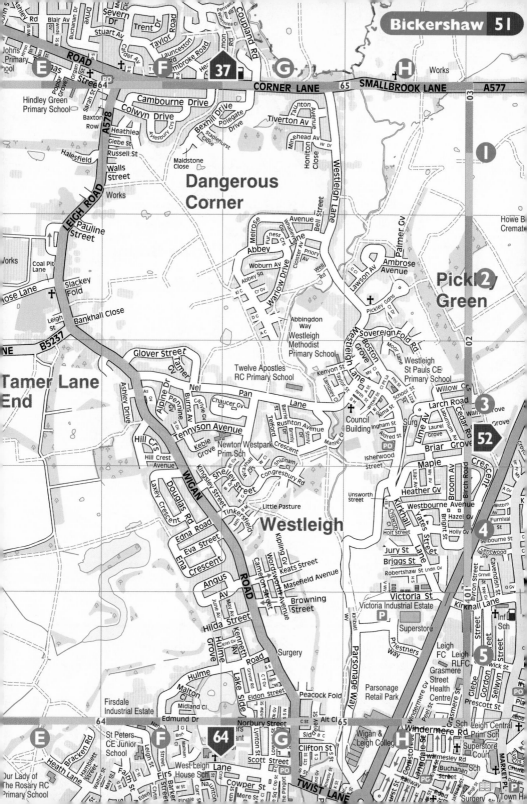

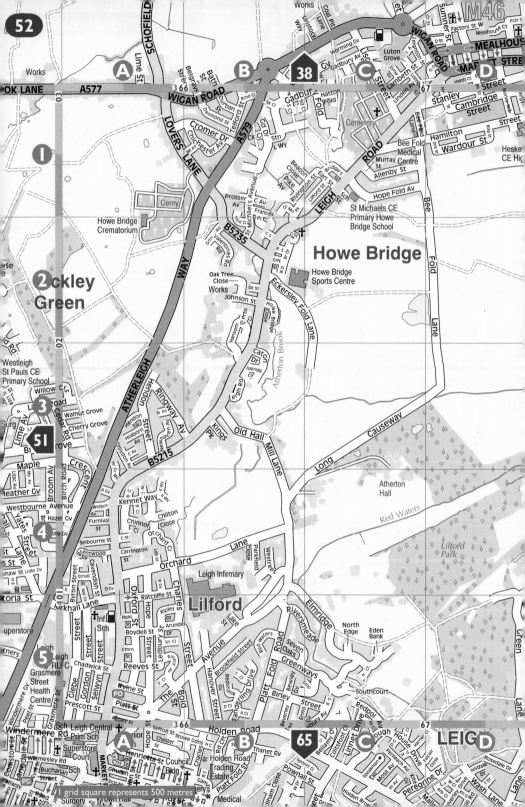

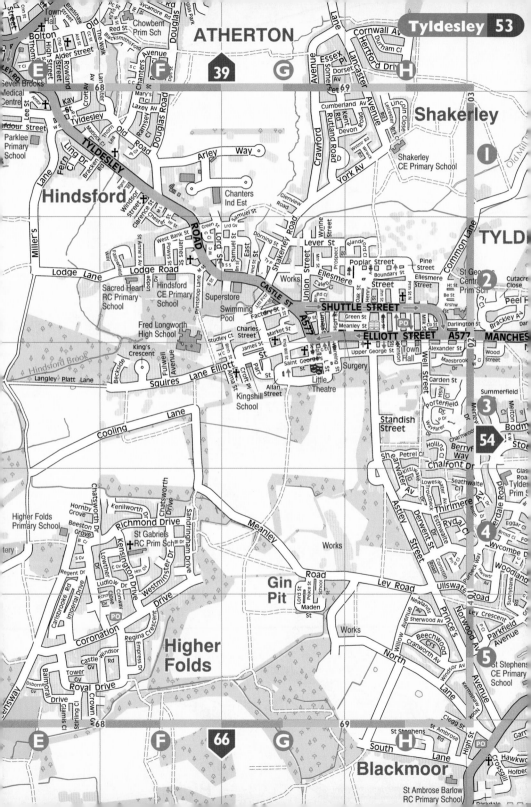

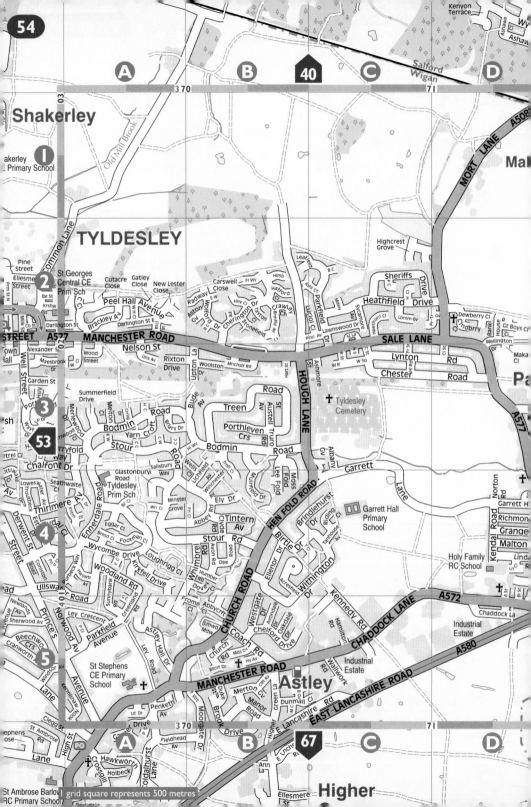

E F **46** G H

54 55

NEWTON ROAD
St. Helens
Leyland Green Road
Birch
Grove
Hawthorn
Poplar Av
Palm Av
Lilac Av
Red
Elm
Cedar
GV
I

B5207
BILLINGE
Garswood
United
FC
**Downall
Green**

BILLINGE
BILLINGE ROAD

**Simm's Lane
End**

ckley Hurst
ll

400

Peebles Close
Selkirk
Stirling Dri
Avenue

Smock
Lane
Thornhill
Road
Oban Drive
Falkland Dr
Dunblane
Close
Argyll Close
Girvan
Forrest
2

Garswood Road

Langholm Road

Daniel
Av
Kinross Avenue
Hamilton
Victoria
Coldstone
GV

Garswood
Prim Sch
Station Rd
Manor
Close
Nwbr Ct

Old Colliery Yard
PO
Surgery
Mnt Cre
School
Lane

Works
Garswood
Garswood Road
3
Garswood Station
60

Arch Lane

Tithebarn
66
4

Old Garswood
Hall Farm

Garswood Old Road

5
3.98

A58
Liverpool Road

54 55

E F G H

ay Grove
LIVERPOOL ROAD
Yer
Tra

E F `48` G H

58 59 BOLTON ROAD Riding Lane

Stubshaw Cross

Antler Ct
Redgate Rd Lockett Road Kestrel Dr Beaver Ct

Ashton Grange Industrial Estate

ROAD

Lockett Business Park

Lockett Road

Bolton Rd Severn Road Trent Rd
Orynz Pl Avon Rd Welland Road
Conway Rd Willow Grove School
Crossway Av Linkway Av Moorland Rd

I
400

Tooth'll Cl
Grasmere Dr Hawes Crs Welbeck
Eskdale Rd Buttermere Av Ennerdale Rd Tittook

Luke St
Hope St John St
Barrow St North St School St
Diane Road Elaine Gv Yonne
Rushmoor Av
Upland Drive White Lodge Dr Heather Gv

The Strand
Alexandra Road
Bowland Avenue Malvern Close
Penrith Crs Kendal
Rydal Close Mr Rd

Wood's La
East St
Recreation Avenue
Thompson
Kilburn Avenue Msn Cl Edge Gn St
Upland Drive Chestnut Gv Lord St

Green

2

ROAD A58

Edward Dr
Queen's Avenue Fairview Av
Grnflds
Longmead Sibley Rd
Cleveland Dr Rutland Dursley Cl
Glendale Av Elwall Rd
Hazlehurst
Ashton Town AFC Cath Prim Sch
St Wilfrids Cath Prim Sch
Fleming Dr Moxon Wy

Town Green

Jameson's Farm

COLBORNE ROAD B5207

Green
Edge
3
`62`
ASH

Hornbeam Crescent
Hooten Drive Orchard St
St Thomas CE Prim Sch
sdale Drive Rigbys
Belvedere Wotton Dr Wotton Drive
Wyatt Grove Salvin Close
Ware Cl Soane Cl
Mansart

ASHTON-IN-MAKERFIELD

WIGAN ROAD
PO PA
Hilton Street Chapel St
Ladywinth Avenue Chelmand
Princess
Walford Rd
Allscott Way
Duke St Peter St
Westnov Taima
Brandale
Drive

Tintern Avenue
Norwich Avenue
Ripon Drive
Chester Drive

99
St
Edge
Helen
4
Manley Av
Farefield Avenue
Milli

BRYN STREET
GERARD STREET
Princess Road
Turhill Dr
York Road Lily Place
Heath
Mitchel Street
Monmouth Crescent
Lincoln
Blenheim Road
Mill ST
Ashton Heath

Wigan
St Helens

WARRINGTON ROAD A49

Violet Street Mnc Ter Lbr St
Flora Street
Glebe Av
Premier Inn Leigh
Bransford Close
Hampson Close
Park View
Windsor
Chiltern
Farndale Grove
Newlyn Drive Chetwode Av
Kiveton Dr
Road

Haydock Park Gardens

Haydock Park Racecourse

Hell Noo'k
St
Mansfield St
Harvey
Halewoo Av
Park
Ringley
Gawsw
Oakeld Av Wa

398

LODGE LANE

58 59
E F `69` G H

Haydock Park

LEIGH

Bedford

Bedford High School

Lately Common

Wood's

EAST LANCS

A580

A574

A572

A574

MANCHESTER RD

WARRINGTON ROAD

SPINNING JENNY WAY

Pennington Brook

Grave Oak La

Jennet's Lane

Hesnall

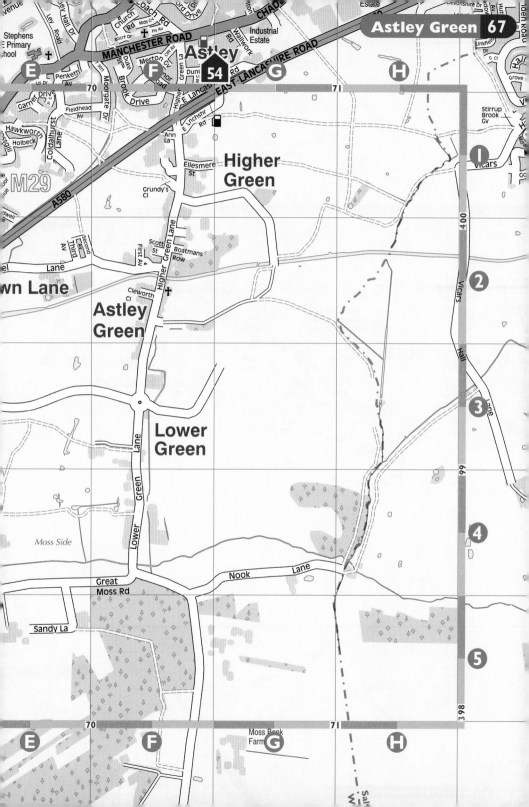

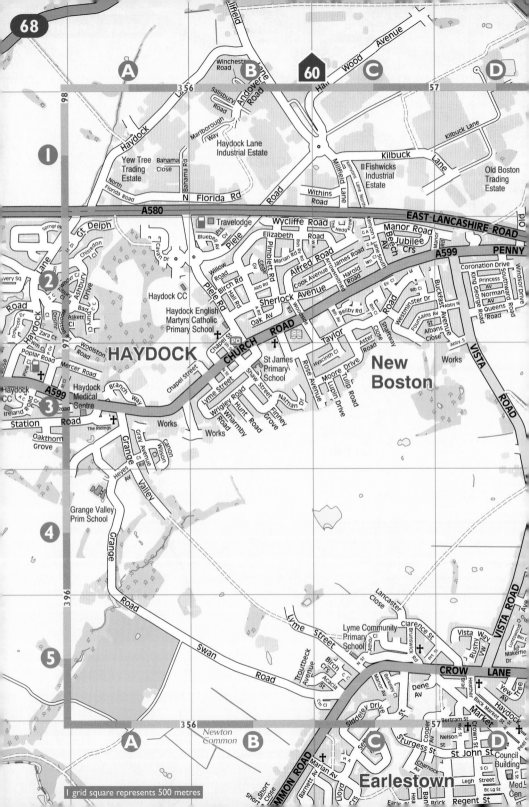

Grave Oak La

La... Common

Jennet's Lane

E **F** **G** **H**

66 67

98

Wood's Farm

Hesnall Close

Hurst Ml La

A574

Warrington to Wigan

I

Warrington Rd

Acreville Grove

Sandfield Crescent

Carr Brook

Walton Av

Lowfield Gdns

Whity Av

Queen's Av

Duke Av

Mowbrn Gd

Crn Av

2

Glazebury CE Primary School

PO

Hurst Lane

Hurst Hall

97

Glazebury

3

Light Oaks Road

WARRINGTON ROAD

Fowley Common

Millbrook Cl

4

Fowley common Lane

Hebden Av

Hawthorne

Hey Shoot La

396

5 Works

Bevin Av

Attlee Av

Gaillet Av

Eden Av

Churchill Avenue

Beaverbrook Av

Cranwell Av

Chatsworth Av

Colclough

Lowther Rd

Culcheth Hall Drive

Clarke Av

Culcheth Primary & High School

Withington Av

E **F** **G** **H**

66 67

Road

A574

B5212

Beech Av

Drive

Council Building

Charnock Rd

HOLCR...

Abram 49 H3
Appley Bridge 8 B2
Ashton-in-Makerfield 61 G3
Ashurst 17 G1
Aspull 13 E5
Aspull Common 64 A5
Astley 54 B5
Astley Green 67 F2
Atherton 39 F5
Bamfurlong 48 D3
Bank Top 19 F1
Bedford 65 H2
Beech Hill 21 G3
Bickershaw 50 B5
Billinge 59 E1
Birch Green 17 H3
Blackmoor 66 D1
Blackrod 7 H4
Blaguegate 16 A4
Boar's Head 10 D4
Boothstown 55 F5
Brownlow 45 E3
Bryn 47 G5
Bryn Gates 49 E4
Chadwick Green 58 D2
Chapel House 16 C3
Chequerbent 26 D4
Chew Moor 26 D1
Clinkham Wood 57 H5
Cooper Turning 14 A5
Coppull Moor 5 E1
Crank 57 F2
Crankwood 62 D1

Crawford 43 H1
Crooke 20 D2
Daisy Hill 38 B2
Dangerous Corner 51 F1
Digmoor 29 H2
Dover 49 G5
Downall Green 59 H1
Edge Green 62 A5
Ellenbrook 55 F5
Elmers Green 18 A2
Far Moor 31 H3
Fernhill Gate 27 G1
Firs Lane 64 C1
Four Gates 25 F1
Fowley Common 73 G4
Garswood 59 G3
Gathurst 20 A2
Gin Pit 53 G4
Glazebury 73 G3
Golborne 70 C2
Goose Green 33 F4
Greenheys 40 C3
Hag Fold 38 C3
Haigh 12 C3
Hall Green 18 D5
Hart Common 37 E1
Hawkley 33 H5
Haydock 68 A3
Higher End 31 F5
Higher Folds 53 F5
Higher Green 67 G1
Highfield 32 D4
Highfield 41 E1

Hilton House 13 H4
Hindley 36 B4
Hindley Green 57 F4
Hindsford 53 E1
Holland Lees 8 A5
Houghwood 45 E5
Howe Bridge 52 C2
Ince-in-Makerfield 3 H7
Kenyon 71 H5
Kings Moss 44 C4
Kitt Green 33 F1
Lamberhead Green 33 E3
Land Gate 47 H4
Lane Head 71 G3
Lark Hill 66 D1
Lately Common 65 H5
Leigh 52 B5
Lilford 52 B5
Little Hulton 41 E4
Little Scotland 7 F5
Longshaw 45 H2
Lostock 14 D4
Lower Green 67 F3
Lowton 71 E1
Lowton Common 71 H1
Lowton Heath 70 D5
Lowton St Mary's 71 H2
Makants 54 D1
Marsh Green 20 D4
Marylebone 22 C2
Middlebrook 14 A2

Mosley Common 55 F4
Moss Bank 57 G5
Mossy Lea 4 A1
New Boston 68 C3
New Bury 41 F1
Newgate 30 D1
New Houses 46 C2
New Springs 23 F4
Newton-le-Willows 69 G4
Newtown 33 F2
Old Boston 69 E2
Orrell 31 G4
Orrell Post 31 G2
Over Hulton 39 H1
Park Hill 42 C1
Parr Brow 54 D3
Pemberton 32 D5
Pennington 64 C3
Pennington Green 24 B5
Pennylands 16 B5
Pickley Green 51 H2
Plank Lane 64 A1
Platt Bridge 49 G1
Pocket Nook 72 B1
Poolstock 33 H2
Prestolee 43 F4
Rainford 43 E1
Rainford Junction 43 E1
Red Rock 11 G2
Roby Mill 19 E2
Scholes 3 F5
Scot Lane End 13 F3
Shakerley 53 H1
Shevington 9 F5

Shevington Moor ....
Shevington Vale ....
Simm's Lane End ....
Skelmersdale ....
Springfield ....
Spring View ....
Standish ....
Standish Lower Ground ...
Stanley ....
Stubshaw Cross ....
Tamer Lane End ....
Tanhouse ....
Tontine ....
Top Lock ....
Town Green ....
Town Lane ....
Town of Lowton ....
Twiss Green ....
Tyldesley ....
Up Holland ....
Water's Nook ....
Westhoughton ....
Westleigh ....
Whelley ....
Whitley ....
Wigan ....
Wingates ....
Winstanley ....
Winstanleys ....
Worsley Hall ....
Worsley Mesnes ....

USING THE STREET INDEX

Street names are listed alphabetically. Each street name is followed by its postal town or area locality, the Postcode District, the page number, and the reference to the square in which the name is found.

Standard index entries are shown as follows:

Abberley Wy *WGNS/IIMK* WN3 ....**32** C4

Street names and selected addresses not shown on the map due to scale restrictions are shown in the index with an asterisk:

Acresfield Cl *HOR/BR* BL6 *............**7** H4

GENERAL ABBREVIATIONS

ACC .... ACCESS
ALY .... ALLEY
AP .... APPROACH
AR .... ARCADE
ASS .... ASSOCIATION
AV .... AVENUE
BCH .... BEACH
BLDS .... BUILDINGS
BND .... BEND
BNK .... BANK
BR .... BRIDGE
BRK .... BROOK
BTM .... BOTTOM
BUS .... BUSINESS
BVD .... BOULEVARD
BY .... BYPASS
CATH .... CATHEDRAL
CEM .... CEMETERY
CEN .... CENTRE
CFT .... CROFT
CH .... CHURCH
CHA .... CHASE
CHYD .... CHURCHYARD
CIR .... CIRCLE
CIRC .... CIRCUS
CL .... CLOSE
CLFS .... CLIFFS
CMP .... CAMP
CNR .... CORNER
CO .... COUNTY
COLL .... COLLEGE
COM .... COMMON
COMM .... COMMISSION
CON .... CONVENT
COT .... COTTAGES
CP .... CAPE
CPS .... COPSE
CR .... CREEK
CREM .... CREMATORIUM
CRS .... CRESCENT
CSWY .... CAUSEWAY
CT .... COURT
CTRL .... CENTRAL
CTS .... COURTS

CTYD .... COURTYARD
CUTT .... CUTTINGS
CV .... COVE
CYN .... CANYON
DEPT .... DEPARTMENT
DL .... DALE
DM .... DAM
DR .... DRIVE
DRO .... DROVE
DRY .... DRIVEWAY
DWGS .... DWELLINGS
E .... EAST
EMB .... EMBANKMENT
EMBY .... EMBASSY
ESP .... ESPLANADE
EST .... ESTATE
EX .... EXCHANGE
EXPY .... EXPRESSWAY
EXT .... EXTENSION
F/O .... FLYOVER
FC .... FOOTBALL CLUB
FK .... FORK
FLD .... FIELD
FLDS .... FIELDS
FLS .... FALLS
FM .... FARM
FT .... FORT
FTS .... FLATS
FWY .... FREEWAY
FY .... FERRY
GA .... GATE
GAL .... GALLERY
GDN .... GARDEN
GDNS .... GARDENS
GLD .... GLADE
GLN .... GLEN
GN .... GREEN
GND .... GROUND
GRA .... GRANGE
GRG .... GARAGE
GT .... GREAT
GTWY .... GATEWAY
GV .... GROVE
HGR .... HIGHER
HL .... HILL

HLS .... HILLS
HO .... HOUSE
HOL .... HOLLOW
HOSP .... HOSPITAL
HRB .... HARBOUR
HTH .... HEATH
HTS .... HEIGHTS
HVN .... HAVEN
HWY .... HIGHWAY
IMP .... IMPERIAL
IN .... INLET
IND EST .. INDUSTRIAL ESTATE
INF .... INFIRMARY
INFO .... INFORMATION
INT .... INTERCHANGE
IS .... ISLAND
JCT .... JUNCTION
JTY .... JETTY
KG .... KING
KNL .... KNOLL
L .... LAKE
LA .... LANE
LDG .... LODGE
LGT .... LIGHT
LK .... LOCK
LKS .... LAKES
LNDG .... LANDING
LTL .... LITTLE
LWR .... LOWER
MAG .... MAGISTRATE
MD .... MEAD
MDW .... MEADOWS
MEM .... MEMORIAL
MKT .... MARKET
MKTS .... MARKETS
ML .... MALL
MNR .... MANOR
MS .... MEWS
MSN .... MISSION
MT .... MOUNT
MTN .... MOUNTAIN
MTS .... MOUNTAINS
MUS .... MUSEUM

MWY .... MOTORWAY
N .... NORTH
NE .... NORTH EAST
NW .... NORTH WEST
O/P .... OVERPASS
OFF .... OFFICE
ORCH .... ORCHARD
OV .... OVAL
PAL .... PALACE
PAS .... PASSAGE
PAV .... PAVILION
PDE .... PARADE
PH .... PUBLIC HOUSE
PK .... PARK
PKWY .... PARKWAY
PL .... PLACE
PLN .... PLAIN
PLNS .... PLAINS
PLZ .... PLAZA
POL .... POLICE STATION
PR .... PRINCE
PREC .... PRECINCT
PREP .... PREPARATORY
PRIM .... PRIMARY
PROM .... PROMENADE
PRS .... PRINCESS
PRT .... PORT
PT .... POINT
PTH .... PATH
PZ .... PIAZZA
QD .... QUADRANT
QU .... QUEEN
QY .... QUAY
R .... RIVER
RBT .... ROUNDABOUT
RD .... ROAD
RDG .... RIDGE
REP .... REPUBLIC
RES .... RESERVOIR
RFC ...... RUGBY FOOTBALL CLUB
RI .... RISE
RP .... RAMP
RW .... ROW
S .... SOUTH
SCH .... SCHOOL

SE .... SOUTH
SER .... SERVICE
SH .... S
SHOP .... SHOP
SKWY .... SK
SMT .... SU
SOC .... SO
SP ....
ST .... SF
SQ .... SQ
ST .... ST
STN .... STA
STR .... STF
STRD .... STF
SW .... SOUTH Y
TDG .... TRA
TER .... TER
THWY .... THROUGH
TNL .... TU
TOLL .... TOL
TPK .... TURN
TR .... T
TRL ....
TWR .... TC
U/P .... UNDER
UNI .... UNIVE
UPR .... U
V ....
VA .... VA
VIAD .... VIA
VIL ....
VIS ....
VLG VIL
VLS ....
W ....
WD ....
WHF .... W
W ....
WKS .... W
WY ....
YD ....
YHA .... YOUTH H(

POSTCODE TOWNS AND AREA ABBREVIATIONS

AIMK .... Ashton-in-Makerfield
ATH .... Atherton
BOL .... Bolton
BOLS/LL .... Bolton south/
                                  Little Lever
BRSC .... Burscough
CHLY/EC .... Chorley/Eccleston

CHLYE .... Chorley east/
                                  Adlington/
                                  Whittle-le-Woods
FWTH .... Farnworth
GOL/RIS/CUL ...... Golborne/Risley/
                                  Culcheth
HOR/BR .... Horwich/Blackrod

LEIGH .... Leigh
LHULT .... Little Hulton
NEWLW ...... Newton-le-Willows
ORM .... Ormskirk
RNFD/HAY .... Rainford/
                                  Haydock
SKEL .... Skelmersdale

TYLD .... Tyldesley
WALK .... Walkden
WARRN/WOL ... Warrington north/
                                  Woolston
WGN .... Wigan
WGNE/HIN .... Wigan east/
                                  Hindley

WGNNW/ST .... Wigan northw
                                  Sta
WGNS/IIMK .... Wigan so
                                  Ince-in-Make
WGNW/BIL/OR ..... Wigan w
                                  Billinge/
WHTN .... Westhous

3

WGNE/HIN WN2 .... 48 D4
WGNE/HIN WN2 .... 49 E4

A

ey Wy WGNS/IIMK WN3 .... 32 C4
t SKEL WN8 .... 31 F1
ct WGNNW/ST WN6 ...... 21 F5
roft Cl TYLD M29 .... 54 B5
WGNNW/ST WN6 .... 8 C3
ale Gdns WALK M28 ...... 41 H4
WGNW/BIL/OR WN5 ...... 31 H2
ields WGNNW/ST WN6 .... 21 G3
La LEIGH WN7 .... 51 G2
ea Dr WHTN BL5 .... 26 B3
d COL/RIS/CUL WA3 ...... 73 H2
D/HAY WA11 .... 68 B2
M29 .... 54 B4
q LEIGH WN7 .... 51 G2
tead SKEL WN8 .... 29 G1
t SKEL WN8 .... 52 A5
way North
/HAY WA11 .... 68 D2
way South
wood SKEL WN8 .... 68 D3
ton Wy LEIGH WN7 ...... 51 G2
cft WHTN BL5 .... 38 A2
Fold Rd WALK M28 ...... 55 C4
ford Cl
 .... 63 E5
on TYLD M29 .... 66 D2
t WGNE/HIN WN2 .... 35 H2
s Wy
W/BIL/OR WN5 .... 58 C3
r Rd AIMK WN4 .... 60 D2
n Dr WGNE/HIN WN2 .... 49 F2
Crs WGNNW/ST WN6 .... 21 G2
t NEWLW WA12 .... 68 C5
t La
W/BIL/OR WN5 .... 20 A3
Cl LEIGH WN7 .... 65 E5
LEIGH WN7 .... 65 E4
MK WN4 .... 61 E4
ale HOR/BR BL6 .... 15 H4
ghale CHLY/EC PR7 ...... 7 F4
M29 .... 54 B4
eld Cl HOR/BR BL6 * 7 H4
eld Rd LHULT M38 ...... 41 G4
wood Av WGNE/HIN WN2 . 36 D4
eld Rd COL/RIS/CUL WA3 . 73 H2
t WGN WN1 .... 2 D3
er WGN WN1 .... 2 D2
r St AIMK WN4 .... 33 G5
on St AIMK WN4 .... 60 D5
rton Cl WGNE/HIN WN2 . 36 A4
ton Rd BOLS/LL BL3 .... 27 G2
Dr LHULT M38 .... 41 G3
Gv LHULT M38 .... 41 G3
t WGNNW/ST WN6 ...... 5 F5
Cl COL/RIS/CUL WA3 ...... 71 H1
ghs Ct LEIGH WN7 ...... 64 D2
e Av HOR/BR BL6 .... 15 E2
d HOR/BR BL6 .... 7 C4
rth St WHTN BL5 .... 25 H2
Pl WGNS/IIMK WN3 ...... 34 A5
t LHULT M38 .... 41 G3
Gv TYLD M29 .... 54 C3
v LEIGH WN7 .... 51 F5
el WGN WN1 .... 11 E1
Av AIMK WN4 .... 60 C1
Wy WGNW/BIL/OR WN5 . 33 E2
s GOL/RIS/CUL WA3 ...... 71 G2
Cl WGN WN1 .... 11 E1
rook Rd LHULT M38 ...... 41 E5
Cl LEIGH WN7 .... 65 E4
eld St ATH M46 .... 39 E5
a RNFD/HAY WA11 ...... 57 G2
eld St ATH M46 .... 38 D3
Wy WGNNW/ST WN6 .... 10 B2
t SKEL WN8 .... 51 H3
Rd ATH M46 .... 36 A4
Ce Cl WGNS/IIMK WN3 .. 34 A5
der Briant Ct
BL4 .... 41 H1
der St TYLD M29 .... 53 H3
dra Cl SKEL WN8 .... 16 D5
dra Crs
WGNE/HIN WN2 .... 33 F2
dra Rd AIMK WN4 ...... 61 E2
/BR BL6 .... 23 H3
t M28 .... 41 H3
dra St WGNE/HIN WN2 .. 49 F3

Alexandria Dr WHTN BL5 .... 26 C5
Alfred Rd GOL/RIS/CUL WA3 . 71 H1
RNFD/HAY WA11 .... 68 C5
Alfred St RNFD/HAY WA11 ... 43 E4
TYLD M29 .... 53 G2
WGN WN1 .... 22 A3
WGNE/HIN WN2 .... 35 F5
WGNS/IIMK WN3 .... 34 C2
Algernon Rd WALK M28 ...... 41 H4
Algernon St WGNE/HIN WN2 . 36 A3
WGNS/IIMK WN3 .... 33 H4
Allan St WGNE/HIN WN2 .... 33 G2
Allan St TYLD M29 .... 53 G2
Allen Av GOL/RIS/CUL WA3 .. 73 H5
Allenby Gv WHTN BL5 ...... 37 H1
Allenby St ATH M46 .... 52 C1
Allerby Wy GOL/RIS/CUL WA3 . 71 G1
Allerton Cl WHTN BL5 ...... 26 B4
Allesley Cl WHTN BL5 ...... 26 B4
Alliance St WGN WN1 ...... 2 E4
All Saints Ct RNFD/HAY WA11 . 56 B1
All Saints Gv WHTN BL5 .... 38 B1
Allscott Wy AIMK WN4 ...... 61 F3
Alma Cl SKEL WN8 .... 31 F1
Alma Ct SKEL WN8 .... 31 F1
Alma Gv WGNS/IIMK WN3 .. 47 F1
Alma Hl SKEL WN8 .... 31 F1
Alma Rd SKEL WN8 .... 31 F1
WHTN BL5 .... 26 A5
Alma St ATH M46 .... 38 D5
LEIGH WN7 .... 51 H3
 .... 53 C3

Almond Brook Rd
WGNNW/ST WN6 .... 9 H1
Almond Cl WGNNW/ST WN6 . 10 C3
Almond Gv
WGNW/BIL/OR WN5 ...... 33 F2
Alnwick Cl WGNE/HIN WN2 . 13 C5
Alpine Dr LEIGH WN7 ...... 51 F5
Alston Lea ATH M46 .... 39 F4
Alston Rd WGNE/HIN WN2 .. 3 K1
Alt Cl LEIGH WN7 .... 64 C1
Alt Cl AIMK WN4 .... 60 D2
Alvanley Cl
WGNW/BIL/OR WN5 ...... 20 A4
Alwyn Cl WGNS/IIMK WN3 .. 65 E5
Alwyn St WGN WN1 .... 3 F2
Alwyn Ter WGN WN1 ...... 3 K7
Amar St WGNE/HIN WN2 .... 36 B4
Amathyst Cl WGNE/HIN WN2 . 36 B4
Amber Gdns WGNE/HIN WN2 . 36 B4
Ambergate ATH M46 .... 53 E1
SKEL WN8 .... 29 G1
Amber Gv WHTN BL5 ...... 26 A3
Amberley Cl WGNE/HIN WN2 . 3 K1
Amberswood Cl
 .... 35 G1
Amblecote Dr East LHULT M38 . 41 F2
Amblecote Dr West
LHULT M38 .... 41 F2
Ambleside Av WGNE/HIN WN2 . 23 G5
Ambrose Av LEIGH WN7 .... 51 H2
Amersham St WGN WN1 .... 29 G1
Amesbury Dr WGNS/IIMK WN3 . 46 D1
Amis Gv GOL/RIS/CUL WA3 . 71 F1
Anchor La FWTH BL4 ...... 41 E1
Ancroft Dr WGNE/HIN WN2 . 36 B5
Anderby Wy WHTN BL5 .... 25 H5
Anderton St WGNE/HIN WN2 . 3 K6
Anderton Wy WGNE/HIN WN2 . 3 K6
Andover Crs WGNS/IIMK WN3 . 46 D1
Andover Rd RNFD/HAY WA11 . 68 B1
Andrew Av
WGNW/BIL/OR WN5 ...... 59 E1
Angus Av LEIGH WN7 ...... 51 F5
Anjou Bvd WGNW/BIL/OR WN5 . 45 F2
Annandale Gdns SKEL WN8 .. 30 D1
Anneslay Gv WGNE/HIN WN2 . 23 G5
Annesley Crs WGNS/IIMK WN3 . 33 G5
Annette Av NEWLW WA12 .... 68 D4
Ann La TYLD M29 .... 54 A4
Ann St SKEL WN8 .... 51 H3
SKEL WN8 .... 31 F1
Ansdell Rd WGNW/BIL/OR WN5 . 33 E5
Ansford Av WGNE/HIN WN2 . 49 G5
Anson Pl WGNW/BIL/OR WN5 . 20 D5
Anson St WGNE/HIN WN2 .. 33 G1
Anthorn Rd WGNS/IIMK WN3 . 33 F5
Antier Ct AIMK WN4 ...... 48 A5
Antrim Ct WGNS/IIMK WN3 . 31 G3
Anvil Cl WGNW/BIL/OR WN5 . 31 G3
Apple Dell Av
GOL/RIS/CUL WA3 .... 62 B5
Apple Hey WGNNW/ST WN6 . 8 C2
Apple La WGNNW/ST WN6 .. 8 C2
Applethwaite WGNE/HIN WN2 . 23 G5
Appleton La WHTN BL5 .... 26 A4
Appleton Rd SKEL WN8 .... 17 E3
Appleton St WGNS/IIMK WN3 . 2 B5
Appley La North
 .... 8 B3
Appley La South SKEL WN8 . 16 B4
Arbor Gv LHULT M38 ...... 40 D4
Arbory Cl LEIGH WN7 ...... 65 H1
Arbour La WGNNW/ST WN6 . 10 B2
Arcade St WGN WN1 .... 2 D5
Archer St LEIGH WN7 ...... 65 G4
WALK M28 .... 55 H5
Arch La AIMK WN4 .... 59 F3
Arena Ap HOR/BR BL6 .... 14 B3
Argyle Av WALK M28 ...... 55 H1
Argyle St ATH M46 .... 52 D1
ATH M46 .... 37 H2
WGNE/HIN WN2 .... 35 G2
Argyll Gv AIMK WN4 ...... 59 H2
Arkholme WALK M28 ...... 55 F3
Arley Cl WGNE/HIN WN2 .. 23 G3
Arley La WGN WN1 .... 11 G1
Arley St WGNS/IIMK WN3 .. 34 A5
Arley Wy ATH M46 .... 36 A4
Arlington Dr LEIGH WN7 .... 72 B1
Armadale Rd BOLS/LL BL3 . 27 F1
Armitage Av LHULT M38 .... 41 E4
Armitage St LHULT M38 .... 41 E4
Armitstead St WGNE/HIN WN2 . 36 A2
Armoury Bank AIMK WN4 .. 61 E3
Armstrong St
WGNE/HIN WN2 * 23 F2

Arncliffe Cl WGNE/HIN WN2 . 35 H4
WGNE/HIN WN2 .... 55 C5
Arnian Rd RNFD/HAY WA11 . 43 E4
Arnian Wy RNFD/HAY WA11 . 43 E4
Arnside Av WGNE/HIN WN2 . 35 F1
Arnside Rd WGNE/HIN WN2 . 36 D3
WGNE/HIN WN2 .... 32 C1
Arrowsmith Rd
RNFD/HAY WA11 .... 68 C2
Arrow St LEIGH WN7 ...... 65 G3
Arthur La WALK M28 ...... 41 H5
Arthur St LEIGH WN7 ...... 64 D2
WGNE/HIN WN2 .... 36 B3
Arundale WHTN BL5 ...... 26 A3
Arundel Dr LEIGH WN7 .... 52 A5
Arundel St ATH M46 ...... 36 B3
WGNW/BIL/OR WN5 ...... 33 C2
Ascot Dr ATH M46 .... 39 F4
Ascroft St WGN WN1 ...... 3 G6
Ashawe Cl LHULT M38 .... 40 D5
Ashawe Gv LHULT M38 .... 41 E5
Ashawe Ter LHULT M38 .... 40 D5
Ashbourne Av WGNE/HIN WN2 . 3 K1
WGNE/HIN WN2 .... 36 C4
Ashbourne Cl LEIGH WN7 .. 51 G2
Ashburn Cl HOR/BR BL6 .... 14 C2
Ashbury Dr RNFD/HAY WA11 . 68 A2
Ashby Gv LEIGH WN7 ...... 51 F1
Ashby Rd WGNS/IIMK WN3 . 34 A5
Ash Cl WGNNW/ST WN6 .... 8 C3
Ashcroft Av WGNNW/ST WN6 . 21 G2
Ashcroft Rd LEIGH WN7 .... 52 B4
Ashdale Rd WGNE/HIN WN2 . 36 C5
Ashdene WGNE/HIN WN2 .. 47 H1
Ashdown Dr WALK M28 .... 55 F4
Ashfield ATH M46 .... 38 D4
WGNE/HIN WN2 .... 36 C4
Ashfield Crs
WGNW/BIL/OR WN5 ...... 58 D1
Ashfield Dr WGNE/HIN WN2 . 12 D5
WGNE/HIN WN2 .... 36 C4
Ashfield House Gdns
WGNNW/ST WN6 .... 10 C3
Ashfield Park Dr
WGNNW/ST WN6 .... 10 C2
Ashford Av WALK M28 .... 55 E5
Ashford Ri WGN WN1 ...... 22 A1
Ash Gv GOL/RIS/CUL WA3 .. 70 D1
WGNE/HIN WN2 .... 43 E5
SKEL WN8 .... 16 C4
WGNNW/ST WN6 .... 32 A2
WHTN BL5 .... 37 H1
Ash Grove Crs
WGNW/BIL/OR WN5 ...... 45 H5
Ashington Cl
WGNW/BIL/OR WN5 ...... 20 C4
 .... 2 D1
Ashlands Av WALK M28 .... 55 F4
Ash La WGNE/HIN WN2 .... 35 F1
Ashley Dr SKEL WN8 ...... 51 F3
Ashley St SKEL WN8 ...... 17 G2
WGNE/HIN WN2 .... 37 E5
Ashling Ct TYLD M29 ...... 53 H2
Ashmead Rd SKEL WN8 .... 17 F1
Ashmore St TYLD M29 .... 54 B3
Ashridge Cl HOR/BR BL6 .. 15 E4
Ashridge Wy
WGNW/BIL/OR WN5 ...... 20 C4
Ash Rd RNFD/HAY WA11 .. 68 B2
Ash St GOL/RIS/CUL WA3 .. 62 C4
TYLD M29 .... 53 H2
WGNE/HIN WN2 .... 36 B3
Ashton Field Dr WALK M28 . 41 H4
Ashton Heath AIMK WN4 .. 61 E4
Ashton Rd GOL/RIS/CUL WA3 . 62 A4
NEWLW WA12 .... 69 F5
WGNE/HIN WN2 .... 46 C3
Ashurst Cl SKEL WN8 ...... 17 F1
Ashurst Gdns SKEL WN8 .. 17 G2
Ashurst Rd SKEL WN8 .... 17 G2
WGNNW/ST WN6 .... 45 C5
Ashwall St SKEL WN8 ...... 16 C5
Ashwell Av GOL/RIS/CUL WA3 . 63 E5
Ashwood SKEL WN8 ...... 17 H2
Ashwood Av AIMK WN4 .... 60 D3
GOL/RIS/CUL WA3 .... 71 E2
WALK M28 .... 41 H3
WGNE/HIN WN2 .... 49 H4
Ashworth St WGNE/HIN WN2 . 24 B2
Askrigg Cl ATH M46 .... 52 B5
Askwith Rd WGNE/HIN WN2 . 36 C5
Aspen Cl WHTN BL5 ...... 26 A3
Aspen Wk WGNNW/ST WN6 * . 1 F1
Aspenwood Av AIMK WN4 . 60 D4
Aspinall Cl HOR/BR BL6 .... 14 B3
Aspinalls Wk WALK M28 .. 55 E1
Aspinall Rd WGNNW/ST WN6 . 9 G1
Aspinall St HOR/BR BL6 .... 14 C1
Aspinall Wy HOR/BR BL6 .. 14 B2
Aspull Common LEIGH WN7 . 64 B5
Aspull Ct LEIGH WN7 ...... 64 B5
Assheton Cl NEWLW WA12 . 68 D5
Astbury Cl GOL/RIS/CUL WA3 . 72 A1
Aster Rd RNFD/HAY WA11 . 68 C3
Astley Cl RNFD/HAY WA11 . 68 A4
Astley Hall Dr TYLD M29 .. 54 A5
Astley St LEIGH WN7 ...... 65 G2
TYLD M29 .... 53 H4
Aston Gv TYLD M29 .... 53 G5
Athens Dr WALK M28 ...... 55 H1
Atherleigh Gv LEIGH WN7 .. 52 A4
Atherleigh Wy LEIGH WN7 . 64 C5
Atherton Rd WGNE/HIN WN2 . 36 B1
Atherton St CHLY/EC PR7 .. 7 F1
WGNE/HIN WN2 .... 36 C4
WGNS/IIMK WN3 .... 33 G5
Athertons Yd WGN WN1 * .. 22 B1
Athol Cl NEWLW WA12 .... 68 C5
Athol Crs WGNE/HIN WN2 . 37 E4
Atholl Gv WGNS/IIMK WN3 . 33 H5
Atkinson St WGN WN1 .... 49 G5
Attingham Wk
 .... 33 H3
Attlee Av GOL/RIS/CUL WA3 . 73 G5
Aughton Cl
WGNE/HIN WN2 .... 58 D2
Aughton St WGNE/HIN WN2 . 35 H4
Austin Av AIMK WN4 ...... 60 B2

Austin's La HOR/BR BL6 .... 15 E1
Austin St LEIGH WN7 * 64 C1
Avebury Cl GOL/RIS/CUL WA3 . 71 F1
HOR/BR BL6 .... 15 E1
The Avenue LEIGH WN7 .... 52 A5
NEWLW WA12 .... 69 F5
RNFD/HAY WA11 .... 43 E5
WGN WN1 .... 2 E1
WGNE/HIN WN2 .... 21 F1
WGNW/BIL/OR WN5 ...... 31 G5
WHTN BL5 .... 26 A4
Averham Cl AIMK WN4 .... 60 B2
Averhill WALK M28 .... 55 G3
Aviemore Cl AIMK WN4 .... 60 A2
Avocet Cl LEIGH WN7 ...... 52 B5
WGNE/HIN WN2 .... 49 F5
Avon Cl WALK M28 .... 55 G2
Avondale Dr TYLD M29 .... 54 B5
Avondale Rd WGN WN1 .... 2 C1
Avondale St WGNNW/ST WN6 . 5 F5
Avon Rd AIMK WN4 .... 61 H1
TYLD M29 .... 54 B5
WGNW/BIL/OR WN5 ...... 32 D1
WGNW/BIL/OR WN5 ...... 58 C3
Avon St LEIGH WN7 .... 65 G2
Aye Bridge Rd WGNE/HIN WN2 . 62 C1
Aylesbury Crs WGNE/HIN WN2 . 36 D4
Ayrefield Gv WGNNW/ST WN6 . 10 C4
Ayrefield Rd SKEL WN8 .... 19 F1
Ayrton Gv LHULT M38 .... 41 F3

B

Back Common St WHTN BL5 . 37 E1
Back Cross La NEWLW WA12 . 69 E5
Back Hart St WHTN BL5 .... 37 E1
Back Hulton La South
BOLS/LL BL3 * 27 H3
Back Hulton La West
BOLS/LL BL3 * 27 H1
Back La RNFD/HAY WA11 .. 57 G1
SKEL WN8 .... 30 A2
WGNNW/ST WN6 .... 8 D2
NEWLW WA12 .... 69 F5
WGNW/BIL/OR WN5 ...... 45 E5
Back Market St LEIGH WN7 . 65 E1
WHTN BL5 .... 37 H1
Back Mesnes St WGN WN1 . 2 D3
Back Patterson St
BOLS/LL BL3 * 27 H1
Back Railway Vw CHLY/EC PR7 . 7 F1
Back Rw WGN WN1 .... 31 F1
Back St Helens Rd South
BOLS/LL BL3 * 27 H3
Back Salford LEIGH WN7 * . 65 E1
Back School La SKEL WN8 . 16 C4
Back Shakerley Rd TYLD M29 * . 53 G2
Back Short St ATH M46 .... 53 F2
Back Skull House La
WGNNW/ST WN6 .... 8 B2
Back Wigan Rd North
WGNE/HIN WN2 .... 36 A3
Back Wigan Rd South
TYLD M29 .... 53 H2
Baclaw Cl WGN WN1 ...... 3 K5
Badbury Cl RNFD/HAY WA11 . 68 B1
Bag La ATH M46 .... 38 C4
Bagshaw La WGNE/HIN WN2 . 24 B3
Bahama Cl RNFD/HAY WA11 . 68 A1
Bahama Rd RNFD/HAY WA11 . 68 A1
Bailey Fold WHTN BL5 .... 25 H4
Bailrigg Cl ATH M46 .... 52 B5
Bainbridge Av
GOL/RIS/CUL WA3 .... 71 G1
Baker St WGNS/IIMK WN3 . 34 A2
Bakewell Dr WCNNW/ST WN6 . 21 H1
Balcarres Av WGN WN1 .... 3 G2
Balcarres Rd WGNE/HIN WN2 . 23 G1
Baldrine Dr WGNE/HIN WN2 . 37 E5
Baldwin St WGNE/HIN WN2 . 37 E5
 .... 3 F7
Balfern Cl WHTN BL5 ...... 25 H4
Balfern Fold WHTN BL5 .... 25 H4
Balharry Av RNFD/HAY WA11 . 68 C2
Ballantyne Wy
COL/RIS/CUL WA3 .... 71 F1
Balliol Wy AIMK WN4 ...... 60 C2
Ball St WGNNW/ST WN6 .. 21 G5
Balmoral Av GOL/RIS/CUL WA3 . 63 E5
Balmoral Dr LEIGH WN7 .. 35 H4
FWTH BL4 .... 41 H1
Balmoral Rd AIMK WN4 .... 60 D2
Balmore Cl BOLS/LL BL3 .. 27 H1
Balniel Wk WGN WN1 .... 22 D3
Bamber Ct WHTN BL5 .... 25 H2
Bamburgh Pl AIMK WN4 .. 60 D1
Bamford Dr WGNE/HIN WN2 . 3 J2
Bampton Av RNFD/HAY WA11 . 58 A5
Bampton Cl WHTN BL5 .... 25 H4
Banbury Cl LEIGH WN7 .... 45 D5
Banbury Rd
WGNW/BIL/OR WN5 ...... 45 D5
Bangor Fold LEIGH WN7 .. 65 H2
Banham Av WGNS/IIMK WN3 . 33 G5
Bank Av WGNW/BIL/OR WN5 . 31 G3
Bankbrook WGNW/BIL/OR WN5 . 19 F1
Bank Brow SKEL WN8 .... 17 F1
Bank Blds WGNNW/ST WN6 * . 49 F1
Bankes Av WGNW/BIL/OR WN5 . 31 G5
Bankfield SKEL WN8 ...... 29 H1
Bank Hd WHTN BL5 ...... 38 B1
Bankfield Dr WALK M28 .. 55 F5
Bankfield Rd TYLD M29 .. 54 D3
Bankhall Cl WGNE/HIN WN2 . 36 D4
Bank Hey WHTN BL5 * 26 A5
Bank House Cl TYLD M29 . 54 D2
Bank La LHULT M38 .... 41 E2
Bank Pas GOL/RIS/CUL WA3 * . 62 B5
Bank Rd WGNE/HIN WN2 .. 49 E1
Banks Ct LEIGH WN7 ...... 64 C1
Bank Side WHTN BL5 .... 26 A5
Bankside Av AIMK WN4 .. 47 H3

Bank St GOL/RIS/CUL WA3 . 62 B5
WGNE/HIN WN2 .... 35 G5
WGNW/BIL/OR WN5 ...... 33 F2
Bankwood WGNNW/ST WN6 . 8 D4
Banner St WGNE/HIN WN2 . 36 A3
WGNS/IIMK WN3 .... 34 D5
Bannister Wy WGNS/IIMK WN3 . 47 F1
Barbara Rd BOLS/LL BL3 .. 27 H5
Barbrook Cl WGNNW/ST WN6 . 4 C1
Barbury Cl LEIGH WN7 .... 52 A4
Bardale Gv AIMK WN4 .... 60 A3
Bardney Av COL/RIS/CUL WA3 . 62 A4
Bardsley Cl SKEL WN8 .... 30 D1
Bardwell Av WHTN BL5 .. 25 H4
Barford Cl SKEL WN8 ...... 30 D1
Barford Dr COL/RIS/CUL WA3 . 71 H1
Barford Gv HOR/BR BL6 .. 15 E1
Barker St LEIGH WN7 ...... 64 B1
Barlborough Rd
WGNW/BIL/OR WN5 ...... 33 E3
Barley Brook St
 .... 2 A2
Barnabys Rd WHTN BL5 .. 25 G2
Barn Acre HOR/BR BL6 .. 13 F1
Barnes Rd LEIGH WN7 .... 16 D4
Barnfield Cl TYLD M29 .... 53 G2
Barnfield Dr SKEL WN8 .... 30 B1
WALK M28 .... 55 G5
WHTN BL5 .... 25 G3
Barngill Gv WGNS/IIMK WN3 . 33 F5
Barnham Cl COL/RIS/CUL WA3 . 70 B1
Barn Hill Ter WHTN BL5 .. 25 H4
Barn La COL/RIS/CUL WA3 . 70 B1
Barnsley St WGNNW/ST WN6 . 21 H2
Barnton Cl GOL/RIS/CUL WA3 . 71 E2
Barnwell Av GOL/RIS/CUL WA3 . 72 C5
Baron Fold Crs LHULT M38 . 41 F3
Baron Fold Gv LHULT M38 . 41 E3
Baron Fold Rd LHULT M38 * . 41 E3
Barrack Sq WGN WN1 * 2 D5
Barracks Rd WGNE/HIN WN2 . 50 A2
Barracks St WGN WN1 * .. 21 H2
Barrie St LEIGH WN7 ...... 51 C3
Barrington Cl WGNS/IIMK WN3 . 47 E1
Barron Meadow LEIGH WN7 . 51 G4
Barrowcroft Cl WGN WN1 . 11 E1
Barrowdale Rd
GOL/RIS/CUL WA3 .... 70 C1
Barrowshaw Cl WALK M28 . 55 C2
Barrow St AIMK WN4 ...... 61 G2
Barrs Fold Cl WHTN BL5 .. 25 G3
Barrs Fold Rd WHTN BL5 .. 25 G3
Barry Crs WALK M28 ...... 41 F2
Bar St WGNE/HIN WN2 .... 49 F2
Barton Av WGN WN1 ...... 22 A3
Barton Clough
WGNW/BIL/OR WN5 ...... 58 D1
Barton Rd FWTH BL4 ...... 41 C1
Barton St GOL/RIS/CUL WA3 . 70 B1
WGNE/HIN WN2 .... 35 C5
WGNW/BIL/OR WN5 ...... 32 C5
Barwell Cl GOL/RIS/CUL WA3 . 62 D5
Baslow Av WGNE/HIN WN2 . 36 C3
Bassett Gv WGNS/IIMK WN3 . 46 C2
Basswood Gn WGNE/HIN WN2 . 36 D1
Batheaston Gv LEIGH WN7 . 51 G4
Bath St ATH M46 .... 38 D5
WGNE/HIN WN2 .... 23 E3
Battersby St LEIGH WN7 .. 65 G2
WGNE/HIN WN2 .... 33 G5
Baucher Rd WGNS/IIMK WN3 . 33 G5
Baverstock Cl WGNS/IIMK WN3 . 34 C1
Baxter's Rw WGNE/HIN WN2 . 54 C1
Bayliff Cl WGNNW/ST WN6 . 10 C1
Baycliff Cl WHTN BL5 ...... 26 B3
Baysdale Av BOLS/LL BL3 . 27 G1
Baytree Rd WGNNW/ST WN6 . 21 H2
Beacon Cl ATH M46 .... 52 B1
Beacon Hl
WGNW/BIL/OR WN5 * 45 G4
Beacon La SKEL WN8 ...... 18 C3
Beacon Rd WGNE/HIN WN2 . 50 D3
WGNNW/ST WN6 .... 4 C5
WGNW/BIL/OR WN5 ...... 8 C5
The Beacons WGNNW/ST WN6 . 8 B2
Beacon View Dr SKEL WN8 . 31 E1
Beaford Cl WGNW/BIL/OR WN5 . 33 E3
Beal Dr WGNE/HIN WN2 .. 23 H5
Beardsmore Dr
GOL/RIS/CUL WA3 .... 63 E5
Bearncroft WGNNW/ST WN6 . 8 B1
Beatty Dr WHTN BL5 ...... 25 H4
Beaufort St WGNE/HIN WN2 * . 36 A3
WGNW/BIL/OR WN5 ...... 33 F2
Beaumaris Cl LEIGH WN7 . 52 B5
Beaumaris Rd WGNE/HIN WN2 . 36 A3
Beaumont Cha BOLS/LL BL3 . 27 G2
Beaumont Gv
 .... 20 C5
Beaverbrook Av
GOL/RIS/CUL WA3 .... 73 G5
Beaver Ct AIMK WN4 ...... 48 B5
Beavers La SKEL WN8 .... 30 D2
Beckside TYLD M29 .... 53 C3
Beckwith WGNE/HIN WN2 . 55 H2
Bedford Av WALK M28 .... 55 H2
Bedford Dr ATH M46 ...... 52 B2
Bedford Pl AIMK WN4 .... 60 D1
Bedford St LEIGH WN7 .... 65 F1
WGN WN1 .... 3 C3
Beech Av ATH M46 .... 39 E5
GOL/RIS/CUL WA3 .... 71 G2
HOR/BR BL6 .... 14 D1
RNFD/HAY WA11 .... 68 C2
WALK M28 .... 55 F3
Beech Cl SKEL WN8 ...... 16 D4
Beech Crs LEIGH WN7 .... 64 D3
Beech Dr LEIGH WN7 ...... 65 F2
The Beeches ATH M46 * .. 39 E5
Beechfield Av LHULT M38 . 41 F5
WGNE/HIN WN2 .... 36 D4
Beechfield Dr LEIGH WN7 . 51 H4
Beech Gdns RNFD/HAY WA11 . 42 D4
Beech Gv LEIGH WN7 ...... 64 D3
LHULT M38 .... 40 D5
WGNE/HIN WN2 .... 49 H4

WGNNW/ST WN6 21 F2
Beech Hall St WGNNW/ST WN6 21 H3
Beech Hill Av WGNNW/ST WN6 21 F2
Beech Hill La WGNNW/ST WN6 21 F2
Beech Rd GOL/RIS/CUL WA3 62 B5
Beech St AIMK WN4 47 H5
ATH M46 39 F5
Beech Tree Av
WGNNW/ST WN6 8 C2
Beech Tree Houses
WGNE/HIN WN2 48 D5
Beechtrees SKEL WN8 29 H1
Beech Wk LEIGH WN7 64 D4
WGNNW/ST WN6 10 A2
WGNS/IIMK WN3 46 D1
Beechwood SKEL WN8 17 H2
Beechwood Av AIMK WN4 60 D4
NEWLW WA12 69 G5
WGNNW/ST WN6 9 E5
Beechwood Crs TYLD M29 53 H5
WGNW/BIL/OR WN5 31 H2
Beechwood La
GOL/RIS/CUL WA3 72 C5
Bee Fold La ATH M46 52 C1
Beeford Dr
WGNW/BIL/OR WN5 31 H3
Beehive Gn WHTN BL5 26 C4
Beeston Gv LEIGH WN7 53 E4
Beilby Rd RNFD/HAY WA11 68 C2
Belcroft Dr LHULT M38 40 D2
Belcroft Gv LHULT M38 * 40 D3
Belfield SKEL WN8 30 A2
Belfry Crs WGNNW/ST WN6 5 G5
Belgrave Cl LEIGH WN7 72 B1
WGNS/IIMK WN3 33 E5
Belgrave St ATH M46 38 B5
Bellamy Dr LEIGH WN7 65 G1
Belldean WGNE/HIN WN2 23 F5
Belle Green La WGNE/HIN WN2 23 F5
Belle Vue St
WGNW/BIL/OR WN5 33 E3
Bellingham Av WGN WN1 22 C3
Bellingham Dr WGN WN1 22 C3
Bellingham Mt WGN WN1 22 C2
Bell La WGNW/BIL/OR WN5 20 C5
Bellpit Cl WALK M28 55 H4
Bell St LEIGH WN7 51 G2
WGNE/HIN WN2 36 B2
Bellwood WHTN BL5 37 F1
Belmont Av ATH M46 39 G4
GOL/RIS/CUL WA3 62 D5
WGNE/HIN WN2 50 C2
WGNW/BIL/OR WN5 31 G5
Belmont Dr WGNE/HIN WN2 12 D5
Belmont Pl CHLY/EC PR7 4 D1
Belmont Rd WGNE/HIN WN2 36 C3
Belton Cl GOL/RIS/CUL WA3 70 B2
Belvedere Av ATH M46 39 G4
Belvedere Cl LEIGH WN7 53 E4
Belvedere Pl WGNS/IIMK WN3 33 G3
Belvedere Rd AIMK WN4 61 F3
NEWLW WA12 69 E5
Belvoir St WGN WN1 3 F5
Bembridge Ct
WGNS/IIMK WN3 47 F1
Bengairn Cl WGN WN1 3 J3
Bengal St LEIGH WN7 65 E1
Benjamin Fold AIMK WN4 61 E1
Ben La ORM L39 42 A1
Ben Lane Ct ORM L39 42 A1
Bennett Dr
WGNW/BIL/OR WN5 31 G4
Bentham Pl WGNNW/ST WN6 5 G5
Bentham Rd WGNNW/ST WN6 10 B1
Bent Hill St BOLS/LL BL3 * 27 H1
Bentinck St WGNS/IIMK WN3 33 G4
Bentworth Cl WHTN BL5 38 A2
Beresford St WGNNW/ST WN6 21 H4
Berkeley Av WGNS/IIMK WN3 47 E1
Berkeley Cl LEIGH WN7 72 B1
Berkeley Ct NEWLW WA12 68 C5
Berrington Gv AIMK WN4 60 D3
Berrington's La
RNFD/HAY WA11 56 D4
Berry Cl SKEL WN8 17 E3
Berryfold Wy TYLD M29 53 H3
Berry St SKEL WN8 16 D3
Berwick Cl WALK M28 55 E4
Berwick Pl WGN WN1 3 H2
Bessie's Well Pl
WGNNW/ST WN6 * 10 C2
Bessybrook Cl HOR/BR BL6 15 H4
Bethany Ms WGNE/HIN WN2 37 E4
Bethersden Rd WGN WN1 22 A1
Bettison Av LEIGH WN7 65 H3
Beulah Av WGNW/BIL/OR WN5 58 C2
Beverley Av LEIGH WN7 65 F1
WGNW/BIL/OR WN5 45 H2
Beverley Rd
WGNW/BIL/OR WN5 20 C5
Bevin Av GOL/RIS/CUL WA3 73 G5
Bevington St AIMK WN4 60 C1
Bewerley Cl WGNS/IIMK WN3 34 A2
Bewley Gv LEIGH WN7 52 B5
Bexhill Dr LEIGH WN7 51 F1
Bexley Dr LHULT M38 41 H5
Bexley St WGNE/HIN WN2 37 E5
Bickershaw Dr WALK M28 55 H1
Bickershaw La
WGNE/HIN WN2 49 H2
Bickley Gv TYLD M29 54 B5
Bidford Cl TYLD M29 54 B2
Billinge Rd AIMK WN4 59 G1
WGNS/IIMK WN3 32 D4
WGNW/BIL/OR WN5 33 E3
Billington Av NEWLW WA12 69 F4
Birchall Av GOL/RIS/CUL WA3 72 C5
Birch Av WGNNW/ST WN6 10 C2
WHTN BL5 38 A1
Birch Crs NEWLW WA12 68 C5
Birchfield Av ATH M46 38 C4
Birchfield Dr WALK M28 55 F4
Birchfield Gv BOLS/LL BL3 27 F1
Birchfold Cl LHULT M38 41 G4
Birch Green Rd SKEL WN8 17 G2
Birch Gv AIMK WN4 59 H1
Birchley Av
WGNW/BIL/OR WN5 58 B3
Birchley Rd RNFD/HAY WA11 58 A3
Birchley Vw RNFD/HAY WA11 58 A4
Birch Rd ATH M46 39 F5
LEIGH WN7 52 A4
RNFD/HAY WA11 68 B2
WGNE/HIN WN2 49 G4
Birch St SKEL WN8 16 D4
TYLD M29 * 53 H2
WGNE/HIN WN2 36 A3
WGNNW/ST WN6 21 H4
Birch Tree Rd
GOL/RIS/CUL WA3 71 G1
Birch Tree Wy HOR/BR BL6 14 D1
Birchwood Cl LEIGH WN7 65 E3
WGNS/IIMK WN3 46 D2
Bird St WGNE/HIN WN2 3 K7
Birkdale Av ATH M46 38 D3
Birkett Bank WGN WN1 3 H5
Birkett St WGN WN1 3 H5
Birkrig SKEL WN8 30 A2
Birkside Cl WGNS/IIMK WN3 47 H2
Birley Cl WGNNW/ST WN6 9 E2
Birley St LEIGH WN7 52 B5
NEWLW WA12 69 G5
Birleywood SKEL WN8 30 A2
Birtle Dr TYLD M29 54 B4
Bishop Reeves Rd
RNFD/HAY WA11 68 B2
Bispham Ct
WGNW/BIL/OR WN5 45 G1
Bispham Dr AIMK WN4 60 C1
Blackberry Dr WGNE/HIN WN2 35 H4
Blackburn Cl GOL/RIS/CUL WA3 71 G1
Blackburne Dr NEWLW WA12 68 D5
Blackcap Cl WALK M28 55 G4
Blackhorse Av HOR/BR BL6 * 7 H5
Blackhorse Cl HOR/BR BL6 7 H4
Black Horse St HOR/BR BL6 7 H4
Blackledge Cl
WGNW/BIL/OR WN5 31 H3
Blackleyhurst Av
WGNW/BIL/OR WN5 58 D1
Blackmoor Av TYLD M29 67 E1
Blackrod Brow HOR/BR BL6 7 G3
Blackrod By-Pass Rd
HOR/BR BL6 13 G2
Blacksmiths Fold ATH M46 39 F5
Blackthorn Av
WGNNW/ST WN6 21 G2
Blaguegate La SKEL WN8 16 A3
Blair Av LHULT M38 41 G4
WGNE/HIN WN2 37 E5
Blairmore Dr BOLS/LL BL3 27 F1
Blake Cl WGNS/IIMK WN3 33 H3
Blakehall SKEL WN8 30 A1
Blakemore Pk ATH M46 38 C4
Blakey Cl BOLS/LL BL3 27 G1
Blandford Cl TYLD M29 53 H2
Blandford Ri HOR/BR BL6 15 F1
Blantyre St WGNE/HIN WN2 36 B2
Blaydon Cl WGNE/HIN WN2 13 E5
Blaydon Pk SKEL WN8 30 A1
Bleach St WGNE/HIN WN2 35 H3
Bleakledge Gn WGNE/HIN WN2 36 C1
Bleakledge Gv WGNE/HIN WN2 36 B2
Bleaklow Cl WGNS/IIMK WN3 48 A1
Bleasdale Cl HOR/BR BL6 15 E2
Bleasdale Rd NEWLW WA12 69 E5
Bleasedale Rd WGNE/HIN WN2 36 C3
Blenheim Dr LEIGH WN7 53 F4
Blenheim Rd AIMK WN4 61 G4
WGNW/BIL/OR WN5 20 D5
Blenheim St TYLD M29 53 G3
Blewberry Cl LEIGH WN7 52 A4
Bligh Rd WHTN BL5 25 H4
Blindsill Rd FWTH BL4 41 G1
Blissford Cl WGNE/HIN WN2 36 A4
Bloomfield Dr WALK M28 55 F4
Blossom St TYLD M29 53 H2
Bluebell Av RNFD/HAY WA11 68 B2
Blue Bell Av WGNNW/ST WN6 21 G2
Blundell La HOR/BR BL6 7 F5
Blundell Ms WGNS/IIMK WN3 33 E4
Blundells Ct WGNS/IIMK WN3 33 E4
Blythewood SKEL WN8 29 H1
Boars Head Av
WGNNW/ST WN6 10 D3
Boatmans Rw TYLD M29 67 F2
Bodden St GOL/RIS/CUL WA3 63 H5
Bodmin Dr WGNE/HIN WN2 49 F2
Bodmin Rd TYLD M29 54 A3
Bogburn La CHLY/EC PR7 5 E1
Bolderwood Dr
WGNE/HIN WN2 36 A4
Bold St LEIGH WN7 65 E1
WGNW/BIL/OR WN5 33 F3
Bolney St WGNE/HIN WN2 23 F3
Bolton Cl GOL/RIS/CUL WA3 72 A1
Bolton House Rd
WGNE/HIN WN2 50 C4
Bolton Old Rd ATH M46 39 F5
Bolton Rd AIMK WN4 61 E3
ATH M46 39 F4
BOLS/LL BL3 27 E3
WGNE/HIN WN2 24 A1
WHTN BL5 26 A5
Bolton Sq WGN WN1 3 G3
Bolton St AIMK WN4 60 A1
Bombay Rd
WGNW/BIL/OR WN5 20 D5
Bond St ATH M46 53 G2
LEIGH WN7 65 E1
Bonnywell Rd LEIGH WN7 65 E3
Boothsbank Av WALK M28 55 G5
Booth's Brow Rd AIMK WN4 47 E5
Booth's Hall WALK M28 55 G5
Booth's Hall Gv WALK M28 55 G5
Booth's Hall Rd WALK M28 55 G5
Bor Av WGNS/IIMK WN3 34 A4
Borden Cl WGNE/HIN WN2 3 K1
Border Brook La WALK M28 55 F4
Bores Hl WGN WN1 6 B3
Borron Rd NEWLW WA12 69 E4
Borrowdale Rd
WGNW/BIL/OR WN5 * 32 C1
Borsdane Av WGNE/HIN WN2 36 B4
Boscombe Pl WGNE/HIN WN2 36 B4
Boston Cl GOL/RIS/CUL WA3 73 E5
Boston Gv LEIGH WN7 51 H2
Boswell Pl WGNS/IIMK WN3 33 G4
Botany Cl WGNE/HIN WN2 23 F3
Botesworth Cl WGNE/HIN WN2 37 E3
Boughey St LEIGH WN7 64 D1
Boundary La WGNNW/ST WN6 4 B4
Boundary St LEIGH WN7 65 G2
TYLD M29 53 H2
WGN WN1 3 F7
Bournbrook Av LHULT M38 41 F2
Bourne Av GOL/RIS/CUL WA3 71 E1
Bourton Ct TYLD M29 54 C2
Bowden Cl GOL/RIS/CUL WA3 73 E5
LEIGH WN7 65 H4
Bowker St WALK M28 41 G5
Bowland Av AIMK WN4 61 E2
GOL/RIS/CUL WA3 62 D5
The Bowlings WGNNW/ST WN6 21 H3
Bowness Pl WGNE/HIN WN2 23 G5
Bow Rd LEIGH WN7 65 G3
Bowyer Gdns BOLS/LL BL3 27 G2
Boyd Cl WGNNW/ST WN6 10 C2
Boydell St LEIGH WN7 52 A5
Brabazon Pl
WGNW/BIL/OR WN5 20 D5
Bracken Lea WHTN BL5 38 A3
Bracken Rd ATH M46 53 F1
LEIGH WN7 64 A1
Brackley Av TYLD M29 54 A2
Brackley Rd WHTN BL5 27 H5
Brackley St WALK M28 41 H4
Braddyll Rd WHTN BL5 27 G5
Bradford St WGNS/IIMK WN3 2 D7
Bradley La WGNNW/ST WN6 5 G5
Bradshaw Cl WGNNW/ST WN6 10 A1
Bradshawgate LEIGH WN7 65 E1
WGN WN1 3 F5
Bradshaw St ATH M46 39 E5
WGN WN1 3 F1
WGNW/BIL/OR WN5 32 B2
Bradwell Rd GOL/RIS/CUL WA3 71 F2
Braeburn Ct LEIGH WN7 64 C1
Braemar La WALK M28 55 G5
Braemore Cl WGNS/IIMK WN3 46 D1
Braeside Crs
WGNW/BIL/OR WN5 58 C1
Braidhaven WGNNW/ST WN6 8 D3
Braithwaite WGNNW/ST WN6 9 F4
Braithwaite Rd
GOL/RIS/CUL WA3 63 E5
Brakesmere Gv WALK M28 41 F4
Bramble Cft HOR/BR BL6 26 B2
Bramble Gv
WGNW/BIL/OR WN5 33 F1
The Brambles AIMK WN4 60 A1
Bramblewood WGNE/HIN WN2 36 C1
Brambling Dr WHTN BL5 37 G2
Brambling Wy
GOL/RIS/CUL WA3 71 F2
Bramford Cl WHTN BL5 37 H2
Bramhall Rd SKEL WN8 17 E3
Brampton Cl WGNE/HIN WN2 49 E2
Brampton Rd BOLS/LL BL3 27 H2
Brampton St ATH M46 * 39 E5
Brancaster Dr
GOL/RIS/CUL WA3 71 H2
Branch St WGNE/HIN WN2 35 F1
Branch Wy RNFD/HAY WA11 68 A3
Brancker St WHTN BL5 26 D5
Brandon Cl SKEL WN8 30 D1
Brandreth Pl WGNNW/ST WN6 10 C1
Brandwood Cl WALK M28 55 F3
Bransdale Cl BOLS/LL BL3 27 G1
Bransdale Dr AIMK WN4 61 G3
Bransfield Cl WGNS/IIMK WN3 33 H5
Bransford Cl AIMK WN4 61 F4
Branson Cl GOL/RIS/CUL WA3 62 B4
Branthwaite WGNE/HIN WN2 23 G4
Bratton Cl WGNS/IIMK WN3 46 D2
Brayford Dr WGNE/HIN WN2 12 D5
Brayton Ct WGNE/HIN WN2 36 A2
Brazley Av HOR/BR BL6 14 D1
Breaktemper WHTN BL5 25 H4
Breaston Av LEIGH WN7 65 H3
Brecon Cl WGNE/HIN WN2 49 G1
Brecon Dr WGNE/HIN WN2 36 D5
Breeze Hl ATH M46 39 G3
WGNNW/ST WN6 11 E3
Breeze Hill Rd ATH M46 39 H3
Brentwood
WGNW/BIL/OR WN5 33 E3
Brentwood Gv LEIGH WN7 52 A4
Bretherton Rw WGN WN1 2 C5
Bretherton St WGNE/HIN WN2 35 H3
Brett Rd WALK M28 55 E5
Brewery La LEIGH WN7 65 F1
Briar Cl AIMK WN4 60 D2
WGNE/HIN WN2 37 E4
Briarcroft Dr ATH M46 52 B2
Briar Gv LEIGH WN7 51 H3
Briar Hill Av LHULT M38 40 D4
Briar Hill Cl LHULT M38 40 D4
Briar Hill Gv LHULT M38 40 D4
Briarly WGNNW/ST WN6 10 D3
Briar Rd GOL/RIS/CUL WA3 70 C1
WGNW/BIL/OR WN5 33 E1
Briars Gn SKEL WN8 17 F1
Briary Dr TYLD M29 54 A3
Brick Kiln La WGN WN1 2 D3
Brideoake St LEIGH WN7 65 G2
Bridge End WGNS/IIMK WN3 2 A5
Bridgehall Dr SKEL WN8 31 E1
Bridgeman Ter WGN WN1 2 C2
Bridge's St ATH M46 52 C1
Bridge St GOL/RIS/CUL WA3 70 B2
WGNE/HIN WN2 36 A2
WGNS/IIMK WN3 2 C7
Bridgewater Rd WALK M28 55 F4
Bridgewater St LHULT M38 41 G4
WGNE/HIN WN2 36 B2
WGNS/IIMK WN3 2 B6
WGNW/BIL/OR WN5 33 G2
Brierfield SKEL WN8 30 A3
Brierfield Av ATH M46 38 D4
Briggs St LEIGH WN7 51 H4
Bright St LEIGH WN7 51 H4
Brignall Gv GOL/RIS/CUL WA3 63 E5
Briksdal Wy HOR/BR BL6 15 H3
Brimfield Av TYLD M29 54 B2
Brindlehurst Dr TYLD M29 54 C4
Brindle St TYLD M29 53 H2
WGNE/HIN WN2 36 C1
Brindley Av WALK M28 55 F5
Brindley Cl ATH M46 52 B1
Brindley St WALK M28 55 E5
WGNW/BIL/OR WN5 32 D3
Brinksway BOL BL1 15 H3
Brinsop Hall La WHTN BL5 13 H4
Bristle Hall Wy WHTN BL5 26 A3
Britannia Rd
WGNW/BIL/OR WN5 20 D5
Broadacre SKEL WN8 30 D2
WGNNW/ST WN6 4 B5
Broadheath Cl WHTN BL5 26 B4
Broadhurst La
WGNNW/ST WN6 4 A1
Broadlands WGNNW/ST WN6 9 G4
Broad La RNFD/HAY WA11 58 A4
Broadley Av GOL/RIS/CUL WA3 70 D2
Broadoak Av WALK M28 55 E4
Broadriding Rd
WGNNW/ST WN6 8 D4
Broad Wk WHTN BL5 37 H1
Broadway ATH M46 39 G3
WGNE/HIN WN2 36 D3
Broadwell Dr LEIGH WN7 64 D5
Broadwood HOR/BR BL6 15 H3
Brockhurst Wk
WGNS/IIMK WN3 33 H3
Brock Mill La WGN WN1 22 B1
Brock Pl WGNE/HIN WN2 49 E1
Brockstedes Av AIMK WN4 47 F5
Brock St WGN WN1 3 H5
Brocstedes Rd AIMK WN4 47 E4
Brogden Av GOL/RIS/CUL WA3 72 D5
Bromilow Rd SKEL WN8 16 B4
Bromley Av GOL/RIS/CUL WA3 71 E2
Bromley Cl WGNE/HIN WN2 23 F3
Bromley Dr LEIGH WN7 51 G3
Bronte Cl WGNS/IIMK WN3 33 H3
Brook Cl TYLD M29 53 H1
Brookdale ATH M46 39 G2
Brookdale Pk LHULT M38 * 41 G2
Brookdale Rd WGNE/HIN WN2 36 C3
Brook Dr TYLD M29 54 B5
Brookfield Dr WALK M28 55 E5
Brookfield Rd
GOL/RIS/CUL WA3 72 B5
SKEL WN8 31 E1
WGNNW/ST WN6 4 C5
Brookfields
WGNW/BIL/OR WN5 * 32 C3
Brookfield St LEIGH WN7 52 B5
Brookhouse Av FWTH BL4 41 H2
Brookhouse St WGN WN1 2 E6
Brookhouse Ter WGN WN1 2 E6
Brookhurst La LHULT M38 40 D2
Brookland Av FWTH BL4 41 H1
WGNE/HIN WN2 36 A3
Brookland Rd WGN WN1 22 A2
Brooklands Av AIMK WN4 61 G4
ATH M46 39 E4
LEIGH WN7 64 D3
Brooklands Dr
WGNW/BIL/OR WN5 31 G3
Brooklands Rd SKEL WN8 31 F1
Brook La RNFD/HAY WA11 44 C4
WGNW/BIL/OR WN5 32 C3
Brook Lynn Av
GOL/RIS/CUL WA3 63 G5
Brook Meadow WHTN BL5 * 26 B5
Brooks Houses LEIGH WN7 51 H3
Brookside WGNS/IIMK WN3 * 33 H3
Brookside Av AIMK WN4 47 G4
FWTH BL4 41 H1
RNFD/HAY WA11 42 D5
Brookside Cl ATH M46 39 F4
WGNW/BIL/OR WN5 58 D2
Brookside Rd WGN WN1 11 E1
Brook St AIMK WN4 61 F4
ATH M46 38 C5
GOL/RIS/CUL WA3 63 H5
GOL/RIS/CUL WA3 70 B2
WGNE/HIN WN2 35 F1
WGNS/IIMK WN3 33 G4
WHTN BL5 * 26 A4
Brookvale WGNNW/ST WN6 21 H4
Brookview WGNE/HIN WN2 36 A4
Broom Av LEIGH WN7 51 H4
Broomfield Pl
WGNNW/ST WN6 10 B1
Broomfield Rd
WGNNW/ST WN6 10 B1
Broomfield Ter WGN WN1 * 3 H6
Broomflat Cl WGNNW/ST WN6 10 B1
Broomhey Av WGN WN1 11 F5
Broomhey Ter WGN WN1 3 H6
Broomholme WGNNW/ST WN6 8 C3
Broom Rd WGNW/BIL/OR WN5 33 E1
Broom Wy WHTN BL5 26 B3
Broseley Av GOL/RIS/CUL WA3 72 C5
Broseley La GOL/RIS/CUL WA3 72 C4
Brotherton Wy NEWLW WA12 69 E5
Brougham St WALK M28 55 H1
Brough Cl WGNE/HIN WN2 36 B5
Broughton Av
GOL/RIS/CUL WA3 71 E2
LHULT M38 41 F4
Brown Heath Av
WGNW/BIL/OR WN5 58 C3
Browning Av ATH M46 39 E3
WGNS/IIMK WN3 33 G4
Browning Gv WGNNW/ST WN6 21 F2
Browning St LEIGH WN7 51 G5
Brownlow Av WGNE/HIN WN2 35 G1
Brownlow La
WGNW/BIL/OR WN5 45 F2
Brownmere WGNNW/ST WN6 21 G3
Brown St TYLD M29 * 53 G4
WGNE/HIN WN2 35 F1
WGNE/HIN WN2 50 B2
WGNS/IIMK WN3 2 B6
Brown St North LEIGH WN7 65 F1
Brown St South LEIGH WN7 65 F2
Broxton Av
WGNW/BIL/OR WN5 32 A1
Brunswick Rd NEWLW WA12 68 C5
Brunswick St LEIGH WN7 65 F2
Bryham St WGN WN1 3 F5
Bryn Gates La WGNE/HIN WN2 48 C3
Brynheys Cl LHULT M38 41 F3
Brynn St WGNE/HIN WN2 49 E4
Bryn Rd AIMK WN4 47 H5
Bryn Rd South AIMK WN4 61 F2
Bryn St AIMK WN4
WGNS/IIMK WN3
Bryony Cl WGNW/BIL/OR WN5
Buchanan Dr WGNE/HIN WN2
Buchanan Rd
WGNW/BIL/OR WN5
Buchanan St LEIGH WN7
Buckfast Av RNFD/HAY WA11
Buckingham Cl
WGNW/BIL/OR WN5
Buckland Dr
WGNW/BIL/OR WN5
Buckley La FWTH BL4
Buckley Sq FWTH BL4
Buckley St WGNNW/ST WN6
Buckley St West
WGNNW/ST WN6
Buck St LEIGH WN7
Buckthorn Cl WHTN BL5
Bude Av TYLD M29
Buer Av WGNS/IIMK WN3
Buile Hill Av LHULT M38
Buile Hill Gv LHULT M38
Bullcroft Dr TYLD M29
Bullough St ATH M46
Bullows Rd LHULT M38
Bulteel St WALK M28
WGNW/BIL/OR WN5
Bunting Cl GOL/RIS/CUL WA3
Bunting Ms WALK M28
Burgess St WGNS/IIMK WN3
Burghley Wy WGNS/IIMK WN3
Burland St WGNW/BIL/OR WN5
Burley Av GOL/RIS/CUL WA3
Burley Crs WGNS/IIMK WN3
Burlington St WGNE/HIN WN2
Burlton Gv WGNE/HIN WN2
Burnaston Gv
WGNW/BIL/OR WN5
Burnden Wy HOR/BR BL6
Burnet Cl TYLD M29
Burnfell GOL/RIS/CUL WA3
Burnham Cl GOL/RIS/CUL WA3
Burnham Gv WGNE/HIN WN2
Burnhill Ct WGNNW/ST WN6 *
Burnsall Av GOL/RIS/CUL WA3
Burns Av ATH M46
LEIGH WN7
Burns Cl AIMK WN4
WGNS/IIMK WN3
WGNW/BIL/OR WN5
Burnside Cl TYLD M29
Burns Rd LHULT M38
WGNE/HIN WN2
Burnvale WGNS/IIMK WN3
Burrington Dr LEIGH WN7
Bursar Cl NEWLW WA12
Burwell Cl LEIGH WN7
Bushey La RNFD/HAY WA11
Butcher St AIMK WN4
Butler St WGN WN1
Buttercup Av WALK M28 *
Buttercup Cl ATH M46
Butterfield Rd WHTN BL5
Buttermere Av AIMK WN4
Buttermere Crs
RNFD/HAY WA11
Buttermere Rd
WGNW/BIL/OR WN5
Butts Av LEIGH WN7
Butts Ct LEIGH WN7
Butts St LEIGH WN7
Buxton Cl ATH M46
Byfleet Cl WGNS/IIMK WN3
Byley Ri WGNNW/ST WN6
Byrness Cl ATH M46
Byrom La GOL/RIS/CUL WA3
Byron Av WGNE/HIN WN2
Byron Cl WGNE/HIN WN2
WGNNW/ST WN6
WGNW/BIL/OR WN5
Byron Gv LEIGH WN7
Byron St LEIGH WN7
Byron Wk FWTH BL4

C

Cadman Gv WGNE/HIN WN2
Cadman's Yd
WGNW/BIL/OR WN5
Cadogan Dr WGNS/IIMK WN3
Caernarvon Rd
WGNE/HIN WN2
Cairn Brae NEWLW WA12
Caister Cl SKEL WN8
Caldbeck Cl AIMK WN4
Caldbeck Dr FWTH BL4
Caldbeck Gv RNFD/HAY WA11
Calder Av WGNE/HIN WN2
Calderbank St
WGNW/BIL/OR WN5
Calderburn Cl HOR/BR BL6
Calder Dr WALK M28
WGNE/HIN WN2
Calder Pl WGNW/BIL/OR WN5
Caldew Cl WGNE/HIN WN2
Caldford Cl WGNE/HIN WN2
Caldwell Av TYLD M29
Caldwell Cl TYLD M29
Caldwell St WHTN BL5
Caleb Cl TYLD M29
Cale La WGNE/HIN WN2
Calico Wood Av
WGNNW/ST WN6
Callander Ct
WGNW/BIL/OR WN5
Calow Dr LEIGH WN7
Calton Cl WGNS/IIMK WN3
Calveley Wk WGNNW/ST WN6
Calverhall Wy AIMK WN4
Calver Hey Cl WHTN BL5
Calverleigh Cl BOLS/LL BL3
Camberwell Crs
WGNE/HIN WN2
Cambourne Dr
WGNE/HIN WN2
Cambrian Crs WGNS/IIMK WN3

idge Rd HOR/BR BL6 15 E2
. WN8 16 D4
IW/BIL/OR WN5 19 H5
idge St ATH M46 52 D1
V WN1 3 F6
idge Wy WGN WN1 3 F6
ot Cl NEWLW WA12 68 C5
on Pl
IW/BIL/OR WN5 21 F5
on St LEIGH WN7 51 G4
St WGNE/HIN WN2 49 F3
ell Rd BOLS/LL BL3 27 H3
ell St
IW/BIL/OR WN5 33 E3
ell Wy WALK M28 41 H5
on Gv AIMK WN4 60 C2
Rd AIMK WN4 60 B3
n GOL/RIS/CUL WA3 72 B1
it CHLY/EC PR7 7 F1
IE/HIN WN2 35 E2
NNW/ST WN6 21 G4
fer WGN WN1 3 H6
rra Rd
IW/BIL/OR WN5 20 D4
re Cl BOLS/LL BL3 27 H2
Fold WALK M28 55 G4
g Cl WGNE/HIN WN2 35 H4
n St ATH M46 39 E5
Cl WGNNW/ST WN6 5 G5
Wilson Cl
D/HAY WA11 68 A3
eld Gv AIMK WN4 60 D2
bury Av
/RIS/CUL WA3 63 E5
bury Cl ATH M46 39 F4
docia Wy WHTN BL5 37 G1
St WGNE/HIN WN2 35 G5
n Fold Rd LHULT M38 41 E3
n Lees Gdns WHTN BL5 26 B5
n Lees Rd WHTN BL5 26 B4
n's La AIMK WN4 61 F3
ood Cl WGNNW/ST WN6 8 C3
nk Av ATH M46 39 E4
nk Sq ATH M46 39 E4
nk St ATH M46 38 C4
s Cl LEIGH WN7 64 D2
St SKEL WN8 16 C4
ss La WGNE/HIN WN2 3 K6
Cl WGNS/IIMK WN3 47 E1
d SKEL WN8 30 B2
rooke Rd LEIGH WN7 53 E5
e St WGNE/HIN WN2 * 36 B2
IW/BIL/OR WN5 33 E2
n Av BOLS/LL BL3 27 H1
L WN8 30 D1
n Cl WALK M28 55 H2
n Gv HOR/BR BL6 14 C1
IE/HIN WN2 36 C5
n Rd GOL/RIS/CUL WA3 63 E5
K M28 55 H2
n St WGNS/IIMK WN3 34 A2
Gv LEIGH WN7 51 F3
ie Dr AIMK WN4 60 D1
rth Av WGNE/HIN WN2 36 D4
istie BOLS/LL BL3 27 H2
e St WGN WN1 3 J5
IS/IIMK WN3 2 B6
ion Dr WGNNW/ST WN6 10 B1
rook Dr ATH M46 39 F4
ommon Rd
IE/HIN WN2 37 G5
eld Av LHULT M38 40 D4
ld Gv LHULT M38 40 D4
gton Gv LEIGH WN7 * 52 A4
gton Rd CHLY/EC PR7 7 E1
gton St LEIGH WN7 52 A4
GOL/RIS/CUL WA3 71 H2
GH WN7 64 D5
IS/IIMK WN3 33 H5
ill Crs
IW/BIL/OR WN5 58 D2
ill Rd
IW/BIL/OR WN5 58 D2
LEIGH WN7 64 B1
IE/HIN WN2 36 A2
WGNE/HIN WN2 49 F2
ell Cl TYLD M29 54 B2
Av RNFD/HAY WA11 56 B1
St WGNS/IIMK WN3 34 D2
ach Gv WALK M28 55 F1
ach La WALK M28 55 E1
el Av WGN WN1 22 A2
el Cl BOLS/LL BL3 27 E3
right Gv LEIGH WN7 51 G2
e Gv WGNE/HIN WN2 37 E4
od Gv HOR/BR BL6 14 C1
les SKEL WN8 * 29 H1
d RNFD/HAY WA11 68 A3
ore Dr WGNE/HIN WN2 36 A4
Dr CHLY/EC PR7 6 D1
Gv LEIGH WN7 53 E5
ney SKEL WN8 30 B2
Hl NEWLW WA12 69 H5
Hill Pk WGNE/HIN WN2 36 C1
Hill Rd WGNE/HIN WN2 36 B2
House La CHLY/EC PR7 6 D1
mere Cl WGNS/IIMK WN3 47 E2
Ri WGNE/HIN WN2 36 B3
St ATH M46 53 G2
IE/HIN WN2 36 B2
ton Wy WGNS/IIMK WN3 46 D1
way WGNE/HIN WN2 36 C3
am Av BOLS/LL BL3 27 G3
ine St LEIGH WN7 52 A5
ine Ter WGN WN1 3 G5
Dr ATH M46 52 B3
e Av GOL/RIS/CUL WA3 70 B2
e Rd WGN WN1 3 G4
e St WGN WN1 3 G5
n Dr RNFD/HAY WA11 68 A2
dish Dr WGNS/IIMK WN3 47 E1
dish St LEIGH WN7 52 A4
r St LEIGH WN7 65 E2
IE/HIN WN2 36 B3
IW/BIL/OR WN5 33 G2
Av GOL/RIS/CUL WA3 72 D5
Cl WGNS/IIMK WN3 47 G1
MK WN4 61 E4
WGNNW/ST WN6 21 H3
LEIGH WN7 65 F2
WGN WN1 3 H5
WGNS/IIMK WN3 34 D4
Cedar Av ATH M46 38 C4
GOL/RIS/CUL WA3 71 G2
HOR/BR BL6 14 D1
WGNE/HIN WN2 36 D4
WGNNW/ST WN6 10 C2
Cedar Dr WGN WN1 22 C3
Cedar Gv AIMK WN4 60 A1
RNFD/HAY WA11 68 B2
SKEL WN8 16 D4
WGNW/BIL/OR WN5 32 A2
WHTN BL5 37 H1
Cedar Rd LEIGH WN7 51 H3
Celandine Wk WGNS/IIMK WN3 32 C4
Cemetery Rd WGNS/IIMK WN3 34 D4
Cemetery St WHTN BL5 25 H4
Cemetery Vw CHLY/EC PR7 7 E1
Central Av ATH M46 39 F4
LEIGH WN7 * 65 H3
WALK M28 41 H3
Central Dr RNFD/HAY WA11 43 E4
WGNNW/ST WN6 9 G4
WHTN BL5 25 H4
Central Flats WGNE/HIN WN2 * 3 K6
Central Park Wy WGN WN1 2 E2
Centre Ct LEIGH WN7 64 A5
Chadbury Cl HOR/BR BL6 26 D2
Chaddock La TYLD M29 54 C5
Chadwick St LEIGH WN7 52 A5
WGNE/HIN WN2 36 B2
WGNS/IIMK WN3 34 A2
Chalbury Cl WGNE/HIN WN2 * 36 A4
Chalfont Dr TYLD M29 53 H4
Challenge Wy
WGNW/BIL/OR WN5 20 D4
Chancery Cl TYLD M29 54 A3
Chandler Wy
GOL/RIS/CUL WA3 71 F1
Chanters Av ATH M46 39 F5
The Chanters WALK M28 55 H4
Chantry Cl WHTN BL5 38 A3
Chantry Wk AIMK WN4 60 C1
Chapel Cl WGNS/IIMK WN3 34 C2
Chapelfield Dr WALK M28 41 G5
Chapel Fields La
WGNE/HIN WN2 36 B3
Chapel Green Rd
WGNE/HIN WN2 36 B2
Chapel La WGNS/IIMK WN3 2 C7
Chapel Meadow WALK M28 55 G4
Chapel Pl AIMK WN4 * 61 E3
Chapelstead WHTN BL5 38 A3
Chapel St AIMK WN4 61 E3
ATH M46 39 E5
CHLY/EC PR7 7 E1
LEIGH WN7 65 F2
RNFD/HAY WA11 68 B3
TYLD M29 * 53 H2
WALK M28 55 E5
WGNE/HIN WN2 23 F2
WGNE/HIN WN2 49 F1
WGNS/IIMK WN3 2 C7
WGNW/BIL/OR WN5 32 C3
Chapel Vw RNFD/HAY WA11 57 G2
Charity St LEIGH WN7 64 B1
Charles St GOL/RIS/CUL WA3 62 B5
LEIGH WN7 65 F1
TYLD M29 53 G2
WGN WN1 3 G2
WGNE/HIN WN2 36 B1
Charlesworth Av
WGNE/HIN WN2 36 C4
Charlock Av WHTN BL5 37 G2
Charlock Cl LEIGH WN7 65 E3
Charlotte Dr WGNS/IIMK WN3 33 E4
Charlton Cl AIMK WN4 60 D2
Charlton Fold WALK M28 41 H3
Charmouth Cl NEWLW WA12 69 E5
Charnock St WGNE/HIN WN2 49 G2
Charnwood Cl TYLD M29 54 A3
WALK M28 55 H1
Charterhouse Rd
WGNS/IIMK WN3 34 C2
Chatburn Av GOL/RIS/CUL WA3 62 D5
Chatham St LEIGH WN7 52 A4
WGN WN1 3 G6
Chatsworth Av
GOL/RIS/CUL WA3 73 E5
WGNS/IIMK WN3 35 E4
Chatsworth Cl AIMK WN4 60 C2
Chatsworth Dr LEIGH WN7 53 F4
Chatsworth St
WGNW/BIL/OR WN5 32 D3
Chatteris Cl WGNE/HIN WN2 36 B4
Chaucer Gv LEIGH WN7 51 F3
Chaucer Pl WGN WN1 22 B2
WGNE/HIN WN2 49 G2
Chedworth Crs LHULT M38 41 F2
Cheetham Gv WGNS/IIMK WN3 33 G3
The Cheethams HOR/BR BL6 13 F3
Chelburn Cl WGNE/HIN WN2 50 B2
Chelford Av GOL/RIS/CUL WA3 71 E2
Chelford Cl WGNS/IIMK WN3 47 G1
Chelford Dr TYLD M29 54 B5
Chelmarsh Av AIMK WN4 61 F3
Chelmer Cl WHTN BL5 26 B4
Chelmorton Gv
WGNS/IIMK WN3 46 D1
Chelmsford Dr
WGNS/IIMK WN3 33 H4
Chelmsford Ms WGN WN1 22 B3
Chelsea Cl WHTN BL5 37 H1
Chelsea Ct WHTN BL5 * 37 G3
Cheltenham Av
WGNS/IIMK WN3 34 C2
Cheltenham Dr NEWLW WA12 69 F4
WGNW/BIL/OR WN5 45 G1
Cheltenham St
WGNE/HIN WN2 23 E3
Chelwood Ms HOR/BR BL6 * 15 G3
Chelwood Pk AIMK WN4 61 E5
Chepstow Gv LEIGH WN7 53 F4
Chequer Cl SKEL WN8 30 C3
Chequer La SKEL WN8 30 C2
Chequers St WGN WN1 2 B5
Cherington Dr TYLD M29 54 B2
Cherrybrook Dr
WGNS/IIMK WN3 47 E2
Cherry Cl NEWLW WA12 68 C5
Cherrycroft SKEL WN8 30 B2
Cherry Gv LEIGH WN7 52 A3
WGNNW/ST WN6 21 G2
Cherry Tree Gv LEIGH WN7 51 G5
ATH M46 38 C4
Cherry Tree La
RNFD/HAY WA11 57 H4
Cherry Tree Rd
GOL/RIS/CUL WA3 71 G1
Cherry Tree Wy HOR/BR BL6 14 D1
Cherrywood Av WHTN BL5 39 H1
Cherrywood Cl WALK M28 55 G3
Chervil Wk WGNS/IIMK WN3 32 D4
Cherwell Cl WGNE/HIN WN2 12 D4
Cherwell Rd WHTN BL5 26 A3
Chester Av GOL/RIS/CUL WA3 71 E1
Chester Dr AIMK WN4 61 G4
Chester Rd TYLD M29 54 C3
Chester St ATH M46 53 F1
LEIGH WN7 65 E1
Chesterton Cl WGNS/IIMK WN3 33 H3
Chestnut Av ATH M46 * 38 D4
LEIGH WN7 64 D3
Chestnut Dr LEIGH WN7 65 E3
WHTN BL5 38 A1
Chestnut Dr South LEIGH WN7 65 E5
Chestnut Gv AIMK WN4 61 G2
GOL/RIS/CUL WA3 71 G1
WGNE/HIN WN2 36 D4
Chestnut La LEIGH WN7 65 E4
Chestnut Rd WGN WN1 3 F1
Chetwode Av AIMK WN4 61 E5
Cheviot Cl WGNS/IIMK WN3 46 D1
Chew Moor La WHTN BL5 26 B3
Chichester Av ATH M46 52 B1
Chilgrove Av HOR/BR BL6 13 E1
Chilham St
WGNW/BIL/OR WN5 32 B2
Chillingham Dr LEIGH WN7 65 G2
Chiltern Av ATH M46 39 G3
Chiltern Cl AIMK WN4 61 E4
Chiltern Dr WGNS/IIMK WN3 32 D5
Chiltern Rd GOL/RIS/CUL WA3 72 D5
Chiltern Wy TYLD M29 54 A3
Chilton Cl LEIGH WN7 52 A4
Chimes Rd AIMK WN4 47 G5
Chinnor Cl LEIGH WN7 52 A4
Chip Hill Rd BOLS/LL BL3 27 H1
Chirton Cl RNFD/HAY WA11 68 A2
Chisacre Dr WGNNW/ST WN6 8 C3
Chisholm Cl WGNNW/ST WN6 4 C5
Chisledon Cl RNFD/HAY WA11 68 A2
Chisnall Av WGNNW/ST WN6 4 A2
Chisnall La WGNNW/ST WN6 4 B2
Chiswell St
WGNW/BIL/OR WN5 32 D3
Chisworth Cl LEIGH WN7 51 H4
Chorley New Rd HOR/BR BL6 14 C1
Chorley Rd HOR/BR BL6 7 F2
WGNNW/ST WN6 11 E4
WHTN BL5 25 F1
Chorley St WGNS/IIMK WN3 34 D2
Chowbent Cl ATH M46 39 F5
Christleton WGNNW/ST WN6 9 G4
Christopher St
WGNS/IIMK WN3 35 E2
Chulsey Gate La HOR/BR BL6 26 B1
Church Av WGNE/HIN WN2 50 C3
Church Dr WGNW/BIL/OR WN5 31 G3
Churchfield WGNNW/ST WN6 9 F4
Church Gates WGN WN1 2 C5
Church Gn SKEL WN8 17 E4
Church Green Gdns
GOL/RIS/CUL WA3 62 B5
Church Gv WGN WN1 * 3 G5
Churchill Av GOL/RIS/CUL WA3 73 G5
Churchlands La
WGNNW/ST WN6 10 C1
Church La GOL/RIS/CUL WA3 71 E2
WGNNW/ST WN6 9 F4
WHTN BL5 25 H2
Church Rd RNFD/HAY WA11 56 B2
RNFD/HAY WA11 68 B3
SKEL WN8 17 E4
TYLD M29 54 B5
WGNE/HIN WN2 35 G5
Churchside FWTH BL4 41 G1
Church St GOL/RIS/CUL WA3 62 C5
HOR/BR BL6 7 H5
LEIGH WN7 65 E1
NEWLW WA12 69 H5
SKEL WN8 31 F1
WGN WN1 2 D4
WGNE/HIN WN2 12 C4
WGNE/HIN WN2 36 A3
WGNNW/ST WN6 10 B1
WGNS/IIMK WN3 35 E2
WGNW/BIL/OR WN5 31 G3
WHTN BL5 25 H4
Churnett Cl WHTN BL5 26 A3
Churton Gv WGNNW/ST WN6 4 C5
Cinnamon Av WGNE/HIN WN2 36 C4
Cinnamon Brow SKEL WN8 31 F2
Cirencester Cl LHULT M38 41 F2
City Rd WALK M28 55 F3
WGNW/BIL/OR WN5 32 C1
Clanwood Cl WGNS/IIMK WN3 47 F1
Clap Gate La WGNS/IIMK WN3 33 F5
Claremont Av WGNE/HIN WN2 36 C3
Claremont Dr LHULT M38 41 G3
Claremont Rd
GOL/RIS/CUL WA3 72 C5
WGNW/BIL/OR WN5 58 D1
Clarence St AIMK WN4 60 C2
ATH M46 53 F2
GOL/RIS/CUL WA3 62 B5
LEIGH WN7 65 G2
NEWLW WA12 68 C5
WGNE/HIN WN2 35 F1
Clarence Yd WGN WN1 2 C5
Clarington Gv WGN WN1 3 G6
Clarke Av GOL/RIS/CUL WA3 73 E5
Clarke Crs LHULT M38 40 C2
Clarke St LEIGH WN7 64 D2
Claude St WGNW/BIL/OR WN5 33 E2
Claughton Av WALK M28 55 H3
Claybridge Cl
WGNW/BIL/OR WN5 20 C4
Claybrook Cl ATH M46 52 B1
Clay Brow Rd SKEL WN8 30 B2
Claydon Dr WGNS/IIMK WN3 35 E4
Clayhill Gv GOL/RIS/CUL WA3 72 A1
Claypool Rd HOR/BR BL6 14 D1
Clayton Av GOL/RIS/CUL WA3 71 F1
Clayton House LEIGH WN7 64 B1
Clayton Ms SKEL WN8 16 C4
Clayton St SKEL WN8 16 C4
WGNS/IIMK WN3 2 A5
Clegg's La LHULT M38 41 F3
Clegg St SKEL WN8 16 C4
TYLD M29 53 H5
Clement Av ATH M46 52 B1
Clevedon Dr WGNS/IIMK WN3 32 D4
Cleveland Av WGNS/IIMK WN3 46 D1
Cleveland Dr AIMK WN4 61 F2
GOL/RIS/CUL WA3 71 E1
Cleworth Cl TYLD M29 67 F2
Clifford Rd BOLS/LL BL3 * 27 H3
Clifford St LEIGH WN7 65 G2
Clifton Av TYLD M29 54 B5
Clifton Crs WGN WN1 22 B3
Clifton Dr HOR/BR BL6 7 G4
Cliftonmill Mdw
GOL/RIS/CUL WA3 70 A1
Clifton Rd AIMK WN4 47 G5
LEIGH WN7 64 D5
WGNW/BIL/OR WN5 58 C2
Clifton St LEIGH WN7 64 C1
TYLD M29 54 D3
WGN WN1 2 D2
Clive Rd WHTN BL5 37 H2
Clock Tower Cl WALK M28 41 E5
Cloister Av LEIGH WN7 51 G2
The Cloisters WHTN BL5 37 H3
Clondberry Cl TYLD M29 54 D2
Closebrook Rd
WGNW/BIL/OR WN5 33 E2
Close La WGNE/HIN WN2 36 C5
Close St WGNE/HIN WN2 36 C2
The Close ATH M46 39 G3
Cloudstock Gv LHULT M38 40 D3
Clough Av WHTN BL5 26 A5
Clough Gv AIMK WN4 60 C1
Clough House Dr LEIGH WN7 65 G1
The Clough AIMK WN4 60 A2
Cloughwood Crs
WGNNW/ST WN6 8 C3
Clovelly Av LEIGH WN7 52 A3
Cloverdale Dr AIMK WN4 61 F4
Clover St WGNNW/ST WN6 21 H3
Club St RNFD/HAY WA11 57 H5
Clyde Rd TYLD M29 54 B4
Clyde St LEIGH WN7 * 65 G2
Coach House Dr
WGNNW/ST WN6 9 G4
Coach Rd TYLD M29 54 B5
Coach St ATH M46 39 E5
Coal Pit La ATH M46 38 C5
ORM L39 28 B4
WGNE/HIN WN2 51 E2
Cobden St NEWLW WA12 69 G5
TYLD M29 53 H2
Cob Moor Av
WGNW/BIL/OR WN5 45 G2
Cob Moor Rd
WGNW/BIL/OR WN5 45 G2
Cocker St LHULT M38 41 F4
Code La WHTN BL5 25 E1
Colburn Cl WGNS/IIMK WN3 47 H1
Colby Rd WGNS/IIMK WN3 34 A5
Coldalhurst La TYLD M29 67 E1
Coldstone Dr AIMK WN4 60 A2
Cole Av NEWLW WA12 69 F5
Coleclough Pl
GOL/RIS/CUL WA3 73 E5
Coleridge Av
WGNW/BIL/OR WN5 32 B2
Coleridge Rd
WGNW/BIL/OR WN5 45 G2
Colerne Wy WGNS/IIMK WN3 47 E1
Colesbourne Cl LHULT M38 41 F2
Coleshill Ri WGNS/IIMK WN3 46 D1
Colin St WGN WN1 2 E2
Colinton SKEL WN8 30 B1
Collard St ATH M46 38 C4
College Av WGN WN1 2 D6
College Rd SKEL WN8 19 E4
College St LEIGH WN7 65 F1
Collett Cl WGN WN1 3 G5
Colliers Cl LEIGH WN7 64 D3
Collier St WGNE/HIN WN2 36 A2
Colliery La ATH M46 38 B4
Collinge St WGNE/HIN WN2 49 F1
Collingwood St
WGNNW/ST WN6 10 B1
Collingwood Wy WHTN BL5 25 H4
Collins La WHTN BL5 38 A2
Collisdene Rd
WGNW/BIL/OR WN5 31 G2
Colnbrook WGNNW/ST WN6 9 G1
Coltsfoot Cl LEIGH WN7 65 G1
Colwyn Dr WGNE/HIN WN2 51 F1
Colwyn Gv ATH M46 38 D3
Combermere Cl TYLD M29 54 A2
Comet Rd WGNW/BIL/OR WN5 20 D5
Commodore Pl
WGNW/BIL/OR WN5 21 F4
Common End CHLY/EC PR7 6 D3
Common La GOL/RIS/CUL WA3 72 C5
LEIGH WN7 64 A2
TYLD M29 53 H2
Common Nook
WGNE/HIN WN2 35 F2
Common Side Rd WALK M28 55 E4
Common St WHTN BL5 37 E1
The Common CHLY/EC PR7 6 D2
Commonwealth Cl LEIGH WN7 65 F3
Concord Av WGNS/IIMK WN3 34 A5
Congresbury Rd LEIGH WN7 51 G4
Coningsby Gdns
GOL/RIS/CUL WA3 71 F1
Coniston Av AIMK WN4 61 E2
ATH M46 39 E3
FWTH BL4 40 D1
LHULT M38 41 F4
WGN WN1 22 A2
WGNE/HIN WN2 35 G1
WGNW/BIL/OR WN5 32 A1
Coniston Dr WGNE/HIN WN2 49 G3
Coniston Gv LHULT M38 41 F4
Coniston Park Dr
WGNNW/ST WN6 10 D3
Coniston Rd TYLD M29 53 H4
WGNE/HIN WN2 36 B4
Coniston St LEIGH WN7 64 D1
Coniston Wy RNFD/HAY WA11 43 E1
Conrad Cl WGNS/IIMK WN3 34 A3
Constantia St WGNS/IIMK WN3 35 E5
Conway Cl LEIGH WN7 53 F4
Conway Crs
WGNW/BIL/OR WN5 45 H5
Conway Dr WGNE/HIN WN2 24 A1
WGNW/BIL/OR WN5 59 E1
Conway Rd AIMK WN4 61 H1
WGNE/HIN WN2 36 C4
Conway St
WGNW/BIL/OR WN5 32 D3
Cook Av RNFD/HAY WA11 68 B2
Cooke St AIMK WN4 47 G5
Cook St LEIGH WN7 65 E1
WGNE/HIN WN2 49 F2
Cooling La TYLD M29 53 E3
Coombe Cl TYLD M29 54 A3
Co-operative St LEIGH WN7 64 C1
LHULT M38 * 40 D3
Coopers Gin WGNE/HIN WN2 23 F5
Coop St WGN WN1 3 F3
Copeland Dr WGNNW/ST WN6 5 G5
Copesthorne Cl
WGNE/HIN WN2 12 D4
Coplow Dl WGNE/HIN WN2 36 B5
Copperas Cl WGNNW/ST WN6 9 F3
Copperas La WGNE/HIN WN2 12 B4
Copperbeech Dr
WGNNW/ST WN6 11 E3
Copperfield WGN WN1 2 C1
Copperfields HOR/BR BL6 26 C2
Coppice Cl HOR/BR BL6 26 B2
Coppice Dr WGNS/IIMK WN3 33 G5
WGNW/BIL/OR WN5 45 G1
Coppull La WGN WN1 2 E1
Coppull Moor La CHLY/EC PR7 5 E1
The Copse NEWLW WA12 68 D5
WGNW/BIL/OR WN5 32 B2
Coral Gv LEIGH WN7 64 D2
Coralin Wy AIMK WN4 47 G5
Coral St WGNNW/ST WN6 21 H2
Corfe Cl WGNE/HIN WN2 13 E5
Corhampton Crs ATH M46 39 F3
Cormorant Cl LHULT M38 41 H5
Cornbrook SKEL WN8 30 B1
Cornbrook Cl WHTN BL5 37 G2
Cornelian Gv AIMK WN4 60 C1
Corner Brook HOR/BR BL6 26 B2
Cornergate WHTN BL5 37 H3
Corner La LEIGH WN7 51 G1
Cornlea Dr WALK M28 55 H4
Corn St LEIGH WN7 64 C1
Cornwall Av TYLD M29 39 H5
WHTN BL5 27 G5
Cornwall Crs WGN WN1 11 E1
Cornwall Dr WGNE/HIN WN2 36 C2
Cornwallis Rd WGNS/IIMK WN3 33 H3
Cornwall Pl
WGNW/BIL/OR WN5 32 D2
Coronation Av ATH M46 38 D3
GOL/RIS/CUL WA3 73 H2
Coronation Dr LEIGH WN7 53 E5
RNFD/HAY WA11 68 D2
Coronation Rd
WGNNW/ST WN6 21 E2
Coronation St AIMK WN4 47 F5
WGNS/IIMK WN3 34 A2
Coronation Wk
WGNW/BIL/OR WN5 58 C2
Coronet Cl WGNNW/ST WN6 8 B3
Corporation St
WGNS/IIMK WN3 34 A2
Corrie St LHULT M38 41 F4
Corsey Rd WGNE/HIN WN2 36 B4
Corsock Dr WGN WN1 3 H2
Corston Gv HOR/BR BL6 13 E1
Cosgate Cl WGNW/BIL/OR WN5 31 H3
Costessey Wy WGNS/IIMK WN3 32 D5
Cosworth Cl LEIGH WN7 65 G2
Cotswold Av GOL/RIS/CUL WA3 71 E3
WGNW/BIL/OR WN5 32 C3
Cottesmore Wy
GOL/RIS/CUL WA3 62 C5
Cotton St LEIGH WN7 64 C1
Coultshead Av
WGNW/BIL/OR WN5 45 H5
Council Av AIMK WN4 61 E3
County Police St
WGNE/HIN WN2 3 K6
County Rd LHULT M38 41 F4
Coupes Gn WHTN BL5 37 H2
Coupland Rd WGNE/HIN WN2 37 E4
Courier Pl WGNW/BIL/OR WN5 21 F4
Courtyard Dr WALK M28 41 F5
Coverdale Cl WGNE/HIN WN2 49 E1
Coverdale Rd WHTN BL5 25 G5
The Coverts WGNNW/ST WN6 21 G3
Cowburn St LEIGH WN7 64 C1
WGNE/HIN WN2 36 C1
Cowdals Rd HOR/BR BL6 26 C1
Cow Lees WHTN BL5 26 B4
Cowling St WGNS/IIMK WN3 34 A2
Cowper St LEIGH WN7 64 C1
Coxfield WGNNW/ST WN6 8 C3
Cox Wy ATH M46 39 E5
Crab Tree La ATH M46 53 E1
Crabtree Rd
WGNW/BIL/OR WN5 33 E1
Crag Gv RNFD/HAY WA11 58 A5
Cramond Cl WGNS/IIMK WN3 33 E4
Cranberry Av WGNNW/ST WN6 21 G2
Cranberry Dr BOLS/LL BL3 27 G1
Cranborne Cl HOR/BR BL6 15 E1
WGNNW/ST WN6 10 A1
Cranbrook Av AIMK WN4 60 D2
Cranbrook Wy WGN WN1 22 A1
Cranby St WGNE/HIN WN2 36 A3
Crane St CHLY/EC PR7 5 E1
Cranfield Rd HOR/BR BL6 14 C3
WGNS/IIMK WN3 33 H5
Cranham Av GOL/RIS/CUL WA3 71 F2
Cranham Close Crs
LHULT M38 * 41 F2
Crank Hl RNFD/HAY WA11 57 F2

Crank Rd RNFD/HAY WA11 ....57 F4
WCNW/BIL/OR WN5 ....45 G2
Crankwood Rd LEIGH WN7 ....63 F2
WCNE/HIN WN2 ....49 C5
Cranleigh WGNNW/ST WN6 ......10 C2
Cranleigh Cl HOR/BR BL6 ....13 E1
Cranleigh Dr TYLD M29 ....54 A3
Cranshaw St TYLD M29 ....54 C5
Cranstal Dr WCNE/HIN WN2 ......36 D3
Cranwell Av GOL/RIS/CUL WA3 ...73 E5
Cranworth Av TYLD M29 ....53 H5
Craven Av GOL/RIS/CUL WA3 .....71 F2
Crawford Av CHLY/EC PR7 ....6 D2
   TYLD M29 ....9 H5
   WCNE/HIN WN2 ....12 D5
Crawford Pl WCN WN1 * 22 C2
Crawford Rd SKEL WN8 ....44 A1
Crawford St WCN WN1 ....2 C5
   WCNE/HIN WN2 ....23 H1
Crawley Cl TYLD M29 ....54 B2
Crediton Dr WCNE/HIN WN2 ......49 F2
Crescent Av AIMK WN4 ....60 D2
   FWTH BL4 ....41 H2
   WHTN BL5 ....27 H5
Crescent Dr LHULT M38 ....41 G3
Crescent Rd BOLS/LL BL6 ....14 D2
The Crescent HOR/BR BL6 ....16 C1
   WCNE/HIN WN2 ....35 G1
   WCNW/BIL/OR WN5 ....31 H1
   WHTN BL5 ....37 H1
Cressell Pk WGN WN1 ....4 B5
Cressingham Rd BOLS/LL BL3 ....27 H2
Crestfield Gv WCNE/HIN WN2 ....21 G3
Crestfold LHULT M38 ....41 F4
Crestwood Av
   WCNS/IIMK WN3 ....33 F5
Creswick Cl WCNE/HIN WN2 ......35 H4
Cricketers Wy WHTN BL5 ....26 D5
Cricketfield La WALK M28 ....41 H5
Cricket St WCNNW/ST WN6 ....21 H5
Cringle Cl BOLS/LL BL3 ....27 F1
Crippen St ATH M46 ....52 B2
Cripple Ga WCNNW/ST WN6 ......14 B5
Croal Av WCNE/HIN WN2 ....49 F1
Croft Av ATH M46 ....39 E5
   GOL/RIS/CUL WA3 ....62 A4
   WCNW/BIL/OR WN5 ....31 G3
Croft Ct LEIGH WN7 ....64 B1
Croft Gv LHULT M38 ....41 E5
Croftlands WCNW/BIL/OR WN5 ...31 C4
Croft Pl TYLD M29 ....53 G3
Croft St GOL/RIS/CUL WA3 * 70 B1
   LHULT M38 ....41 E3
   WHTN BL5 ....25 H2
The Croft WCNW/BIL/OR WN5 ....31 G4
Croftwood Sq
   WCNE/HIN WN5 ....20 D3
Crombouke Dr LEIGH WN7 ....51 H2
Crombouke Fold WALK M28 ......55 G4
Cromedale Crs
   WCNNW/ST WN6 ....10 D3
Cromer Dr ATH M46 ....52 B1
Cromer Rd WCNS/IIMK WN3 .....33 F5
Cromford Dr
   GOL/RIS/CUL WA3 ....32 C3
Crompton Rd HOR/BR BL6 ....15 E2
Crompton St WCN WN1 ....2 D4
   WCNE/HIN WN2 ....35 E5
Crompton Wy
   GOL/RIS/CUL WA3 ....72 A1
Cromwell Cl NEWLW WA12 ......68 D5
Crookall St AIMK WN4 ....61 F2
Crooke Rd WCNNW/ST WN6 ......5 D3
Crookhurst Av
   WCNW/BIL/OR WN5 ....45 G5
Crook St WGN WN1 ....2 E4
   WCNE/HIN WN2 ....36 A4
Cropton Wy WCNE/HIN WN2 .....36 C5
Crosby St ATH M46 ....39 E5
Crossdale Rd WCNE/HIN WN2 ....36 D4
Crossdale Wy RNFD/HAY WA11 ...58 A5
Crossfield Dr WCNE/HIN WN2 ....37 F5
Crossfield Rd SKEL WN8 ....17 H5
Crossford Cl WCNS/IIMK WN3 ....33 E4
Crossford Dr BOLS/LL BL3 ....27 F1
Crossgill TYLD M29 ....67 H1
Crosslands Rd WALK M28 ....55 E4
Cross La WCNW/BIL/OR WN5 ....31 G5
Cross Pit La RNFD/HAY WA11 ....43 E5
Cross St ATH M46 ....38 C4
   GOL/RIS/CUL WA3 ....70 B2
   LEIGH WN7 ....65 F2
   TYLD M29 * 53 H2
   WCNE/HIN WN2 ....36 A3
   WCNNW/ST WN6 ....10 B1
   WCNS/IIMK WN3 ....2 C7
   WCNW/BIL/OR WN5 * 32 C2
Crossway WALK WN4 ....61 H1
Croston St WCNE/HIN WN2 ......35 H2
Crowborough Cl HOR/BR BL6 ....15 F1
Crowhurst Dr WCN WN1 ....22 A2
Crow La SKEL WN8 ....18 C2
Crow La East NEWLW WA12 .....69 E5
Crow La West NEWLW WA12 ....68 D5
Crown Fields Cl NEWLW WA12 ...69 E5
Crown Gdns NEWLW WA12 ......69 E5
Crown Gv LEIGH WN7 ....53 E5
Crown Park Dr NEWLW WA12 ...64 A5
Crown St ATH M46 ....38 D5
   WCNS/IIMK WN3 ....34 A2
Crow Orchard Rd
   WCNNW/ST WN6 ....4 A5
Crowther Dr WCNS/IIMK WN3 ...47 F2
Crow Wood Rd
   GOL/RIS/CUL WA3 ....63 E5
Croxteth Dr RNFD/HAY WA11 ...43 E4
Croydon Av LEIGH WN7 ....52 A3
Crummock Dr
   WCNS/IIMK WN3 ....33 C5
Crummock Rd FWTH BL4 ....40 D1
Crystal Cl WCNE/HIN WN2 ....49 G2
Culcheth Av WCNE/HIN WN2 ....49 G2
Culcheth Hall Dr
   GOL/RIS/CUL WA3 ....73 E5
Culcross Av WCNS/IIMK WN3 ...32 D4
Cullen Cl WCNE/HIN WN2 ....23 F5
Culraven WCNE/HIN WN2 * 12 C3
Culvert St WCNNW/ST WN6 .....21 H3
Culzean Cl LEIGH WN7 ....65 G2

Cumberbatch Pl
   WCNS/IIMK WN3 ....35 E4
Cumberland Av TYLD M29 ....53 C1
Cumberland Rd ATH M46 ....39 F4
Cumberland St WGN WN1 ....3 G2
Cumbrian Cl WCNE/HIN WN2 ....49 G1
Cunliffe Av NEWLW WA12 ....69 E4
Cunliffe Ct LEIGH WN7 ....63 H2
Cunliffe St LEIGH WN7 ....64 B1
Cunningham Rd WHTN BL5 ......37 F1
Curlew Cl GOL/RIS/CUL WA3 ....71 E1
Curtis St WCNW/BIL/OR WN5 ....33 E2
Cutacre Cl TYLD M29 ....44 A2
Cutacre La WHTN BL5 ....40 C2
Cuthbert St BOLS/LL BL3 ....27 H5
Cygnet St WCNS/IIMK WN3 ......34 A2
Cypress Rd
   WCNW/BIL/OR WN5 ....33 F2

D

Dagmar St WALK M28 ....41 H4
Dalton Rd SKEL WN8 ....30 D1
Dairy Farm Rd
   RNFD/HAY WA11 ....42 C4
Daisybank Cl WCNE/HIN WN2 ....36 A3
Daisyfield HOR/BR BL6 * 14 C1
Daisy Hall Dr WHTN BL5 ....37 H5
Daisyhill Ct WHTN BL5 ....38 A5
Daisy Rd WCNW/BIL/OR WN5 ....33 F2
Dakins Rd LEIGH WN7 ....65 G4
Dalbeatie Ri WGN WN1 ....3 J2
Dalby Rd WCNE/HIN WN2 ....37 E3
Dalebank ATH M46 ....55 H1
Dalecrest WCNW/BIL/OR WN5 ...45 G2
Dalegarth Av BOL BL1 ....15 H3
Dale Gv LEIGH WN7 ....64 B2
Dalehead Gv LEIGH WN7 ....64 B2
Dalehead Pl RNFD/HAY WA11 ...58 A5
Dale Lee WHTN BL5 ....38 A5
Dale Rd GOL/RIS/CUL WA3 ......70 B2
Dalesford Ct LEIGH WN7 ....72 B1
Daleside Av AIMK WN4 ....47 H5
Dale St LEIGH WN7 ....64 B1
   WCNS/IIMK WN3 ....38 B5
   WHTN BL5 ....38 A5
Dale St East HOR/BR BL6 ....14 C1
Dale Vw NEWLW WA12 ....69 H5
Dalkeith Rd WCNE/HIN WN2 ....36 D3
Dalston Dr RNFD/HAY WA11 .....58 A5
Dalston Gv WCNS/IIMK WN3 ....33 F5
Dalton Dr WGNS/IIMK WN3 .....33 C1
Dalton Fold WHTN BL5 ....26 A5
Dalton Gv WCNE/HIN WN2 ......49 F5
Dalwood Cl WCNE/HIN WN2 ....36 C4
Damian Dr NEWLW WA12 ....68 D4
Dam La AIMK WN4 ....62 A3
Dams Head Fold WHTN BL5 ....26 A4
Danbers SKEL WN8 ....30 C2
Danebury Ct WCNE/HIN WN2 * ..36 A4
Danes Av WCNE/HIN WN2 ....36 B2
Danes Brook Cl
   WCNE/HIN WN2 ....36 B2
Danesbury Cl
   WCNW/BIL/OR WN5 ....58 D2
Danes Gn WCNE/HIN WN2 ......36 B1
Danesway WGN WN1 ....22 A2
Daniels La SKEL WN8 ....29 H1
Darby La WCNE/HIN WN2 ....36 C1
Darfield SKEL WN8 ....30 C1
Daric Cl LEIGH WN7 ....64 B5
Dark La HOR/BR BL6 ....7 G4
Darley Rd WCNS/IIMK WN3 .....34 A5
Darlington St TYLD M29 ....53 H2
Darlington St East TYLD M29 ....54 A2
   WGN WN1 ....3 F6
Darnhall St WGNS/IIMK WN3 * ..35 E4
Darnley Av WALK M28 ....55 H2
Darran Av WCNS/IIMK WN3 .....33 F5
Dartington Rd WCNE/HIN WN2 ..35 G1
Darvel Av AIMK WN4 ....49 H2
David Brow BOLS/LL BL3 ....27 H3
Davies Av NEWLW WA12 ....69 F5
Dashes St WCNE/HIN WN2 ......49 F1
Dawber Delph
   WCNNW/ST WN6 ....8 C2
Dawber St AIMK WN4 ....61 G2
Dawley Cl AIMK WN4 ....60 D5
Dawlish Wy GOL/RIS/CUL WA3 ..69 F5
Dawnwood Sq
   WCNW/BIL/OR WN5 ....20 D3
Dawson Av WGNNW/ST WN6 ....35 H2
Dawson St ATH M46 ....38 D5
Daybrook SKEL WN8 ....30 C1
Dayfield SKEL WN8 ....30 C1
Deakin St WGNS/IIMK WN3 * ...34 D5
Dealey Rd BOLS/LL BL3 ....27 H1
Dean Cl SKEL WN8 ....31 F1
   WCNW/BIL/OR WN5 ....58 C5
Dean Crs WCNW/BIL/OR WN5 ...20 B5
Dean Meadow NEWLW WA12 ...69 E5
Dean Rd GOL/RIS/CUL WA3 .....70 B2
Deansgate WCNE/HIN WN2 .....36 A4
Dean Wood Av
   WCNW/BIL/OR WN5 ....19 H4
Dearden Av LHULT M38 ....41 F3
Debdale La TYLD M29 ....66 C2
Deben Cl WCNE/HIN WN2 ....10 A1
Deepdale LEIGH WN7 ....65 H5
Deepdale Av
   RNFD/HAY WA11 * 58 B5
Defiance St ATH M46 ....38 D5
De-Haviland Wy SKEL WN8 .....18 B5
Delamere Av
   GOL/RIS/CUL WA3 ....71 F3
Delamere Rd SKEL WN8 ....17 E3
Delamere Wy SKEL WN8 ....30 D1
Delegarte St WCNW/BIL/OR WN5 ..32 A3
Delfhaven Ct WCNNW/ST WN6 ..10 D3
Dell Av WCNW/ST WN6 * 27 G5
Dellside Cl AIMK WN4 ....47 F1
The Dell SKEL WN8 ....31 E1

WGNNW/ST WN6 ....8 C3
Delph Gv LEIGH WN7 ....51 G2
Delph Meadow Gdns
   WCNW/BIL/OR WN5 ....58 B2
Delphside Cl
   WCNW/BIL/OR WN5 ....31 G3
Delphside Rd
   WCNW/BIL/OR WN5 ....31 F3
Denbigh Gv ATH M46 ....38 D3
Dene Av NEWLW WA12 ....68 C5
Dene Gv LEIGH WN7 ....64 A2
Dene St LEIGH WN7 ....64 A2
Denford Cl WCNW/BIL/OR WN5 ..33 C5
Denham Av WCNS/IIMK WN5 ....33 H5
Denholme SKEL WN8 ....30 D1
Denton Gv
   WCNW/BIL/OR WN5 ....20 C5
Derby Dr RNFD/HAY WA11 ......56 B1
Derby Rd GOL/RIS/CUL WA3 ....62 D5
   SKEL WN8 ....16 B5
Derbyshire Rd
   WCNS/IIMK WN3 ....47 E2
Derby St ATH M46 ....38 D4
   HOR/BR BL6 ....13 H1
   LEIGH WN7 ....65 F2
   WCNS/IIMK WN3 ....35 E4
   WHTN BL5 ....26 A4
Dereham Wy WCNS/IIMK WN3 ..33 E5
Derngate Dr WGNNW/ST WN6 ..10 D3
Derwent Av GOL/RIS/CUL WA3 ..62 D5
   WCNE/HIN WN2 ....35 G1
   WCNS/IIMK WN3 ....47 G1
   WALK M28 ....55 G1
Derwent Pl
   WCNW/BIL/OR WN5 ....32 D1
Derwent Rd AIMK WN4 ....61 H1
   FWTH BL4 ....41 E1
   WCNE/HIN WN2 ....36 B3
   WCNS/IIMK WN3 ....20 A5
Derwent St LEIGH WN7 ....64 B1
   TYLD M29 ....53 H4
Derwent Wy LEIGH WN7 ....64 A5
Desmond St ATH M46 ....52 B1
De Trafford Dr
   WCNE/HIN WN2 ....23 G5
Devoke Av RNFD/HAY WA11 ....57 H5
Devon Av SKEL WN8 ....31 F1
Devon Cl WCNW/BIL/OR WN5 ...11 E5
   WCNS/IIMK WN3 ....33 E2
Devon Rd TYLD M29 ....53 G1
Devonshire Dr AIMK WN4 ......60 D5
Devonshire Rd ATH M46 ....38 D3
   WALK M28 ....41 H2
Devon St LEIGH WN7 ....66 B2
Dewberry Cl TYLD M29 ....54 D2
Dewberry Flds SKEL WN8 ....15 E5
Dewhirst La WHTN BL5 ....26 A4
Diamond St WCNE/HIN WN2 ....64 D2
Diane Rd AIMK WN4 ....61 H2
Dicconson Crs WGN WN1 ....2 C5
Dicconson La WHTN BL5 ....24 D1
Dicconson St WGN WN1 ....2 C2
Dicconson Ter WGN WN1 ....2 C2
Dickens Dr WCNE/HIN WN2 .....49 G3
Dickenson St WCNE/HIN WN2 ..36 A3
Dickens Pl WCNS/IIMK WN3 ....33 G4
Didsbury Gv WCNE/HIN WN2 ...36 A3
Diggle St WGNNW/ST WN6 .....21 H4
Digmoor Dr SKEL WN8 ....29 G1
Digmoor Rd SKEL WN8 ....30 A1
Dingle Av SKEL WN8 ....19 E5
Dingle Rd SKEL WN8 ....31 E1
Dingle Wk WGNNW/ST WN6 ....21 E1
Ditton Brook WHTN BL5 ....26 A4
Dixon Av NEWLW WA12 ....69 G5
Dixon Cl RNFD/HAY WA11 ......68 D1
Dixon Dr WGNNW/ST WN6 ......9 F5
Dixon St WHTN BL5 ....25 H2
Dobb Brow WHTN BL5 ....37 G1
Dobson Pkwy WCNE/HIN WN2 ..53 F1
Doctor's Nook LEIGH WN7 .....65 E1
Dodd La WHTN BL5 ....25 E4
Dodd's Farm La
   WCNE/HIN WN2 ....24 B2
Dodhurst Rd WCNE/HIN WN2 ..36 A3
Doefield Av WALK M28 ....55 H3
Doeford Cl GOL/RIS/CUL WA3 ..72 D4
Donnington Rd LEIGH WN7 ....64 C5
Dootson St WCNE/HIN WN2 ....49 F2
Dorchester Rd SKEL WN8 ......30 A5
Doric Gn WCNW/BIL/OR WN5 ...31 G5
Dorket Gv WHTN BL5 ....37 G2
Dorning St ATH M46 ....53 G2
   HOR/BR BL6 ....13 F5
   LEIGH WN7 * 64 D1
   WGN WN1 ....2 D5
Dorothy Gv LEIGH WN7 ....64 D2
Dorset Av TYLD M29 ....39 G5
Dorset Cl WCNE/HIN WN2 ......62 A2
Dorset Rd ATH M46 ....36 B2
   WGN WN1 ....11 E1
Dorset St LEIGH WN7 ....66 A2
Dorstone Cl WCNE/HIN WN2 ...37 E3
Dotterel Cl LEIGH WN7 ....58 C5
Douglas Av SKEL WN8 ....31 E1
   WCNW/BIL/OR WN5 ....31 F1
Douglas Bank Dr
   WCNNW/ST WN6 ....21 G4
Douglas Dr WCNNW/ST WN6 ...9 E5
Douglas Pk WCNE/HIN WN2 ....10 B5
Douglas Rd ATH M46 ....39 F5
   LEIGH WN7 ....51 F4
   WCNW/BIL/OR WN5 ....31 F1
Douglas St ATH M46 ....39 F5
   WCNW/BIL/OR WN5 ....34 H4
   WCNS/IIMK WN3 ....35 H1
Douglas Vw HOR/BR BL6 * 11 E4
Dovecote La LHULT M38 ....40 D5
Dovedale Crs AIMK WN4 ....47 H5
Dovedale Rd AIMK WN4 ....47 H3

Dovenby Fold WCNE/HIN WN2 ..35 F1
Dove St GOL/RIS/CUL WA3 .....62 B4
Dovey Cl TYLD M29 ....54 B4
Dower St WCNE/HIN WN2 .....36 B2
Dowling Cl WCNNW/ST WN6 ...21 E2
Downall Green Rd AIMK WN4 ...47 C5
Downing Cl WCNE/HIN WN2 ....49 F2
Downing St LEIGH WN7 * 65 F2
The Downs WGNS/IIMK WN3 ...32 D4
Downton Av WGNE/HIN WN2 ...36 A4
Doyle Rd BOLS/LL BL3 ....27 F2
Dragon Cl SKEL WN8 ....18 B5
Drake Hall WHTN BL5 ....37 C3
Drake St ATH M46 ....52 D1
Drapers Ct WCNW/BIL/OR WN5 ..35 E2
Draycott Cl WCNE/HIN WN2 ....36 C2
The Drive ATH M46 * 38 D2
   LEIGH WN7 ....65 E3
Droxford Gv ATH M46 ....39 F3
Druid St AIMK WN4 ....61 F4
Drummer's La AIMK WN4 ....47 F2
Drummond Sq
   WCNW/BIL/OR WN5 ....33 F1
Drummond Wy LEIGH WN7 .....47 G4
Dryden Av AIMK WN4 ....47 C4
Dryden Cl WGNS/IIMK WN3 ....36 A1
Ducky Av WHTN BL5 ....23 F3
Duddon Dr WGNNW/ST WN6 ...10 D3
Dudley St AIMK WN4 ....60 D1
Duerden St BOLS/LL BL3 * 27 H3
Duke Av GOL/RIS/CUL WA3 ....73 H2
Duke St AIMK WN4 ....61 F3
   GOL/RIS/CUL WA3 ....62 B4
   LEIGH WN7 ....65 F2
   LHULT M38 ....41 F3
   TYLD M29 ....54 B5
   WCNE/HIN WN2 ....2 D1
   WCNS/IIMK WN3 ....33 G4
Duke's Wood La SKEL WN8 ....48 C5
Dukinfield St LEIGH WN7 * 65 F1
Dumbarton Gn
   WCNNW/ST WN6 ....19 F2
Dunbane Cl AIMK WN4 ....59 F2
Duncan Av NEWLW WA12 ......64 A4
Duncan Pl WCNW/BIL/OR WN5 ..33 F1
Dunham Cl WHTN BL5 ....37 C3
Dunham Gr WCNE/HIN WN2 ...53 F1
Dunham La WCNE/HIN WN2 ....65 G1
Dunlin Av NEWLW WA12 ....65 G1
Dunlin Cl RNFD/HAY WA11 .....58 B5
Dunmail Cl TYLD M29 ....54 D5
Dunoon Rd WCNE/HIN WN2 ....13 E5
Dunscore Rd WCNS/IIMK WN3 ..33 C4
Dunsdale Dr AIMK WN4 ....61 F3
Dunster Cl WCNE/HIN WN2 .....49 F2
Dunster Pl WALK M28 ....55 E4
Dunster Rd WALK M28 ....55 E4
Durban St ATH M46 ....52 B1
Durham Rd WCNE/HIN WN2 ....49 F2
Durham St SKEL WN8 ....16 C3
   WGN WN1 ....3 J2
Durrell Wy GOL/RIS/CUL WA3 ..71 F1
Durrington Pl WHTN BL5 ....37 H2
Dursley Dr AIMK WN4 ....61 C2
Dutton Gv LEIGH WN7 ....64 A2
Duxbury Cl RNFD/HAY WA11 ...58 B5
Dyer St GOL/RIS/CUL WA3 .....70 A1

E

Eagle Crs RNFD/HAY WA11 ......43 F5
Earlesdon Crs LHULT M38 ......41 F3
Earl St ATH M46 ....52 C1
   WCNE/HIN WN2 ....35 F1
Earlswood SKEL WN8 ....18 B4
East Av GOL/RIS/CUL WA3 .....62 D5
   WCNE/HIN WN2 ....65 H3
East Bond St LEIGH WN7 ....65 F1
East Bridgewater St
   LEIGH WN7 ....65 F1
Eastgarth WCNE/HIN WN2 ......49 G1
Eastham Wy LHULT M38 ....41 G5
East Lancashire Rd
   GOL/RIS/CUL WA3 ....70 C3
   TYLD M29 ....55 E4
   WALK M28 ....55 E4
East Moor WALK M28 ....55 E4
East Mt WCNW/BIL/OR WN5 ...42 H1
Easton Cl WGNS/IIMK WN3 ....37 E1
East St AIMK WN4 ....53 C2
   ATH M46 ....37 E5
   WCNE/HIN WN2 ....37 E5
Eastwell Rd AIMK WN4 ....48 D5
Eastwood Av WALK M28 ....41 H5
Eastwood Cl BOLS/LL BL3 ......27 H2
Eastwood Gv LEIGH WN7 ......52 A3
Eatock St WCNW/BIL/OR WN5 ..35 C5
Eatock Wy WHTN BL5 ....36 B2
Eaton St WCNE/HIN WN2 ......64 A2
Eavesdale SKEL WN8 ....18 B5
Eccles Rd WCNW/BIL/OR WN5 ..20 C4
Eccleston St WGN WN1 ....2 D2
Eckersley Fold La ATH M46 ....52 B2
Eckersley St WCN WN1 ....1 E5
Edale Cl WCNNW/ST WN6 .....38 D5
Edale Rd BOLS/LL BL3 * 27 H5
   FWTH BL4 ....41 H1
   LEIGH WN7 ....64 A5
Eddisford Dr
   GOL/RIS/CUL WA3 ....72 C4
Eddleston St AIMK WN4 ....60 D5
Eden Av GOL/RIS/CUL WA3 ....73 H5
   RNFD/HAY WA11 ....42 D4
Eden Bank LEIGH WN7 ....65 H3
Edendale Dr WCNE/HIN WN2 ..36 C5
Edenhall Gv WCNE/HIN WN2 ...18 B5
Edenhurst SKEL WN8 ....18 B5
Edensor Cl WCNNW/ST WN6 ...21 H1

Edenvale WALK M28 ....38 D2
Edge Gn WALK M28 * 62 B4
Edge Green La
   GOL/RIS/CUL WA3 ....62 B4
Edge Green Rd AIMK WN4 ......61 H1
Edge Green St AIMK WN4 ......61 H1
Edge Hall Rd
   WCNW/BIL/OR WN5 ....31 E3
Edgerley Pl AIMK WN4 ....61 G3
Edgerton Rd
   GOL/RIS/CUL WA3 ....62 B4
Edge Ware Gv
   WCNS/IIMK WN3 ....33 H5
Edgeway Rd WCNS/IIMK WN3 ...33 G4
Edgewood WGNNW/ST WN6 .....10 D3
Edgeworth Rd
   WCNE/HIN WN2 ....36 C2
Edinburgh Cl WCNE/HIN WN2 ..65 E3
Edinburgh Dr WCNE/HIN WN2 ..36 D2
Edith St WCNS/IIMK WN3 ......34 A5
Edmund Dr LEIGH WN7 ....64 C3
Edna Rd LEIGH WN7 ....65 F2
Edridge Wy WCNE/HIN WN2 ....36 C5
Edstone Cl BOLS/LL BL3 ....27 H3
Edward Dr AIMK WN4 ....61 E1
Edward Steet WGN WN1 ....37 G5
Edward St LEIGH WN7 ....65 F1
   WGN WN1 ....3 J5
   WHTN BL5 ....37 G5
Edwin St WGN WN1 ....3 J5
Egerton SKEL WN8 ....30 D1
Egerton St WCNE/HIN WN2 ....36 A4
Eggar Cl TYLD M29 ....54 B5
Elaine Cl AIMK WN4 ....59 F2
Elcombe Av GOL/RIS/CUL WA3 ..71 H2
   WGN WN1 ....2 D1
Eldercot Gv BOLS/LL BL3 ....27 H5
Eldercot Rd BOLS/LL BL3 ....27 H5
Eldon Gdns AIMK WN4 ....61 F2
Eldon St LEIGH WN7 ....65 F2
Eleanor St WCNS/IIMK WN3 ....33 G4
Elgin Av AIMK WN4 ....61 F3
Elgin Cl WCNE/HIN WN2 ....65 E3
Eliot Dr WCNS/IIMK WN3 ......33 F5
Elizabethan Dr
   WCNE/HIN WN2 ....35 H1
Elizabeth Av AIMK WN4 ....61 E2
Elizabeth Rd RNFD/HAY WA11 ..56 B1
   LEIGH WN7 ....64 B1
Elizabeth St ATH M46 ....38 D4
Elkstone Av LHULT M38 ....41 G3
Elkstone Cl WGNS/IIMK WN3 ...33 E5
Elkwood Cl WGN WN1 ....21 H5
Elland Cl WHTN BL5 ....37 G1
Ellenbrook Rd WALK M28 ......55 H5
Ellendale Gra WALK M28 ....55 G4
Ellenor Dr TYLD M29 ....54 B5
Ellen St WGN WN1 ....2 B2
Ellerbeck Crs WALK M28 ....55 G1
Ellesmere Av WALK M28 ....55 G1
Ellesmere Rd AIMK WN4 ....61 H1
   GOL/RIS/CUL WA3 ....62 D5
   WCNW/BIL/OR WN5 ....33 F1
Ellesmere St LEIGH WN7 ....64 B1
   LHULT M38 ....41 F1
Elliott Av GOL/RIS/CUL WA3 ....69 H4
Elliott St FWTH BL4 ....41 H1
   TYLD M29 ....54 A1
Ellis Crs WALK M28 ....55 G1
Ellis Rd WCNW/BIL/OR WN5 ....32 B4
Ellis St WGN WN1 ....3 J5
Ellonby Ri HOR/BR BL6 ....15 F1
Elm Av AIMK WN4 ....61 E2
   BOLS/LL BL3 ....27 G5
   HOR/BR BL6 ....15 E2
   WCNNW/ST WN6 ....10 B1
Elm Cft WGN WN1 ....3 J6
Elm Dr WCNW/BIL/OR WN5 ....31 F1
Elmers Green La SKEL WN8 ....17 E5
Elmers Wood Rd SKEL WN8 ....17 G5
Elmfield WGNNW/ST WN6 ......10 D3
Elmfield Av ATH M46 ....38 D3
Elm Gdns RNFD/HAY WA11 .....43 E4
Elm Gv SKEL WN8 ....17 G4
Elmhow Gv WCNE/HIN WN2 ...21 G3
Elmridge LEIGH WN7 ....65 H5
Elm Rd RNFD/HAY WA11 * 42 D4
   WCNE/HIN WN2 ....36 C5
Elmsbury St AIMK WN4 ....61 E2
The Elms GOL/RIS/CUL WA3 ....71 F1
Elm St LEIGH WN7 ....64 D1
   TYLD M29 * 54 A1
   WCNE/HIN WN2 ....36 A4
Elm Tree Rd GOL/RIS/CUL WA3 ..62 B4
Elmwood Av AIMK WN4 ....61 E1
Elmwood Dr AIMK WN4 ....61 E1
Elmwood Gv FWTH BL4 ....41 H1
Elnup Av WGNNW/ST WN6 .....8 D5
Elsdon Dr ATH M46 ....52 B1
Elsham Dr WALK M28 ....55 H2
Elsie St FWTH BL4 ....41 H1
Elstead Gv AIMK WN4 ....60 D3
Elston Av NEWLW WA12 ....69 H5
Elswick SKEL WN8 ....30 D1
Elsworth Dr FWTH BL4 ....41 H1
Eltham Cl AIMK WN4 ....59 F2
Elton Cl GOL/RIS/CUL WA3 .....69 H4
Elvington Cl
   GOL/RIS/CUL WA3 ....72 C4
Elvington Crs WALK M28 ....55 G4
Elway Rd AIMK WN4 ....61 F4
Elworthy Gv WGN WN1 ....3 G2
Ely Cl WALK M28 ....55 H5
Ely Dr TYLD M29 ....54 D5
Emerald Av LEIGH WN7 ....65 G2
Emerald St BOLS/LL BL3 ....27 H3
Emlyn St WGNE/HIN WN2 ......49 F1
Empress Dr LEIGH WN7 ....65 G2

Rd WCGN/BIL/OR WN5.....21 F4
s Cha
WCGN/BIL/OR WN5.....45 H2
d RNFD/HAY WA11.....68 B3
: ATH M46.....39 E5
.....3 C6
n Av SKEL WN8 *.....17 H5
l WHTN BL5.....39 C1
eld Rd WALK M28.....55 G3
a GOL/RIS/CUL WA3.....73 C3
Mill La GOL/RIS/CUL WA3.....73 H1
: LEIGH WN7.....22 A2
Dr.....41 H2
n Wy NEWLW WA12.....69 E5
Av WALK M28.....55 F5
Cl GOL/RIS/CUL WA3.....72 D4
Ct SKEL WN8.....16 C4
Rd SKEL WN8.....16 C4
St WGN WN1.....5 H4
ry WCNS/IIMK WN3.....33 H3
Rd CHLY/EC PR7.....7 F1
Cl RNFD/HAY WA11.....68 C3
rs WCNS/IIMK WN5.....4 D4
WCNS/IIMK WN5.....33 H3
f WALK M28.....55 H1
nite Av WALK M28.....55 H1
Brow RNFD/HAY WA11.....43 F3
st BOLS/LL BL3 *.....27 H1

I

ase Cl WALK M28.....41 E5
n Dr WCGNE/HIN WN2.....24 C2
Dr LEIGH WN7.....53 E5
een La WCGNE/HIN WN2.....3 J7
l Av WCNE/HIN WN2.....3 K5
d SKEL WN8.....17 C5
ial St WHTN BL5.....38 A1
Rd HOR/BR BL6.....14 D2
: LEIGH WN7.....51 H3
Cl WCGNW/ST WN6.....5 E5
N BL5.....26 A3
bss Dr RNFD/HAY WA11.....43 F4
Fold WALK M28.....55 G3
am Cl LEIGH WN7.....64 D5
n Cl NEWLW WA12 *.....69 E5
Dr RNFD/HAY WA11.....58 A5
hite Av WGN WN1.....3 G6
hite Crs WGN WN1.....22 B3
ood Av WGN WN1.....3 G6
ood Rd
RNFD/HAY WA11.....56 D5
: SKEL WN8.....17 C4
St WCGNE/HIN WN2.....35 F5
N WN6.....21 C4
SKEL WN8.....17 F5
La ORM L39.....42 B1
Dr WCGNW/ST WN6.....5 E5
ld WHTN BL5.....38 A2
WCGNW/ST WN6.....10 C3
nger La
WCNS/IIMK WN3.....2 C7
v WALK M28.....55 F5
y LEIGH WN7.....52 A5
SKEL WN8.....17 F2
d WCGNW/BIL/OR WN5.....32 D2
sq WGN WN1.....3 G4
ood St LEIGH WN7.....51 H3
ge SKEL WN8.....17 C3
Dr.....17 C3
: Dr LEIGH WN7.....65 H1
n Gdns
RIS/CUL WA3.....72 C5
LHULT M38.....41 E4
se Rd
RIS/CUL WA3.....63 E5
GOL/RIS/CUL WA3.....70 C1
N BL5.....38 A1
IMK WN4.....61 E3
.....2 B5

J

La WHTN BL5.....36 D1
n St WALK M28.....41 H4
Dr WCGNE/HIN WN2.....35 F1
t WCGNE/HIN WN2.....36 A2
SE LEIGH WN7.....53 C3
Cl WCNS/IIMK WN3.....2 C7
Pl WCGNW/ST WN6.....5 E5
RNFD/HAY WA11.....68 C2
sq WCGNW/ST WN6.....5 E5
ATH M46.....53 C3
:/HIN WN2.....48 D4
NS/IIMK WN3.....34 C2
N BL5.....25 H3
e Rd
W/BIL/OR WN5 *.....33 E1
LEIGH WN7.....64 D4
on St WCGNE/HIN WN2.....23 F5
on St WCGNE/HIN WN2.....36 A2
Hey AIMK WN4.....47 C5
s La GOL/RIS/CUL WA3.....65 H1
v Av NEWLW WA12.....69 E4
E/HIN WN2.....50 B2
n Cl LEIGH WN7.....64 A2
St ATH M46.....64 A2
Dr.....53 H2
W/BIL/OR WN5.....32 C2
AIMK WN4.....61 C1
WHTN BL5.....70 B1
t WN7.....53 H2
/E/HIN WN2.....37 E5
/BIL/OR WN5.....33 E3

Jonathan Fold LEIGH WN7 *.....66 A1
Jonquil Dr WALK WN28.....41 E5
Jubilee Av WCGNW/BIL/OR WN5.....31 C4
Jubilee Crs RNFD/HAY WA11.....68 B3
Jubilee Dr.....16 D5
Jubilee Houses WALK M28 *.....41 H5
Junction Rd RNFD/HAY WA11.....42 D3
Junction Rd West HOR/BR BL6.....15 H5
Junction St WCNS/IIMK WN3.....34 D2
June Av LEIGH WN7.....51 F5
Juniper Dr WCGNE/HIN WN2.....36 C5
Jupiter Gv WCNS/IIMK WN3.....47 F1
Jury St LEIGH WN7.....51 H4
Justene Cl GOL/RIS/CUL WA3.....62 B4
Jutland Gv WHTN BL5.....25 H4

K

Kane Cl GOL/RIS/CUL WA3.....63 H5
Karen Rd LEIGH WN7.....3 H5
Kay Cl WGN WN1.....3 F5
Kay St ATH M46.....53 E1
Kearsley St LEIGH WN7.....
WCGNW/ST WN6.....2 A3
Keats Av WCGNW/ST WN6.....21 F2
WCNS/IIMK WN3.....33 H3
WCGNW/BIL/OR WN5.....45 C2
Keats St LEIGH WN7.....51 C4
Keble Gv WCGNE/HIN WN2.....49 C2
Keble Gv LEIGH WN7.....51 F5
Keble St WCGNE/HIN WN2.....3 K6
Kellaton Cl WCNS/IIMK WN3 *.....34 D2
Kelibank Rd WCNS/IIMK WN3.....33 F5
Kellet Cl WCGNW/BIL/OR WN5.....21 E3
Kells Gv WCGNW/ST WN6.....21 C5
Kelso Gv WCGNE/HIN WN2.....36 A4
Kelvin Av AIMK WN4.....60 A2
Kelvin Gv WCNS/IIMK WN3.....47 C1
Kelway Ter WGN WN1.....3 F2
Kempton Cl NEWLW WA12.....69 C4
Kendal Cl RNFD/HAY WA11.....43 E2
Kendal Gv AIMK WN4.....61 C1
LEIGH WN7.....64 C1
Kendal Rd WALK M28.....54 D4
WCGNE/HIN WN2.....23 F5
Kendal St WCGNW/ST WN6.....2 A3
Kendrew Rd BOLS/LL BL3.....27 H1
Kendrick Pl WGN WN1.....3 C4
Kenford Dr WCNS/IIMK WN3.....47 F1
Kenhall Rd LEIGH WN7.....65 H2
Kenilworth Dr LEIGH WN7.....53 E4
WCGNE/HIN WN2.....36 C4
Kenilworth Rd
GOL/RIS/CUL WA3.....71 F2
Kenmore Av AIMK WN4.....60 A2
Kennedy Rd TYLD M29.....54 C4
Kennet Cl WHTN BL5.....26 A4
Kenneth Av LEIGH WN7.....51 C5
Kenneth Gv LEIGH WN7.....51 C5
Kennet Wy LEIGH WN7.....52 A4
Kensington Dr LEIGH WN7.....66 A2
WGN WN1.....3 F6
Kensington Rd
WCGNW/BIL/OR WN5 *.....33 E3
Kent Av WCGNE/HIN WN2.....49 F1
Kent Cl WALK M28.....55 F1
Kentmere Av RNFD/HAY WA11.....58 B5
Kentmere Dr TYLD M29.....54 C4
Kentmere Gv FWTH BL4.....41 E1
Kent Rd ATH M46.....38 D4
TYLD M29.....53 H2
Kent St LEIGH WN7.....51 H3
WGN WN1.....3 F6
Kenway RNFD/HAY WA11.....43 F5
Kenwood Av LEIGH WN7.....64 D4
Kenwood Cl LEIGH WN7.....65 H1
Kenwood Cl LEIGH WN7.....65 H2
Kenyon Gv LHULT M38.....40 D4
Kenyon La GOL/RIS/CUL WA3.....71 C3
Kenyon Rd WGN WN1.....3 G4
Kenyons La North
RNFD/HAY WA11.....68 C1
Kenyon's La South
RNFD/HAY WA11.....68 C1
Kenyon St LEIGH WN7.....51 C3
Kenyon Ter LEIGH WN7.....40 D5
Kenyon Wy LHULT M38.....40 D5
Kerans Dr WHTN BL5.....25 H4
Kerfoot's La SKEL WN8.....16 B5
Kerfoot St LEIGH WN7.....65 H2
Kermishaw Nook TYLD M29.....53 H5
Kershaw Av LHULT M38.....41 F3
Kershaw St TYLD M29.....53 H2
WCGNW/ST WN6.....32 C2
Kershaw Wy NEWLW WA12.....69 F4
Kestral Pk SKEL WN8.....17 H1
Kestral Av FWTH BL4 *.....41 E1
LHULT M38.....41 F3
Kestrel Dr AIMK WN4.....48 B5
Kestrel Ms SKEL WN8.....17 H1
Keswick Pl WCGNE/HIN WN2.....35 F1
Keswick Wy RNFD/HAY WA11.....43 E1
Kid Glove Rd
GOL/RIS/CUL WA3.....62 B5
Kielder Cl WALK M28.....41 C4
Kilbuck La RNFD/HAY WA11.....68 C1
Kilburn Av AIMK WN4.....61 C1
Kilburn Clase LEIGH WN7.....51 C2
Kilburn Dr WCGNW/ST WN6.....9 C3
Kilburn Rd WCNS/IIMK WN3.....33 C5
Kildale Cl BOLS/LL BL3.....27 F1
Kildare St LEIGH WN7.....41 H1
WCGNE/HIN WN2.....35 H3
WCNS/IIMK WN3.....33 F4
Killington Cl WCNS/IIMK WN3.....48 A1
Killingworth Ms HOR/BR BL6 *.....14 C1
Kiln La SKEL WN8.....33 E3
The Kilphin HOR/BR BL6.....15 C2
Kilsby Cl HOR/BR BL6.....14 C1
Kilshaw St WCGNW/BIL/OR WN5.....32 D3
Kimberley Pl AIMK WN4.....61 F3
Kimberly St WCGNW/ST WN6.....9 C3
Kincraig Cl BOLS/LL BL3.....27 H1
Kinder Gv AIMK WN4.....48 C5
Kingfisher Ct AIMK WN4.....48 A5
Kingfisher Dr FWTH BL4.....41 E1

Kingfisher Pk SKEL WN8.....17 H1
Kingfisher Wy WCGNW/BIL/OR WN5.....31 C4
King George Cl AIMK WN4.....61 E3
King George Rd
RNFD/HAY WA11.....68 D2
King's Av GOL/RIS/CUL WA3.....71 C2
Kingsbury Ct SKEL WN8.....17 H1
King's Crs TYLD M29.....53 F3
Kingscroft Cl WGN WN1.....3 F6
Kingsdown Crs WGN WN1.....22 B1
Kingsdown Rd
WCGNE/HIN WN2.....49 C4
Kingsfield Wy TYLD M29.....54 A3
Kings Fold ATH M46.....39 F5
Kings's Gdns LEIGH WN7.....65 H1
Kingshill Ct WCGNW/ST WN6.....10 C3
Kingsley Av WCNS/IIMK WN3.....33 C5
Kingsley Rd WALK M28.....55 F1
WCGNE/HIN WN2.....36 C5
Kingsley St LEIGH WN7.....51 F4
Kings Moss La
WCGNW/BIL/OR WN5.....44 C4
Kingsoak Cl WGN WN1.....2 E4
Kings Pk ATH M46.....52 B3
King's Rd AIMK WN4.....60 D1
King's Rd GOL/RIS/CUL WA3.....70 B2
Kings St WHTN BL5.....26 A4
Kingston Cl WCNS/IIMK WN3.....34 A5
King St LEIGH WN7.....65 C2
WGN WN1.....2 D1
.....35 F1
King St West WGN WN1.....2 C5
Kingsway WGN WN1.....2 E1
King William St TYLD M29.....53 C2
Kingwood Crs
WCGNW/BIL/OR WN5.....33 E2
Kinlet Rd WCNS/IIMK WN3.....32 D4
Kinnerly Gv WALK M28.....55 F2
Kinniside Cl WCNS/IIMK WN3.....47 H1
Kinross Av AIMK WN4.....59 H2
Kinsley Dr WALK M28.....55 H1
Kintbury St WCGNE/HIN WN2.....49 E4
Kipling Av WCNS/IIMK WN3.....33 H4
Kipling Gv LEIGH WN7.....51 C4
Kirby Av ATH M46.....38 D3
Kirby Rd LEIGH WN7.....64 D1
Kiribati Wy LEIGH WN7.....51 H5
Kirkdale Gdns WCGNE/HIN WN2.....30 C1
Kirkebrok Rd BOLS/LL BL3.....27 H1
Kirkfell Dr TYLD M29.....54 A3
Kirkhall La LEIGH WN7.....51 H5
Kirkham Av
GOL/RIS/CUL WA3 *.....71 F3
Kirkham Rd LEIGH WN7.....64 D3
Kirkham St LHULT M38.....41 F3
WCGNE/HIN WN2.....49 C3
Kirkhill Gra WHTN BL5.....26 B3
Kirkless St WGN WN1.....3 H4
Kirkless St WCGNE/HIN WN2.....23 F2
Kirkless Vis WCGNE/HIN WN2 *.....23 F3
Kirkpatrick St WCGNE/HIN WN2.....37 E5
Kirkstead Wy
GOL/RIS/CUL WA3.....70 B1
Kirkstile Crs WCNS/IIMK WN3.....47 F1
Kirkstone WCGNE/HIN WN2.....32 D1
Kirkwood Cl WCGNE/HIN WN2.....37 E5
Kite Gv LEIGH WN7.....65 C1
Kitt Green Rd
WCGNW/BIL/OR WN5.....20 D5
Kittiwake Cl TYLD M29.....53 H4
Kiveton Cl WALK M28.....55 H1
Kiveton Dr AIMK WN4.....61 F4
Knaresborough Rd
WCGNE/HIN WN2.....36 B4
Knightscliffe Crs
WCGNW/ST WN6.....8 D4
Knightshill Crs
WCGNW/ST WN6.....21 C4
Knightswood BOLS/LL BL3.....27 C2
Knowles Av WCNS/IIMK WN3.....33 C4
Knowles Pl WGN WN1.....3 H4
Knowsley St WCNS/IIMK WN3 *.....34 C2
Knowsley Av ATH M46.....38 D5
GOL/RIS/CUL WA3.....62 C5
Knowsley Dr LEIGH WN7.....64 D4
Knowsley Gv HOR/BR BL6.....14 C1
Knowsley Rd WCGNW/ST WN6.....21 H2
Knowsley St LEIGH WN7.....64 D4
Knowsley Crs RNFD/HAY WA11.....42 D3
Knutshaw Crs BOLS/LL BL3.....27 E3

L

Laburnum Av ATH M46.....39 F5
LEIGH WN7.....51 F4
WCNS/IIMK WN3.....35 E2
Laburnum Dr SKEL WN8.....16 C4
WCGNW/ST WN6.....21 H1
Laburnum Gv HOR/BR BL6.....14 D1
TYLD M29.....54 C2
Laburnum Rd
GOL/RIS/CUL WA3.....71 C1
Laburnum St AIMK WN4.....61 E4
ATH M46.....39 F5
Laches Cl WCGNE/HIN WN2.....36 A4
Ladybarn Av GOL/RIS/CUL WA3.....70 A2
Ladybridge Av WALK M28.....55 H3
Ladyhill Vw WALK M28.....55 H3
Lady La WCNS/IIMK WN3.....33 F4
Ladysmith Av AIMK WN4.....61 F3
Ladywell Av LHULT M38.....41 F4
Ladywell Gv LHULT M38.....41 F3
Lafford La SKEL WN8.....19 F2
Laithwaite Rd
WCGNW/BIL/OR WN5.....33 E1
Lakeland Av AIMK WN4.....61 F2
Lakes Dr WCGNW/BIL/OR WN5.....31 C5
Lake Side LEIGH WN7.....51 C5
Lakeside Av
RNFD/HAY WA11.....43 F5
Lakeside Ct RNFD/HAY WA11.....31 H5
Lakeside Gdns
RNFD/HAY WA11.....43 F5
Lakes Ter WCGNE/HIN WN2.....35 F1

Lake St LEIGH WN7.....52 B5
Lamberhead Rd
WCGNW/BIL/OR WN5.....32 C2
Lambeth St ATH M46.....38 C5
Lambley Cl LEIGH WN7.....51 C3
Lamborne SKEL WN8.....17 C1
Lamb St WGN WN1.....3 C2
Lambton St
WCGNW/BIL/OR WN5.....32 D3
Lancaster Av ATH M46.....39 E5
GOL/RIS/CUL WA3.....70 D1
TYLD M29.....39 H5
Lancaster Cl NEWLW WA12.....68 C5
Lancaster Crs SKEL WN8.....16 D4
Lancaster Rd WCGNE/HIN WN2.....36 B2
WCGNW/BIL/OR WN5.....20 D4
Lancaster St WCNS/IIMK WN3.....34 C2
Lancaster Wy WCGNE/HIN WN2.....36 B2
Lancaster Wy WHTN BL5.....25 C3
Lance Wood Pl
WCGNW/BIL/OR WN5.....33 E2
Landau Dr WALK M28.....41 E5
Landedmans WHTN BL5.....38 A1
Land Gate La AIMK WN4.....47 H4
Landor Cl GOL/RIS/CUL WA3.....71 F1
Landrace Dr WALK M28.....55 C5
Landside LEIGH WN7.....65 E4
Land St WCGNW/ST WN6.....2 A4
Lane Head Av
LEIGH WN7.....71 C1
Langdale Av GOL/RIS/CUL WA3.....62 D5
LEIGH WN7.....64 C1
Langdale Crs WCGNE/HIN WN2.....20 C5
WCGNW/BIL/OR WN5.....20 C5
Langdale Dr RNFD/HAY WA11.....49 C2
Langdale Gv WCGNE/HIN WN2.....35 C5
WCGNE/HIN WN2.....36 B3
Langdale Rd TYLD M29.....53 H1
Langdale St FWTH BL4.....41 H1
LEIGH WN7.....64 D1
Langden Cl GOL/RIS/CUL WA3.....72 C5
Langfield WCGNW/ST WN6.....10 B3
Langford Dr LEIGH WN7.....64 D4
Langham Rd WCGNW/BIL/OR WN5.....10 A1
Langham St WCNS/IIMK WN3.....33 F4
Langholm Rd AIMK WN4.....59 H2
Langley Cl GOL/RIS/CUL WA3.....62 D5
Langley Dr WALK M28.....54 D5
Langley Platt La TYLD M29.....53 F1
Langley St WCGNW/BIL/OR WN5.....33 E2
Langset Av WCGNE/HIN WN2.....36 A2
Langside BOLS/LL BL3.....27 F1
Langton Av WCGNW/ST WN6.....10 B1
Langton Cl NEWLW WA12.....68 D5
Langton Pl WCGNW/ST WN6.....10 B1
Langtree SKEL WN8.....17 C2
Langtree Cl WALK M28.....55 C3
Langtree La WCGNW/ST WN6.....5 E4
Langwood La RNFD/HAY WA11.....43 H2
Langworthy Av LHULT M38.....41 C4
Lansbury St
WCGNE/HIN WN2.....32 B2
Lansdowne Cl BOLS/LL BL3.....27 E3
Lansdowne Rd ATH M46.....39 C5
Lapwing Cl GOL/RIS/CUL WA3.....71 E1
Larch Av WCGNW/BIL/OR WN5.....33 C2
Larch Cl GOL/RIS/CUL WA3.....71 C3
SKEL WN8.....16 D4
Larch Gv ATH M46.....38 C1
Larch Rd LEIGH WN7.....51 H3
RNFD/HAY WA11 *.....68 B2
Larchwood AIMK WN4.....60 D3
Larchwood Dr WGN WN1.....22 A1
Larkfield Av LHULT M38.....41 E3
Larkfield Ms LHULT M38.....41 E3
Larkhill SKEL WN8.....17 C1
Larkhill Av WCGNW/ST WN6.....10 C2
Larkspur Cl LEIGH WN7.....65 E3
Latham Av NEWLW WA12.....69 F5
Latham La WCGNW/BIL/OR WN5.....20 D5
Latham Rd HOR/BR BL6.....7 H4
Lathom Dr RNFD/HAY WA11.....43 E4
Latimer Cl
WCGNW/BIL/OR WN5 *.....32 A1
Launceston Rd
WCGNE/HIN WN2.....37 F5
Laurel Crs WCGNE/HIN WN2.....36 D5
Laurel Dr LHULT M38.....41 F4
SKEL WN8.....16 D3
Laurel Gv AIMK WN4.....61 F1
GOL/RIS/CUL WA3.....71 E1
LEIGH WN7.....51 H3
Laurel St WCGNW/BIL/OR WN5.....33 C1
Lavender Rd WCGNW/ST WN6.....21 C1
Lawns Av WCGNE/HIN WN2.....31 F3
Lawnswood Dr TYLD M29.....53 C2
Lawrence Ct WCGNE/HIN WN2.....49 C2
Lawson Av LEIGH WN7.....51 F2
Laxey Av ATH M46.....53 F1
Laxey Crs LEIGH WN7.....51 F4
Layland Av GOL/RIS/CUL WA3.....72 C5
Layton Cl WCGNW/BIL/OR WN5.....33 E3
Lazenby Crs AIMK WN4.....60 C3
Lazonby Av WCGNE/HIN WN2.....24 C2
Leadale Cl AIMK WN4.....47 F5
Leadale Cl WCGNW/ST WN6.....10 A1
Leader St WGN WN1.....3 H5
WCGNW/BIL/OR WN5.....32 D2
Leafield TYLD M29.....54 B2
Lea Gate Cl WCNS/IIMK WN3 *.....33 F5
Leal Holme Av WCGNE/HIN WN2.....23 F2
Lea St WCNS/IIMK WN3.....34 A4
Leavale Cl LHULT M38.....41 E4
Lea Vw WGN WN1.....3 J5
Leaway WCGNE/HIN WN2.....35 F2
Leckenby Cl WALK M28.....55 F5
Ledburn SKEL WN8.....17 C2
Ledbury St LEIGH WN7.....52 A3
Ledmore Gv AIMK WN4.....60 A3
Lee Bank WHTN BL5.....26 B5
Leeds St WCNS/IIMK WN3.....2 A6
Lee Fold TYLD M29.....54 B3
Lee La WCGNE/HIN WN2.....49 C3
Lee St ATH M46.....53 C1
Leeswood SKEL WN8.....17 C2
Legh St AIMK WN4.....61 E4
GOL/RIS/CUL WA3.....70 B1
Leicester Av WCGNE/HIN WN2.....36 C3
Leicester Rd TYLD M29.....53 H1

Leigh Rd ATH M46.....52 B3
WALK M28.....55 F5
WCGNE/HIN WN2.....51 E2
WHTN BL5.....38 A1
Leigh St LEIGH WN7.....64 B1
WGN WN1.....3 F5
Leighton Av ATH M46.....38 C5
Leighton Dr LEIGH WN7.....64 A5
Leighton St ATH M46.....38 B5
Lemon St TYLD M29.....53 C3
Lentworth Dr WALK M28.....41 H3
Leopold St
WCGNW/BIL/OR WN5.....32 C3
Lessingham Av WGN WN1.....22 A2
Lester Rd LHULT M38.....40 D3
Levengreave Cl
WCGNE/HIN WN2.....37 F5
Levens Pl WCGNE/HIN WN2.....23 F5
WCGNW/BIL/OR WN5.....32 D1
Lever St TYLD M29.....53 C2
WHTN BL5.....25 H2
Lewis Cl CHLY/EC PR7.....6 D1
WCGNE/HIN WN2.....33 H3
Leyburn Cl WGN WN1.....3 J3
Ley Crs TYLD M29.....54 A5
Leyland Av WCGNE/HIN WN2.....36 A5
Leyland Green Rd AIMK WN4.....59 H1
Leyland Mill La WGN WN1.....22 C1
Leyland Rd RNFD/HAY WA11.....68 A5
Leyland St WCGNE/HIN WN2.....49 C2
Ley Rd TYLD M29.....53 H4
Library St WGN WN1.....2 D5
WCGNE/HIN WN2.....26 A5
Lichfield Av GOL/RIS/CUL WA3.....71 E1
TYLD M29.....54 B4
Lichfield Gv AIMK WN4.....61 F4
Lichfield St
WCGNW/BIL/OR WN5.....32 D3
Lidgate Cl WCNS/IIMK WN3.....33 E5
Lidgett Cl LHULT M38.....41 H3
Lightbourne Av LEIGH WN7.....64 A1
Light Oaks Rd
GOL/RIS/CUL WA3.....73 H3
Lightshaw La
GOL/RIS/CUL WA3.....62 C2
Lightwood WALK M28.....55 G3
Lilac Av AIMK WN4.....60 A1
LEIGH WN7.....51 H4
WCGNW/ST WN6.....21 H2
Lilac Gdns WCGNE/HIN WN2.....35 E4
Lilac Gv SKEL WN8.....16 D4
WCGNW/BIL/OR WN5.....32 C3
Lilac Rd GOL/RIS/CUL WA3.....62 B5
Lilford St ATH M46.....52 C1
WGN WN1.....3 H4
Lilian Dr WCGNW/ST WN6.....22 A2
Lily La WCGNE/HIN WN2.....49 F3
Lily Pl AIMK WN4.....61 F4
Lily St AIMK WN4.....61 H1
Lime Cl WCGNE/HIN WN2.....49 C4
Limefield WGN WN1.....2 E4
Limefield Dr SKEL WN8.....30 B1
Lime Gv GOL/RIS/CUL WA3.....71 E1
RNFD/HAY WA11.....43 E5
SKEL WN8.....16 D4
WCGNE/HIN WN2.....36 C5
Limes Av WCGNW/ST WN6.....21 H1
The Limes GOL/RIS/CUL WA3.....71 E3
RNFD/HAY WA11.....10 D4
Lime St ATH M46.....38 A5
TYLD M29.....53 C2
WGN WN1.....3 H3
Lime V WCNS/IIMK WN3.....35 E4
Lime Vale Rd
WCGNW/BIL/OR WN5.....58 B3
Linwood Meadow TYLD M29.....54 B3
Linbeck Gv GOL/RIS/CUL WA3.....63 E5
Lincoln Av GOL/RIS/CUL WA3.....63 E5
Lincoln Cl LEIGH WN7.....72 B1
TYLD M29.....53 H1
Lincoln Dr AIMK WN4.....61 H1
WCGNE/HIN WN2.....13 C5
Lincoln Pl WCGNE/HIN WN2.....20 D5
Lincoln Rd WCGNE/HIN WN2.....36 B3
Lindale Cl WALK M28.....54 D4
Lindale Rd WALK M28.....54 D4
Linden Av AIMK WN4.....60 C1
ATH M46.....52 C1
WCGNW/BIL/OR WN5.....31 H2
Linden Gv LEIGH WN7.....51 H4
WCGNE/HIN WN2.....31 H2
WCGNW/BIL/OR WN5.....31 H2
Linden Ms WALK M28.....55 E5
Linden Rd WALK M28.....55 E5
WCGNE/HIN WN2.....36 B1
Linden St WGN WN1.....3 H5
Linden St WCGNW/BIL/OR WN5.....32 D3
Lindholme SKEL WN8.....17 C1
Lindisfarne Av
GOL/RIS/CUL WA3.....72 B1
Lindisfarne Dr WCGNW/BIL/OR WN5.....31 F3
Lindley St LEIGH WN7 *.....65 C1
Lindow St LEIGH WN7.....64 C1
Lindsay St HOR/BR BL6.....14 C1
Lindsay Ter WCGNE/HIN WN2.....12 C5
Lingards Dr TYLD M29.....66 D2
Lingards La TYLD M29.....66 D2
Lingard St LEIGH WN7.....65 C2
Ling Dr ATH M46.....53 E1
Lingfield Cl FWTH BL4.....41 H1
Lingfield Crs WCGNW/ST WN6.....31 F3
Lingmell Av RNFD/HAY WA11.....58 A5
Lingmoor Cl WCNS/IIMK WN3.....47 H2
Lingmoor Dr TYLD M29.....54 A4
Linkfield Dr WALK M28.....55 F5
Links Dr HOR/BR BL6.....15 C3
Links Rd HOR/BR BL6.....15 C3
Linkway Av ATH M46.....39 E5
The Linkway HOR/BR BL6.....14 D4
Linley Cl WCGNE/HIN WN2.....20 D1
Linley Rd WCGNW/BIL/OR WN5.....33 E3
Linnet Dr LEIGH WN7.....65 C1
Linney Sq WGN WN1.....3 G4
Linstock Wy ATH M46.....38 B5
Linton Av GOL/RIS/CUL WA3.....62 A4
Linwood Gv WCGNE/HIN WN2.....36 A4

Lion La HOR/BR BL6 .... 7 H5
Liptrot St WGNW/BIL/OR WN5 .... 33 G1
Liscard St ATH M46 .... 38 C5
Little Factory St TYLD M29 .... 53 G2
Littlegate WHTN BL5 .... 37 H3
Little La WGNS/IIMK WN3 .... 33 F4
Little London WGN WN1 .... 2 D3
Little Pasture LEIGH WN7 .... 51 G4
Little Scotland HOR/BR BL6 .... 7 G5
Littleton Gv WGNNW/ST WN6 .... 5 F5
Liverpool Rd AIMK WN4 .... 60 D4
RNFD/HAY WA11 .... 59 H5
SKEL WN8 .... 16 B5
WGNE/HIN WN2 .... 35 G5
Liza St LEIGH WN7 .... 51 H3
Lloyd Ct LEIGH WN7 * 51 H4
Local Board St
WGNE/HIN WN2 .... 3 K7
Loch St WGNW/BIL/OR WN5 .... 32 C2
Lockerbie Pl WGNS/IIMK WN3 .... 47 F1
Locker La AIMK WN4 .... 62 A2
Lockett Rd AIMK WN4 .... 61 F1
Lock La HOR/BR BL6 .... 26 D1
Locks Vw WGN WN1 .... 3 J5
Lodge Dr TYLD M29 .... 54 A5
Lodge Gv ATH M46 .... 53 F2
Lodge La ATH M46 .... 53 E2
LEIGH WN7 .... 66 B2
NEWLW WA12 .... 69 E2
ORM L39 .... 42 B2
Lodge Rd ATH M46 .... 53 F2
WGNW/BIL/OR WN5 .... 31 H4
Loeminster Pl WGNE/HIN WN2 .... 3 J7
Logwood Av
WGNW/BIL/OR WN5 .... 33 F1
Logwood Pl
WGNW/BIL/OR WN5 .... 21 F5
Loire Dr WGNW/BIL/OR WN5 .... 21 G5
Lomax St WGNE/HIN WN2 .... 49 F1
Lombard St ATH M46 .... 52 C1
London Cl WGNW/BIL/OR WN5 .... 21 F5
London Flds
WGNW/BIL/OR WN5 .... 58 D1
Longbrook WGNNW/ST WN6 .... 9 G4
Long Cswy ATH M46 .... 52 C4
Longcroft TYLD M29 .... 66 B2
Longendale Rd
WGNNW/ST WN6 .... 10 A2
Longfellow Cl WGNS/IIMK WN3 .... 33 H3
Longhey SKEL WN8 .... 17 H1
Long Heys La SKEL WN8 .... 18 B1
Long Heys Or Back La
SKEL WN8 .... 8 A4
Longhurst Rd WGNE/HIN WN2 .... 36 C4
Long La SKEL WN8 .... 30 B5
WGNE/HIN WN2 .... 36 D3
WHTN BL5 .... 25 F3
Longmead Av AIMK WN4 .... 61 F2
Longridge Av WGNNW/ST WN6 .... 10 C2
Longshaw Av
WGNW/BIL/OR WN5 .... 45 H2
Longshaw Cl
WGNW/BIL/OR WN5 .... 45 H2
Longshaw Common
WGNW/BIL/OR WN5 .... 45 H2
Longshaw Dr LHULT M38 .... 41 F4
Longshaw Old Rd
WGNW/BIL/OR WN5 .... 45 H2
Longshoot Cl WGN WN1 .... 3 F3
Longton Av GOL/RIS/CUL WA3 .... 70 D1
Longton St WGNE/HIN WN2 .... 35 H4
Longwall Av WALK M28 .... 55 H3
Longwood Cl RNFD/HAY WA11 .... 56 C5
Longworth Av HOR/BR BL6 .... 7 H4
Lonsdale Av LEIGH WN7 .... 64 C4
Lonsdale Wk
WGNW/BIL/OR WN5 .... 20 C5
Lord Av ATH M46 * 53 F2
Lord Gv ATH M46 .... 53 G2
Lords Fold RNFD/HAY WA11 .... 42 D4
Lord St ATH M46 .... 53 F2
LEIGH WN7 .... 65 E1
TYLD M29 .... 53 G5
WGN WN1 .... 2 D2
WGNE/HIN WN2 .... 35 F1
WHTN BL5 .... 25 H4
Lordy Cl WGNNW/ST WN6 .... 11 E3
Lorne St WGN WN1 .... 3 G5
Lorton Cl WALK M28 .... 55 E5
Lostock Cl WGNW/BIL/OR WN5 .... 58 D1
Lostock Junction La
HOR/BR BL6 .... 15 H3
Lostock La HOR/BR BL6 .... 14 D4
Lostock Park Dr HOR/BR BL6 .... 15 F3
Lostock Rd WHTN BL5 .... 25 F1
Loughrigg Av RNFD/HAY WA11 .... 58 A5
Loughrigg Cl TYLD M29 .... 54 A4
Louise Gdns WHTN BL5 .... 37 H2
Lovers' La ATH M46 .... 52 A1
Low Bank Rd AIMK WN4 .... 60 C2
Lowcroft SKEL WN8 .... 17 H2
Lowe Av ATH M46 .... 38 D3
Lowe Mill La WGNE/HIN WN2 .... 36 A3
Lowerbrook Cl HOR/BR BL6 .... 14 C1
Lower Drake Fold WHTN BL5 .... 37 H3
Lower Green La TYLD M29 .... 67 F3
Lower House Dr HOR/BR BL6 .... 15 H3
Lower Landedmans
WHTN BL5 .... 38 A1
Lower Leigh Rd WHTN BL5 .... 38 A3
Lower Longshoot WGN WN1 .... 3 F4
Lower Lyndon Av
WGNNW/ST WN6 .... 9 F4
Lower Makinson Fold
HOR/BR BL6 * 14 C1
Lower New Rw WALK M28 .... 55 F2
Lower St Stephen St
WGNNW/ST WN6 .... 21 H5
Lower Southfield WHTN BL5 .... 37 H1
Lower St FWTH BL4 .... 41 H1
Lowe St GOL/RIS/CUL WA3 .... 70 B1
Loweswater Av TYLD M29 .... 53 H4
Loweswater Rd FWTH BL4 .... 41 E1
Lowfield Gdns
GOL/RIS/CUL WA3 .... 73 H2
Low Gn ATH M46 .... 39 G3
Lowood St LEIGH WN7 .... 64 C1
Lowside Av BOL BL1 .... 15 H4
Lowther Av GOL/RIS/CUL WA3 .... 73 E5
Lowther Dr LEIGH WN7 .... 53 E4
Lowton Gdns
GOL/RIS/CUL WA3 .... 70 C4
Lowton Rd GOL/RIS/CUL WA3 .... 62 C5
Loxton Crs WGNS/IIMK WN3 .... 34 A5
Luciol Cl TYLD M29 .... 54 B2
Ludlow SKEL WN8 .... 17 H1
Ludlow Av WGNE/HIN WN2 .... 36 D4
Ludlow Dr LEIGH WN7 .... 53 E4
Ludlow St WGNNW/ST WN6 .... 5 E4
Ludovic Ter WGN WN1 .... 22 B1
Luke St AIMK WN4 .... 61 G1
Lulworth SKEL WN8 .... 17 H1
Lulworth Dr WGNE/HIN WN2 .... 36 D4
Lulworth Rd BOLS/LL BL3 .... 27 H2
Lune Gv LEIGH WN7 .... 64 B1
Lunehurst GOL/RIS/CUL WA3 .... 71 F1
Lune Rd WGNE/HIN WN2 .... 49 F1
Luntswood Gv NEWLW WA12 .... 68 D5
Lupin Dr RNFD/HAY WA11 .... 68 C3
Lurdin La WGNNW/ST WN6 .... 11 E3
Luton Gv ATH M46 .... 38 C5
Lychgate WGNW/BIL/OR WN5 .... 33 F3
Lydford Gn WGNNW/ST WN6 .... 10 C2
Lyefield Av WGN WN1 .... 3 J3
Lymefield Dr WALK M28 .... 55 F4
Lyme St NEWLW WA12 .... 68 B5
Lymm Cl WALK M28 .... 41 F5
Lymn St WGNE/HIN WN2 .... 35 G5
Lynbridge Cl
WGNW/BIL/OR WN5 .... 31 H3
Lyndale SKEL WN8 .... 17 G1
Lyndhurst SKEL WN8 .... 17 G1
Lyndon Av WGNNW/ST WN6 .... 9 G3
Lynmouth Cl WGNNW/ST WN6 .... 21 H3
Lynstock Wy HOR/BR BL6 .... 14 D4
Lynton Av WGNNW/ST WN6 .... 21 H2
Lynton Rd TYLD M29 .... 54 C3
WGNE/HIN WN2 .... 36 C2
Lynton St LEIGH WN7 .... 64 C1
Lynwood Av GOL/RIS/CUL WA3 .... 71 F3
Lynwood Cl SKEL WN8 .... 30 A1
Lynwood Gv ATH M46 .... 38 C5
Lyon Rd WGNNW/ST WN6 .... 21 H3
Lyon St AIMK WN4 .... 47 G4
WGNS/IIMK WN3 .... 2 B6
Lytham Rd AIMK WN4 .... 60 C1

M

Mabel St WGNW/BIL/OR WN5 .... 33 F2
WHTN BL5 .... 38 A2
Maberry Cl WGNNW/ST WN6 .... 8 C3
Macauley Pl WGNS/IIMK WN3 .... 33 G5
Macclesfield Cl
WGNE/HIN WN2 .... 35 H3
Macdonald Av FWTH BL4 .... 41 F1
WGNS/IIMK WN3 .... 33 H5
Macdonald St
WGNW/BIL/OR WN5 .... 32 C2
Mackenzie Av WGNS/IIMK WN3 .... 33 H5
Madams Wood Rd WALK M28 .... 41 F5
Madeley Cl WGNS/IIMK WN3 .... 33 F5
Maden St TYLD M29 .... 53 G5
Madison Gdns WHTN BL5 .... 26 B3
Madison Pk WHTN BL5 .... 26 A3
Maesbrook Dr TYLD M29 .... 53 H3
Mafeking Pl AIMK WN4 .... 61 F3
Magdalen Dr AIMK WN4 .... 60 C2
Maggots Nook Rd
RNFD/HAY WA11 .... 43 F2
Maiden Cl SKEL WN8 .... 16 B3
Maidstone Cl LEIGH WN7 .... 51 F1
Mains Av WGNE/HIN WN2 .... 49 E4
Main St WGNW/BIL/OR WN5 .... 58 D1
Major St WGNW/BIL/OR WN5 .... 32 D2
Makants Cl ATH M46 .... 39 G2
TYLD M29 .... 54 D3
Makerfield Dr NEWLW WA12 .... 68 D5
Makerfield Wy
WGNE/HIN WN2 .... 35 G1
Makinson Ar WGN WN1 .... 2 C4
Makinson Av HOR/BR BL6 .... 14 D1
WGNE/HIN WN2 .... 36 A1
Maldon Cl WGNE/HIN WN2 .... 3 J1
Maldon Rd WGNNW/ST WN6 .... 10 C2
Malham Av WGNS/IIMK WN3 .... 47 H1
Malham Cl LEIGH WN7 .... 64 B1
Malika Pl AIMK WN4 * 47 F5
Mallory Dr LEIGH WN7 .... 65 G1
Mallowdale WALK M28 .... 55 G3
Malpas Av WGN WN1 .... 3 F2
Malton Av BOLS/LL BL3 .... 27 H1
GOL/RIS/CUL WA3 .... 71 F2
Malton Cl LEIGH WN7 .... 51 F5
Malton Rd WALK M28 .... 54 D4
Malverley Dr LEIGH WN7 .... 65 H1
Malvern Av ATH M46 .... 39 G3
WGNE/HIN WN2 .... 36 D4
Malvern Cl AIMK WN4 .... 61 E2
WGNS/IIMK WN3 .... 32 D5
Malvern Crs WGNS/IIMK WN3 .... 35 E4
Malvern St WGNNW/ST WN6 .... 4 D4
Malvern Ter LEIGH WN7 .... 65 E3
Manchester Rd HOR/BR BL6 .... 13 F2
LEIGH WN7 .... 65 H2
TYLD M29 .... 66 D2
WGN WN1 .... 3 J5
WGNE/HIN WN2 .... 35 F1
WHTN BL5 .... 26 A3
Manchester Rd East
LHULT M38 .... 41 F4
Manchester Rd West
LHULT M38 .... 40 D3
Manderville Cl
WGNS/IIMK WN3 .... 47 E1
Manfield SKEL WN8 .... 17 F2
Manley Av GOL/RIS/CUL WA3 .... 62 A4
Manley Cl LEIGH WN7 .... 51 G3
Manley Crs WHTN BL5 .... 26 C4
Manley St WGNS/IIMK WN3 .... 34 D2
Manning Av WGNNW/ST WN6 .... 21 H3
Manor Av GOL/RIS/CUL WA3 .... 70 D1
NEWLW WA12 .... 68 C5
Manor Cl AIMK WN4 .... 59 H3
Manor Ct GOL/RIS/CUL WA3 .... 70 D1
Manor Gv LEIGH WN7 .... 65 H3
SKEL WN8 .... 17 E4
WGNE/HIN WN2 .... 12 C5
WGNW/BIL/OR WN5 .... 20 C5
Manor House Cl
RNFD/HAY WA11 .... 57 H5
Manor House Dr SKEL WN8 .... 30 B5
Manorial Dr LHULT M38 .... 40 D3
Manor Pl WGNS/IIMK WN3 .... 35 E2
Manor Rd RNFD/HAY WA11 .... 68 C2
TYLD M29 .... 54 B5
WGNE/HIN WN2 .... 36 C3
WGNNW/ST WN6 .... 9 F4
Manor St FWTH BL4 .... 41 H1
GOL/RIS/CUL WA3 .... 62 C5
WGN WN1 .... 2 C5
WGNW/BIL/OR WN5 .... 33 G2
Mansart Cl AIMK WN4 .... 61 G3
Manse Av WGNNW/ST WN6 .... 4 A1
Manse Gdns NEWLW WA12 .... 69 G5
Mansell Wy HOR/BR BL6 .... 14 C2
Mansfield St
GOL/RIS/CUL WA3 .... 61 H5
Maple Av ATH M46 .... 38 C4
GOL/RIS/CUL WA3 .... 71 G2
HOR/BR BL6 .... 14 D1
WGNE/HIN WN2 .... 35 E2
WGNE/HIN WN2 .... 36 C5
Maple Cl WGNW/BIL/OR WN5 .... 58 C1
Maple Crs LEIGH WN7 .... 51 H4
Maple Dr WGNE/HIN WN2 .... 49 G4
Maplefield Dr WALK M28 .... 55 F4
Maple Gv WGNNW/ST WN6 .... 21 H2
Maple St AIMK WN4 .... 47 H5
Maplewood SKEL WN8 .... 17 F1
Marbury Gv WGNNW/ST WN6 .... 10 B2
Marchbank WGNE/HIN WN2 .... 23 F3
Marchbank Rd SKEL WN8 .... 16 C4
Mardale Cl ATH M46 .... 38 D3
Margaret Av WGNNW/ST WN6 .... 20 D1
Margaret St WGNE/HIN WN2 .... 36 A2
WGNNW/ST WN6 .... 21 H4
Margrove Cha HOR/BR BL6 .... 15 H5
Marian Rd RNFD/HAY WA11 .... 68 B2
Marigold St
WGNW/BIL/OR WN5 .... 33 E1
Marina Dr WGNW/BIL/OR WN5 .... 33 E3
Marion Pl WGNE/HIN WN2 .... 49 E3
Maritime Cl NEWLW WA12 .... 69 F4
Market Ap AIMK WN4 * 61 E3
Market Pl CHLY/EC PR7 .... 7 F1
LEIGH WN7 .... 65 E1
WGN WN1 .... 2 C5
WGNNW/ST WN6 .... 10 B1
Market St ATH M46 .... 38 D5
CHLY/EC PR7 .... 7 F1
NEWLW WA12 .... 68 D5
TYLD M29 .... 53 G2
WGN WN1 .... 2 C4
WGNE/HIN WN2 .... 36 A3
WGNNW/ST WN6 .... 10 B1
WHTN BL5 .... 25 H5
Marklands Rd TYLD M29 .... 66 D2
Markland St WGN WN1 .... 3 H6
Mark St WALK M28 .... 55 E4
Marland SKEL WN8 .... 17 F1
Marlborough SKEL WN8 .... 17 F1
Marlborough Av
WGNS/IIMK WN3 .... 35 E4
Marlborough Rd ATH M46 .... 39 F4
Marlborough Wy
RNFD/HAY WA11 .... 68 B1
Marlbrook Dr WHTN BL5 .... 37 H3
Marlbrook Ms WHTN BL5 * 38 A3
Marl Gv WGNW/BIL/OR WN5 .... 31 G4
Marlow Ct CHLY/EC PR7 .... 7 E1
Marlowe Cl WGNS/IIMK WN3 .... 33 H3
Marmion Cl GOL/RIS/CUL WA3 .... 63 F5
Marnland Gv BOLS/LL BL3 .... 27 F1
Marnock Cl WGNE/HIN WN2 .... 50 C3
Marple Cl WGNNW/ST WN6 .... 4 B5
Marrick Cl WGNS/IIMK WN3 .... 47 H1
Marsden St WALK M28 .... 55 E5
WGN WN1 .... 2 D4
WGNS/IIMK WN3 .... 34 D4
WGNW/BIL/OR WN5 .... 33 G1
WHTN BL5 .... 25 H5
Marshall St LEIGH WN7 .... 64 D2
Marsham Rd WHTN BL5 .... 38 A2
Marshbank WHTN BL5 .... 25 H4
Marshbrook Cl
WGNE/HIN WN2 .... 36 D2
Marsh Brook Fold WHTN BL5 .... 36 D1
Marsh Gn WGNW/BIL/OR WN5 .... 21 E4
Marsh Hey Cl LHULT M38 .... 41 E2
Marsh La WGN WN1 .... 2 D4
Marsh Rd LHULT M38 .... 41 G4
Marsh Rw WGNE/HIN WN2 .... 36 D4
Marsh St WHTN BL5 .... 25 H4
Marshway Dr NEWLW WA12 .... 69 E5
Marsland Green La TYLD M29 .... 66 B2
Marston Cl HOR/BR BL6 .... 15 E2
Martin Av NEWLW WA12 .... 69 E4
Martindale Crs
WGNW/BIL/OR WN5 .... 33 F2
Martindale Rd
RNFD/HAY WA11 .... 58 A4
Martinsclough HOR/BR BL6 .... 15 H4
Martins Ct WGNE/HIN WN2 .... 36 D2
Martins La SKEL WN8 .... 30 A1
Martin St ATH M46 * 39 E5
Martland Av
GOL/RIS/CUL WA3 .... 71 E2
WGNNW/ST WN6 .... 9 E5
Martland Crs WGNNW/ST WN6 .... 21 F2
Martland Mill La
WGNW/BIL/OR WN5 .... 21 E3
Martlew Dr ATH M46 .... 39 G4
Marton Cl GOL/RIS/CUL WA3 .... 72 D5
Marton Dr ATH M46 .... 39 F5
Marton St WGN WN1 .... 2 C3
Marus Av WGNS/IIMK WN3 .... 33 G5
Marwick Cl WGNNW/ST WN6 .... 5 E5
Maryfield Cl GOL/RIS/CUL WA3 .... 70 B2
Mary Hulton Ct WHTN BL5 .... 26 B5
Marylebone Ct WGN WN1 .... 22 C2
Marylebone Pl WGN WN1 .... 22 C2
Mary St TYLD M29 * 53 H2
Masefield Av LEIGH WN7 .... 51 G4
WGNW/BIL/OR WN5 .... 32 B2
Masefield Dr FWTH BL4 .... 41 G1
WGNS/IIMK WN3 .... 33 H3
Mason Cl AIMK WN4 .... 61 G2
Mason La ATH M46 .... 53 F1
Mason St WGNE/HIN WN2 .... 49 G3
WGNS/IIMK WN3 .... 2 A6
Massam Cl RNFD/HAY WA11 .... 43 F5
Mather Av GOL/RIS/CUL WA3 .... 71 F3
Mather Fold Rd WALK M28 .... 55 G2
Mather La LEIGH WN7 .... 65 F2
Mather St ATH M46 .... 39 E5
Matheson Dr
WGNW/BIL/OR WN5 .... 21 E5
Matlock Cl ATH M46 .... 53 E1
Maunby Gdns LHULT M38 .... 41 H5
May Av LEIGH WN7 .... 51 G5
WGNE/HIN WN2 .... 49 H4
Mayfair Dr ATH M46 .... 39 G4
WGNE/HIN WN2 .... 24 A3
WGNS/IIMK WN3 .... 47 G1
Mayfield Av FWTH BL4 .... 41 H1
Mayfield Dr LEIGH WN7 .... 72 B1
Mayfield Rd SKEL WN8 .... 31 E1
WGNW/BIL/OR WN5 .... 20 C5
Mayfield St AIMK WN4 * 60 D3
ATH M46 .... 38 D5
May St GOL/RIS/CUL WA3 .... 62 C4
LEIGH WN7 .... 64 B1
May Tree Dr WGN WN1 .... 22 A1
Maytree Wk SKEL WN8 .... 17 G1
McCormack Dr WGN WN1 .... 3 F5
Meadowbank Av ATH M46 .... 39 F4
Meadowbank Gdns
GOL/RIS/CUL WA3 .... 73 H2
Meadowbrook Cl HOR/BR BL6 .... 26 D2
Meadow Cl LEIGH WN7 .... 64 D4
SKEL WN8 .... 30 A1
Meadow Clough SKEL WN8 .... 17 G1
Meadowcroft AIMK WN4 .... 47 G5
SKEL WN8 .... 17 G1
WHTN BL5 .... 38 A1
Meadowcroft Wy LEIGH WN7 .... 65 G4
Meadowfield HOR/BR BL6 .... 15 G3
SKEL WN8 .... 30 D1
Meadowfield Dr WALK M28 .... 55 G5
Meadow Pit La
WGNE/HIN WN2 .... 12 B2
Meadows Cl WGNE/HIN WN2 .... 36 A3
Meadowside Av AIMK WN4 .... 47 H3
Meadowside Rd
WGNE/HIN WN2 .... 36 D4
Meadow St WGNNW/ST WN6 .... 21 H4
Meadowvale Dr
WGNW/BIL/OR WN5 .... 32 D2
Meadow Wk FWTH BL4 .... 41 F1
Meadow Wy HOR/BR BL6 .... 13 F1
Meads Gv TYLD M29 .... 54 B5
Meadway GOL/RIS/CUL WA3 .... 71 E1
SKEL WN8 .... 17 F1
TYLD M29 .... 54 C2
WGNE/HIN WN2 .... 3 J7
Mealhouse Ct ATH M46 .... 38 D5
Mealhouse La ATH M46 .... 38 D5
Meanley Rd LEIGH WN7 .... 53 G4
TYLD M29 .... 53 G4
Meanley St TYLD M29 .... 53 G2
Medlar Wy AIMK WN4 .... 60 C1
Medlock Wy WGNE/HIN WN2 .... 49 F1
Medway Cl AIMK WN4 * 47 G5
LEIGH WN7 .... 72 B1
Medway Pl
WGNW/BIL/OR WN5 .... 33 E1
Medway Rd WALK M28 .... 55 G3
Megfield WHTN BL5 .... 37 H2
Melbreck SKEL WN8 .... 17 F1
Melbury Dr HOR/BR BL6 .... 15 E1
Melford Dr AIMK WN4 .... 60 D2
WGNW/BIL/OR WN5 .... 31 G5
Melling Cl LEIGH WN7 .... 65 E5
Mellings Av
WGNW/BIL/OR WN5 * 45 H2
Melling St WGNW/BIL/OR WN5 .... 33 F3
Melling Wy WGNS/IIMK WN3 .... 47 E2
Mellor Brook Dr
WGNE/HIN WN2 * 49 F1
Mellor Cl WGNNW/ST WN6 .... 5 F5
Mellor Dr WALK M28 .... 55 H2
Melmerby Cl AIMK WN4 .... 60 C3
Melrose Av LEIGH WN7 .... 51 G2
Melrose Crs AIMK WN4 .... 59 H3
Melrose Dr WGNS/IIMK WN3 .... 33 E5
Melton Cl TYLD M29 .... 54 A3
WALK M28 .... 55 H1
Melverley St WGNS/IIMK WN3 .... 33 H1
Mendip Av WGNS/IIMK WN3 .... 32 D5
Mercer St NEWLW WA12 .... 69 G5
Merchants Crs
GOL/RIS/CUL WA3 .... 63 F5
Mercury Wy SKEL WN8 .... 18 B5
Mere Av LEIGH WN7 .... 64 C1
Mere Bank Cl WALK M28 .... 41 H5
Mere Cl SKEL WN8 .... 17 E3
Merefield Cl WGNE/HIN WN2 .... 36 B4
Mere Fold WALK M28 .... 41 G5
Mere Gv RNFD/HAY WA11 .... 58 A5
Mereland Cl
WGNW/BIL/OR WN5 .... 31 H2
Mere Rd AIMK WN4 .... 61 F2
NEWLW WA12 .... 70 A5
Mere St LEIGH WN7 .... 64 C1
WGNW/BIL/OR WN5 .... 33 G2
Merewood SKEL WN8 .... 17 F1
Merlewood Dr TYLD M29 .... 53 H3
Mersey Cl WGNE/HIN WN2 .... 37 F5
Mersey Rd WGNE/HIN WN2 .... 49 E1
WGNW/BIL/OR WN5 .... 32 A1
Mersey St LEIGH WN7 .... 64 B2
Merton Gv TYLD M29 .... 54 B5
Merton Rd WGNS/IIMK WN3 .... 32 C4
Mervyn Pl WGNS/IIMK WN3 .... 33 H4
Mesnes Av WGNS/IIMK WN3 .... 33 H3
Mesnes Park Ter WGN WN1 .... 2 C3
Mesnes Rd WGN WN1 .... 22 B3
Mesnes St WGN WN1 .... 2 C3
Mesnes Ter WGN WN1 .... 2 C4
Metcalfe Ct LHULT M38 * 41 E4
The Mews WGNE/HIN WN2 .... 36 A3
Meynell Dr LEIGH WN7 .... 65 E4
Meyrick St
WGNW/BIL/OR WN5 .... 33 G2
Mickleton ATH M46 .... 39 F4
Middlebrook Dr HOR/BR BL6 .... 15 H4
Middlecot Cl
WGNW/BIL/OR WN5 ....
Middlewood GOL/RIS/CUL WA3 ....
SKEL WN8 ....
Midland Cl LEIGH WN7 ....
Miles La WGNNW/ST WN6 ....
Milford Rd WGNE/HIN WN2 ....
Milford St WGNS/IIMK WN3 ....
Milk St TYLD M29 ....
WGNS/IIMK WN3 ....
Mill Bank WGNNW/ST WN6 ....
Millbeck Farm
WGNW/BIL/OR WN5 ....
Millbeck Gv RNFD/HAY WA11 ....
Millbrook Av ATH M46 ....
Millbrook Cl GOL/RIS/CUL WA3 ....
SKEL WN8 ....
Millcroft Av
WGNW/BIL/OR WN5 ....
Milldale Cl ATH M46 ....
HOR/BR BL6 ....
Milldale Rd LEIGH WN7 ....
Miller's La ATH M46 ....
WGNE/HIN WN2 ....
Millers Nook SKEL WN8 ....
Millfield Dr WALK M28 ....
Millfield La AIMK WN4 ....
RNFD/HAY WA11 ....
Millgate WGN WN1 ....
Millgreen Cl SKEL WN8 ....
Mill Hl LHULT M38 ....
Mill House Vw SKEL WN8 ....
Millingford Av
GOL/RIS/CUL WA3 ....
Millingford Gv AIMK WN4 ....
Mill La LEIGH WN7 ....
RNFD/HAY WA11 ....
SKEL WN8 ....
SKEL WN8 ....
WGNE/HIN WN2 ....
WGNNW/ST WN6 ....
WHTN BL5 ....
Mill Rd WGNW/BIL/OR WN5 ....
Mill St AIMK WN4 ....
ATH M46 ....
GOL/RIS/CUL WA3 ....
LEIGH WN7 ....
WALK M28 ....
WGNE/HIN WN2 ....
WGNS/IIMK WN3 ....
WHTN BL5 ....
Millwood Cl AIMK WN4 ....
Milnes Av LEIGH WN7 ....
Milton Crs FWTH BL4 ....
Milton Gv WGN WN1 ....
WGNW/BIL/OR WN5 ....
Milton Rd GOL/RIS/CUL WA3 ....
Milton St LEIGH WN7 ....
Minehead Av LEIGH WN7 ....
Mine Wy RNFD/HAY WA11 * ....
Minster Gv TYLD M29 ....
Minstrel Cl WGNE/HIN WN2 ....
Mirfield Cl GOL/RIS/CUL WA3 ....
Miriam Gv LEIGH WN7 ....
Miry La WGNNW/ST WN6 ....
WGNS/IIMK WN3 ....
WHTN BL5 ....
Mitchell Rd
WGNW/BIL/OR WN5 ....
Mitchell St AIMK WN4 ....
GOL/RIS/CUL WA3 ....
LEIGH WN7 ....
WGNE/HIN WN2 ....
WGNW/BIL/OR WN5 ....
Mitton Cl GOL/RIS/CUL WA3 ....
Moat House St
WGNE/HIN WN2 ....
Molyneux Rd WHTN BL5 ....
Molyneux St WGN WN1 ....
Mona St WGN WN1 ....
Monica Ter AIMK WN4 ....
Monmouth Crs AIMK WN4 ....
Monroe Cl WGNS/IIMK WN3 ....
Montford Ri WGNE/HIN WN2 ....
Montfort Cl WHTN BL5 ....
Montrey Crs AIMK WN4 ....
Montrose Av
WGNW/BIL/OR WN5 ....
Monument Man WGN WN1 * ....
Monument Rd WGN WN1 ....
Monyash Vw WGNE/HIN WN2 ....
Moody St WGNNW/ST WN6 * ....
Moor Av WGNNW/ST WN6 ....
Moor Dr SKEL WN8 ....
Moore Dr RNFD/HAY WA11 ....
Moores La WGNNW/ST WN6 ....
Moore St WGN WN1 ....
Moore St East WGN WN1 ....
Moorfield WALK M28 ....
Moorfield Crs
GOL/RIS/CUL WA3 ....
Moorfield St WGNE/HIN WN2 ....
Moorgate Dr TYLD M29 ....
Moorhey Rd LHULT M38 ....
Moorings Cl WGN WN1 ....
Moorland Dr LHULT M38 ....
Moorland Rd AIMK WN4 ....
WGNE/HIN WN2 ....
Moorlands Av LEIGH WN7 ....
Moorlands Vw BOLS/LL BL3 ....
Moor La LEIGH WN7 ....
Moor Rd WGNW/BIL/OR WN5 ....
Moorside Av FWTH BL4 ....
Moorside Wk
WGNW/BIL/OR WN5 ....
Morano Dr WGNE/HIN WN2 ....
Morden Av AIMK WN4 ....
Moresby Cl LEIGH WN7 ....
Moreton Cl GOL/RIS/CUL WA3 ....
Moreton Dr LEIGH WN7 ....
Morgans Wy
GOL/RIS/CUL WA3 ....
Morley's La TYLD M29 ....
Morley St ATH M46 ....
Mornington Rd ATH M46 ....
WGNE/HIN WN2 ....
Morris Fold Dr HOR/BR BL6 ....
Morris Rd SKEL WN8 ....
Morris St TYLD M29 ....
WGN WN1 ....

E/HIN WN2 .... 36 A3
.../ST WGN WN1 .... 54 D4
e Cl WALK M28 .... 41 E5
.TYLD M29 .... 54 D1
...Cl WGNS/IIMK WN3 .... 34 A3
.Cl WGNS/IIMK WN3 .... 46 D1
.LEIGH WN7 .... 36 D3
.NW/ST WN6 .... 21 H4
.Dr WGNS/IIMK WN3 .... 34 A4
.le Av WGNW/HAY WA11 ...... 58 A5
.le Cl TYLD M29 .... 54 B5
Common Rd
/ M28 .... 54 D4
d LEIGH WN7 .... 65 C1
d WGNW/BIL/OR WN5 .... 31 C5
ank Rd
/HAY WA11 .... 57 H5
rough Rd
.HAY WA11 .... 56 A1
ook Dr LHULT M38 .... 40 D2
row RNFD/HAY WA11 .... 42 D4
le Rd AIMK WN4 .... 47 H5
old TYLD M29 .... 54 B4
d WGNW/ST WN6 .... 10 B2
d Gv BOLS/LL BL3 .... 27 E3
a GOL/RIS/CUL WA3 .... 70 C4
/HAY WA11 .... 59 E2
M29 .... 66 D5
ane Vw SKEL WN8 .... 35 H5
ne Vw SKEL WN8 .... 29 E2
eadow WHTN BL5 .... 25 H3
ook La
/HAY WA11 .... 42 D5
d WGNS/IIMK WN3 .... 31 C5
WGNW/ST WN6 .... 21 H4
/IIMK WN3 .... 35 C5
W/BIL/OR WN5 * 53 C2
d WGNW/BIL/OR WN5 .... 32 C3
ea Fold
ST WN6 .... 4 A4
norres Cl WHTN BL5 .... 39 C1
Pleasant St
/BR BL6 .... 14 C1
Skip La LHULT M38 .... 41 F4
st HOR/BR BL6 .... 14 C1
H WN7 .... 64 B2
unt SKEL WN8 * 7 H5
ue WGNS/IIMK WN3 .... 34 C3
wood SKEL WN8 .... 17 F1
y AIMK WN4 .... 61 G3
d Cl BOLS/LL BL3 .... 27 C2
d TYLD M29 .... 54 B4
ry Cl
RIS/CUL WA3 .... 71 G2
rs Cl
Cl GOL/RIS/CUL WA3 ...... 71 F1
la NEWLW WA12 .... 19 H5
ster Dr RNFD/HAY WA11 ... 43 F4
Av WGNW/BIL/OR WN5 ..... 31 H2
er WGNS/IIMK WN3 .... 33 H5
St ATH M46 .... 52 C1
Cl LEIGH WN7 .... 65 C4
le AIMK WN4 .... 47 C5
H WN1 .... 51 H4
Gv
W/BIL/OR WN5 * 58 C2
st WGN WN1 .... 2 B5

New Hall Ms BOL BL1 .... 15 H1
Newhart Gv WALK M28 .... 55 H1
Newhaven Av LEIGH WN7 ...... 52 A3
Newholme Gdns WALK M28 .... 41 H5
Newhouse Dr WGNS/IIMK WN3 .. 47 E3
Newland Av
WGNW/BIL/OR WN5 .... 33 E3
Newland Dr WHTN BL5 .... 39 C1
Newland Ms
GOL/RIS/CUL WA3 .... 72 D4
Newlands Av LEIGH WN7 ...... 65 C1
Newlands Dr
GOL/RIS/CUL WA3 .... 70 D1
HOR/BR BL6 .... 13 F5
Newlands Rd LEIGH WN7 ...... 64 D3
New Lester Cl TYLD M29 ...... 54 B4
New Lester Way LHULT M38 ... 40 D4
Newsham Wk
WGNW/ST WN6 .... 22 B5
Newlyn Dr AIMK WN4 .... 61 E4
SKEL WN8 .... 30 A1
Newman Av WGNE/HIN WN2 ... 36 D5
Newman Cl WGNE/HIN WN2 ... 35 H2
Newman St AIMK WN4 .... 3 H1
New Market St WGN WN1 ..... 3 F5
New Meadow HOR/BR BL6 .... 15 H3
New Miles La WGNNW/ST WN6 . 9 E4
New Rd WGNE/HIN WN2 ...... 12 B4
Newsham Wk
WGNW/ST WN6 * 21 H4
News La RNFD/HAY WA11 ..... 43 E1
Newstead Dr BOLS/LL BL3 .... 27 H5
Newstead Rd WGNS/IIMK WN3 . 33 F5
New St WGNE/HIN WN2 ...... 49 F2
New Tempest Rd HOR/BR BL6 . 26 D1
Newton Cl WGN WN1 .... 2 E1
Newton Gdns
GOL/RIS/CUL WA3 .... 71 H1
Newton La GOL/RIS/CUL WA3 .. 70 A2
NEWLW WA12 .... 69 H3
Newton Rd GOL/RIS/CUL WA3 .. 71 F3
WGNW/BIL/OR WN5 .... 46 A5
Newton St WGNE/HIN WN2 ... 65 E1
New York BOLS/LL BL3 .... 27 G1
Nicol Mere Dr AIMK WN4 ..... 61 E1
Nicol Rd AIMK WN4 .... 60 D1
Nightingale Rd HOR/BR BL6 .. 7 H4
Nipe La RNFD/HAY WA11 ..... 29 E4
Nixons La SKEL WN8 .... 30 A1
Noble St LEIGH WN7 * 65 F1
Nook La GOL/RIS/CUL WA3 .... 70 C1
TYLD M29 .... 67 G4
The Nook WGNNW/ST WN6 ... 8 D5
Norbreck Crs WGNNW/ST WN6 . 21 H1
Norbury Av
WGNW/BIL/OR WN5 .... 45 G5
Norbury Cl LEIGH WN7 .... 64 C1
Norfolk Av WGNE/HIN WN2 ... 36 D5
Norfolk Rd AIMK WN4 .... 38 D3
WGNW/BIL/OR WN5 .... 45 H2
Norfolk St WGNW/ST WN6 .... 21 H1
WGNW/BIL/OR WN5 .... 33 G2
Norley Hall Av
WGNW/BIL/OR WN5 .... 32 D2
Norley Rd LEIGH WN7 .... 64 D2
WGNW/BIL/OR WN5 .... 32 D2
Norman Av RNFD/HAY WA11 .. 68 D2
Normanby Rd WALK M28 ..... 55 G4
Normanby St
WGNW/ST WN6 .... 32 C2
Normanton Cl
WGNNW/ST WN6 .... 21 F1
Norris St FWTH BL4 .... 41 H1
Northam Cl WGNNW/ST WN6 .. 10 A1
Northcroft WGN WN1 .... 3 K5
North Edge LEIGH WN7 ...... 52 C5
Northfield SKEL WN8 .... 17 G1
North Florida Rd
RNFD/HAY WA11 .... 68 B1
North Dr WALK M28 .... 55 H1
North La TYLD M29 .... 53 H5
Northolt Av SKEL WN8 .... 52 A3
North Rd ATH M46 .... 46 C1
North St AIMK WN4 .... 61 C1
ATH M46 .... 39 F5
LEIGH WN7 .... 65 G2
RNFD/HAY WA11 .... 68 B3
Northumberland St WGN WN1 . 3 H2
Northway SKEL WN8 .... 17 G3
WGN WN1 .... 2 C3
Northways WGNNW/ST WN6 .. 5 E5
Northwell St LEIGH WN7 ..... 51 H3
Northwold Cl WGNS/IIMK WN3 . 33 E5
Northwood Av WGNE/HIN WN2 . 70 A5
Norton Rd WALK M28 .... 54 D4
Norweb Wy LEIGH WN7 ...... 23 F5
Norwich Av AIMK WN4 .... 61 G4
GOL/RIS/CUL WA3 .... 71 E1
Norwick Cl BOLS/LL BL3 ..... 27 F1
Norwood Av AIMK WN4 ...... 47 G5
GOL/RIS/CUL WA3 .... 71 F2
TYLD M29 .... 53 H1
WGNNW/ST WN6 .... 21 H2
Norwood Gv RNFD/HAY WA11 . 43 E5
Nostell Rd AIMK WN4 .... 60 D1
Nottingham Pl WGN WN1 .... 3 H2
Nuttall St ATH M46 .... 39 F5
Nutt St WGN WN1 .... 3 G2

Oak Av GOL/RIS/CUL WA3 ..... 70 C1
RNFD/HAY WA11 .... 68 B2
WGNE/HIN WN2 .... 11 H2
WGNNW/ST WN6 .... 10 C2
Oakbank WGNE/HIN WN2 ..... 11 H2
Oakbarton HOR/BR BL6 ...... 26 D1
Oak Crs SKEL WN8 .... 16 C4
Oakdale Dr TYLD M29 .... 54 B5
Oakenden Cl AIMK WN4 ...... 47 H5
Oakengates WGNNW/ST WN6 .. 10 C1
Oakfield Av ATH M46 .... 38 D4
Oakfield Crs WGNE/HIN WN2 .. 12 D5
Oakfield Dr LHULT M38 ...... 40 D5
Oakfield Gv FWTH BL4 ...... 41 H2

Oakhead LEIGH WN7 .... 65 H3
Oak Hill Cl WGN WN1 * 22 A2
Oakhurst Dr WHTN BL5 ...... 37 H1
Oaklands
GOL/RIS/CUL WA3 .... 71 G2
Oaklea WGNNW/ST WN6 ..... 4 B5
Oakleigh SKEL WN8 .... 44 A1
Oakley Av WGNW/BIL/OR WN5 . 45 C5
Oakley Dr WGNW/BIL/OR WN5 . 33 F2
The Oaklings WGNE/HIN WN2 . 36 D5
Oak St ATH M46 .... 52 B2
LEIGH WN7 .... 65 E3
TYLD M29 .... 53 H5
WGN WN1 .... 3 G5
Oak Tree Cl ATH M46 .... 52 B2
Oak Tree Ct SKEL WN8 ...... 18 A2
Oakwood SKEL WN8 * 18 A2
Oakwood Av AIMK WN4 ...... 60 D4
WGNW/ST WN6 .... 9 C5
Oakwood Dr LEIGH WN7 ..... 64 D5
Oban Dr AIMK WN4 .... 59 H2
Oban Wy WGNE/HIN WN2 * .. 13 E5
Okell Cv LEIGH WN7 .... 64 C1
Okell Gv LEIGH WN7 * 64 C1
Old Beechfield Gdns
.... 10 A1
Old Boston RNFD/HAY WA11 .. 68 D2
Oldbridge Dr WGNE/HIN WN2 . 36 A2
Old Colliery Yd AIMK WN4 ... 61 H5
Old Engine La SKEL WN8 ..... 16 B3
Oldfield Cl WHTN BL5 .... 26 A5
Old Fold WGNW/BIL/OR WN5 . 32 C2
Old Fold Rd WGNE/HIN WN2 .. 13 E5
WHTN BL5 .... 37 E1
Old Greenwood La
.... 14 C1
Old Hall Clough HOR/BR BL6 . 15 H4
Old Hall Dr WGNE/HIN WN2 .. 60 D4
Old Hall Gdns RNFD/HAY WA11 43 H5
Old Hall La HOR/BR BL6 ..... 15 H1
WHTN BL5 .... 37 C3
Old Hall Mill La ATH M46 ... 52 B3
Old Hall St WGNS/IIMK WN3 . 34 D2
Old La LHULT M38 .... 41 E3
RNFD/HAY WA11 .... 43 E4
WGN WN1 .... 9 C4
WGNNW/ST WN6 .... 4 B5
WHTN BL5 .... 25 C5
Old Manor Pk ATH M46 ..... 52 B1
Old Pepper La
WGNNW/ST WN6 .... 4 C5
Old Rd AIMK WN4 .... 61 G3
Old School La CHLY/EC PR7 .. 6 D2
Old School Pl AIMK WN4 .... 60 D3
Oldstead Gv BOLS/LL BL3 ... 27 C1
Old Town Cl SKEL WN8 ..... 16 C5
Old Town Wy SKEL WN8 .... 16 C5
Old Vicarage WHTN BL5 .... 37 H3
Old Wells Cl LHULT M38 .... 41 F2
Olive Gv SKEL WN8 .... 16 D4
WGNW/ST WN6 .... 21 C2
Oliver St ATH M46 .... 39 E5
Ollerton Cl WGNE/HIN WN2 .. 23 F3
Opal Gv LEIGH WN7 .... 64 D2
Orchard Av WALK M28 ...... 55 C4
Orchard Cl LEIGH WN7 ...... 52 A4
.... 9 F3
Orchard Ct
The Orchards
WGNW/BIL/OR WN5 .... 31 H3
Orchard St AIMK WN4 ...... 61 F3
WGN WN1 .... 2 E4
The Orchard WHTN BL5 ..... 25 H4
Orchid Cl SKEL WN8 .... 31 C2
Ordsall Av LHULT M38 ..... 41 G4
Orford Cl GOL/RIS/CUL WA3 . 70 B2
Orford Ct LEIGH WN7 ...... 65 C4
Organ St LEIGH WN7 .... 64 D1
WGNE/HIN WN2 .... 36 D5
Oriel Rd AIMK WN4 .... 47 C5
Oriole Cl WALK M28 .... 55 C4
Oriole Dr WALK M28 .... 55 C3
Ormsby Cl WGNNW/ST WN6 . 10 B1
Ormside Cl WGNE/HIN WN2 . 37 E5
Ormskirk Rd RNFD/HAY WA11 42 C1
SKEL WN8 .... 30 B5
WGNW/ST WN6 .... 32 D2
Ormston Gv LEIGH WN7 .... 52 A4
Orpington St
WGNW/BIL/OR WN5 .... 32 D2
Orrell Av WGN WN1 .... 3 C1
Orrell Gdns
WGNW/BIL/OR WN5 .... 32 A2
Orrell Hall Cl
WGNW/BIL/OR WN5 .... 31 H1
Orrell St WGN WN1 .... 3 F7
Orton Wy AIMK WN4 .... 60 D4
Orwell Cl WGNW/BIL/OR WN5 31 H1
Osborne Ct ATH M46 ...... 52 A2
Osborne Gv LEIGH WN7 .... 53 E5
Osborne Rd AIMK WN4 ..... 60 D2
GOL/RIS/CUL WA3 .... 71 F2
Oscott Av LHULT M38 ...... 41 F3
Osprey Cl LEIGH WN7 ...... 65 F2
The Ospreys WGNS/IIMK WN3 32 D5
Otterwood Sq
WGNNW/ST WN6 .... 20 D3
Oulton Cl LEIGH WN7 ...... 65 F2
The Oval WGNNW/ST WN6 .. 9 E5
Overbeck Cl WGNW/ST WN6 . 31 C2
Overdene Cl HOR/BR BL6 ... 15 C4
Overhill Wy WGNS/IIMK WN3 33 E5
Overton St LEIGH WN7 ..... 64 D2
Owenington Gv LHULT M38 . 41 F3
Owen St LEIGH WN7 * 64 C1
Owlwood Cl LHULT M38 .... 40 D5
Owlwood Dr LHULT M38 .... 40 D5
Oxburgh Rd WGNS/IIMK WN3 35 C4
Oxford Cl WGN WN1 .... 1 F3
Oxford Rd ATH M46 .... 38 D4
HOR/BR BL6 .... 15 E2
SKEL WN8 .... 16 D4
WGN WN1 .... 32 A1
Oxford St CHLY/EC PR7 .... 7 E1
LEIGH WN7 .... 52 A4
WGNE/HIN WN2 .... 49 F2
Ox Hey Cl HOR/BR BL6 .... 14 D2
Ox Hey La HOR/BR BL6 .... 15 E3

Oxhouse Rd
WGNW/BIL/OR WN5 .... 31 F4
Oxlea Gv WHTN BL5 .... 37 H1

Paddock Cl ATH M46 ...... 39 F3
Paddock Ri WGNNW/ST WN6 . 21 F2
Paddock Rd SKEL WN8 ..... 29 H4
The Paddock AIMK WN4 ... 47 G5
Padiham Cl LEIGH WN7 .... 65 F1
Pagefield Cl WGNNW/ST WN6 21 H4
Pagefield St WGNNW/ST WN6 21 H4
Paignton Cl
WGNNW/ST WN6 * 45 H3
Palace Ar AIMK WN4 ...... 61 E3
Palatine Cl WGNS/IIMK WN3 33 F4
Palatine Sq LEIGH WN7 .... 64 C1
Palewood Cl WGN WN1 .... 3 C2
Palin St WGNE/HIN WN2 ... 36 D5
Palm Av AIMK WN4 .... 60 D1
Palm Ct SKEL WN8 .... 16 D3
Palmer Gv LEIGH WN7 .... 51 H2
Palmerston St WGNE/HIN WN2 35 H4
Palm Gv WGNS/IIMK WN3 . 36 B5
Panton St HOR/BR BL6 .... 14 C1
The Parchments NEWLW WA12 69 C5
Paris Av WGNS/IIMK WN3 . 32 D5
Park Av GOL/RIS/CUL WA3 . 62 A4
WGNE/HIN WN2 .... 36 D5
WGNW/BIL/OR WN5 .... 45 H2
Park Bank ATH M46 ...... 39 C2
Parkbrook La WGNNW/ST WN6 9 C3
Park Crs West WGN WN1 .. 2 B2
Park Crs WGN WN1 ...... 2 B2
Parkdale TYLD M29 .... 67 E1
Park Edge WHTN BL5 ..... 38 B1
Parkedge Cl LEIGH WN7 ... 64 C3
Parkend Dr LEIGH WN7 ... 64 C3
Parkfield WGNNW/ST WN6 . 9 C5
Parkfield Av FWTH BL4 ... 41 H1
TYLD M29 .... 54 A5
Parkfield Cl LEIGH WN7 ... 52 B4
TYLD M29 .... 54 A5
Parkfield Dr TYLD M29 ... 54 A5
Parkfields WGNE/HIN WN2 49 G4
Parkham Cl WHTN BL5 .... 38 A2
Park Hey Dr WGNNW/ST WN6 8 D2
Parklands RNFD/HAY WA11 43 E4
SKEL WN8 .... 18 A3
Parklands Dr WGNE/HIN WN2 22 B2
Park La LEIGH WN7 ...... 65 H2
WGNE/HIN WN2 .... 49 G4
Park Meadow WHTN BL5 . 26 B5
Park Rd CHLY/EC PR7 .... 6 D1
WGNE/HIN WN2 .... 49 C4
WALK M28 .... 55 H2
WGNNW/ST WN6 .... 36 B5
WGNNW/ST WN6 .... 10 B2
WGNNW/ST WN6 .... 21 H4
WHTN BL5 .... 26 A5
Parkside WGNW/BIL/OR WN5 36 B2
Parkside Av AIMK WN4 ... 47 G3
SKEL WN8 .... 16 B3
Parkside Crs
WGNW/BIL/OR WN5 .... 32 A2
Parks Nook FWTH BL4 .... 41 H1
The Parks NEWLW WA12 .. 21 E5
Park St ATH M46 .... 39 F4
TYLD M29 .... 53 H2
WGNS/IIMK WN3 .... 34 A2
WGNW/BIL/OR WN5 .... 49 E2
Park Vw AIMK WN4 ...... 47 H5
WGNE/HIN WN2 .... 49 C2
WGNW/BIL/OR WN5 * 58 D5
Parkway LHULT M38 ..... 40 D4
WGNS/IIMK WN3 .... 34 A2
WHTN BL5 .... 37 C3
Parkway Gv LHULT M38 .. 40 D4
Parkwood Cl WGNS/IIMK WN3 34 D2
Parkwood Dr WHTN BL5 .. 39 C1
Parliament St SKEL WN8 .. 17 F5
WGNS/IIMK WN3 .... 34 C2
Parnell Cl TYLD M29 ..... 67 E1
Parr Fold Av WALK M28 .. 55 H2
Parr St TYLD M29 .... 53 C3
Parsonage Brow SKEL WN8 18 C5
Parsonage Cl SKEL WN8 .. 30 D1
Parsonage Dr WALK M28 . 55 H1
Parsonage Rd SKEL WN8 . 30 D1
WALK M28 .... 55 H1
Parsonage Wy LEIGH WN7 55 H1
Parson's Brow
RNFD/HAY WA11 .... 42 D5
Parson's Wk WGN WN1 .. 2 B3
Partington St
Part St WHTN BL5 .... 21 F5
Pasture Cl AIMK WN4 .... 47 F5
Pasture La RNFD/HAY WA11 56 B2
Pateley Sq WGNNW/ST WN6 22 A3
Patricroft Rd WGNE/HIN WN2 35 F2
Patterdale Av LEIGH WN7 . 53 E5
Patterdale Rd AIMK WN4 . 47 H3
LEIGH WN7 .... 65 H2
Patterson St BOLS/LL BL3 . 27 H1
NEWLW WA12 .... 69 E5
WHTN BL5 .... 35 E1
Paulhan St WGNE/HIN WN2 36 A2
Pavilion Gdns WHTN BL5 . 25 H5
Paxton Pl SKEL WN8 ..... 29 H4
Peace St ATH M46 .... 39 F5
TYLD M29 .... 53 H5
Peach Gv RNFD/HAY WA11 * 68 B2
Peacock Fold LEIGH WN7 . 51 C5
Peak Av ATH M46 .... 38 D3
Pearl St WGNNW/ST WN6 . 21 H1
Pear Tree Cl WGNE/HIN WN2 12 D4
Pear Tree Ct SKEL WN8 .. 16 C4
Pear Tree Gv TYLD M29 .. 54 D2
Peebles Cl AIMK WN4 .... 59 H2
Peel Cl AIMK WN4 .... 61 H3
Peel Dr LHULT M38 ...... 41 E4
Peel Hall Av TYLD M29 .. 54 A2
Peel La TYLD M29 .... 67 E2
WALK M28 .... 41 H5
Peel Park Crs LHULT M38 41 E4

Peel Rd SKEL WN8 .... 30 A3
Peel St LEIGH WN7 ...... 64 D1
WGNE/HIN WN2 .... 49 F1
SKEL WN8 .... 25 H4
Peelwood Av LHULT M38 . 41 F4
Peelwood Gv ATH M46 .. 53 F1
Pelham Gv WGNE/HIN WN2 36 A4
Pemberlei Rd WGNE/HIN WN2 24 A3
Pemberton Rd
WGNS/IIMK WN3 .... 46 C2
Pemberton St LHULT M38 41 C4
Pembroke Rd WGNE/HIN WN2 37 F5
WGNW/BIL/OR WN5 ...... 21 C4
Penbury Rd WGN WN1 ... 11 E5
Pendeen Cl TYLD M29 ... 53 H4
Pendennis Crs WGNE/HIN WN2 36 D5
Pendlebury Fold BOLS/LL BL3 27 E3
Pendlebury La WGN WN1 . 11 F4
Pendle Cl WGNW/BIL/OR WN5 45 E3
Pendle Ct LEIGH WN7 .... 65 C2
SKEL WN8 .... 30 A5
Pendle Pl SKEL WN8 ..... 30 A4
Pendle Rd GOL/RIS/CUL WA3 62 D5
Penketh Av TYLD M29 ... 54 A5
Penketh Pl SKEL WN8 ... 29 H5
Penleach Av LEIGH WN7 . 65 C1
Pennell Dr WGNS/IIMK WN3 33 C3
Pennine Cl WGNE/HIN WN2 32 D5
Pennine Gv LEIGH WN7 .. 65 C1
Pennine La GOL/RIS/CUL WA3 62 D5
Pennine Pl SKEL WN8 .... 29 C2
Pennington Av LEIGH WN7 64 D3
Pennington Cl LHULT M38 40 D4
WGNE/HIN WN2 .... 24 D4
Pennington Gdns LEIGH WN7 64 D3
Pennington Green La
WGNE/HIN WN2 .... 24 B3
Pennington La
WGNE/HIN WN2 .... 11 H1
WGNE/HIN WN2 .... 23 F5
Pennington Rd LEIGH WN7 64 D3
Pennington St
WGNE/HIN WN2 .... 36 A2
Pennygate Cl WGNE/HIN WN2 36 A2
Pennyhurst St
WGNS/IIMK WN3 .... 2 A6
Penny La RNFD/HAY WA11 68 D2
Penrhyn Gv ATH M46 .... 38 D3
Penrice Fold WALK M28 . 55 C4
Penrith Crs AIMK WN4 ... 61 E2
Penrose Pl SKEL WN8 .... 30 B4
Penshaw Av WGNS/IIMK WN3 34 A5
Penson St WGN WN1 .... 2 E1
Penswick Rd WGNE/HIN WN2 36 D5
Pepper La WGNNW/ST WN6 4 C4
Pepper Mill La WGN WN1 2 E7
Pepperwood Dr
WGNS/IIMK WN3 .... 47 F1
Pepys Pl WGNS/IIMK WN3 33 H4
Percy St WGN WN1 ...... 3 C5
Percival Wy LEIGH WN7 . 65 C1
Peregrine Dr LEIGH WN7 65 C1
Perryn Pl WGNNW/ST WN6 10 C1
Perry Rd WGNE/HIN WN2 23 F5
Petersfield Gdns
GOL/RIS/CUL WA3 .... 72 D5
Peter St AIMK WN4 ...... 61 F3
GOL/RIS/CUL WA3 .... 70 B1
LEIGH WN7 .... 53 C2
TYLD M29 .... 53 C2
WGNE/HIN WN2 .... 36 A3
WGNW/BIL/OR WN5 ..... 20 C5
WHTN BL5 .... 36 D1
Petrel Cl TYLD M29 ..... 53 H3
Petticoat La WGNE/HIN WN2 23 C5
Petworth Av WGNS/IIMK WN3 47 F1
Pewfist Gn WHTN BL5 ... 37 H2
The Pewfist Spinney
WHTN BL5 .... 37 H1
The Pewfist WHTN BL5 .. 37 H1
Pheasant Cl WALK M28 . 55 C5
Philip Cl WGNW/BIL/OR WN5 33 E3
Phillips St SKEL WN8 .... 31 C2
Phipps St WALK M28 .... 41 H4
Picadilly WGNW/BIL/OR WN5 58 D2
Pickley Gdns LEIGH WN7 . 51 H2
Picksley St LEIGH WN7 .. 51 C2
Pickthorn Cl WGNE/HIN WN2 36 D5
Pickup St WGNE/HIN WN2 3 K7
Piele Rd RNFD/HAY WA11 68 B2
Piggott St FWTH BL4 .... 41 H1
Pigot St WGNW/BIL/OR WN5 32 C2
Pike Av ATH M46 .... 53 F1
Pikelaw Pl SKEL WN8 ... 29 H4
Pilgrims Wy WGNNW/ST WN6 10 D3
Pilkington St RNFD/HAY WA11 43 F5
WGNE/HIN WN2 .... 49 C2
Pilling Pl SKEL WN8 ..... 29 H3
Pilling St LEIGH WN7 .... 64 C1
Pilsley Cl WGNW/BIL/OR WN5 20 B4
Pimblett Rd RNFD/HAY WA11 68 B2
Pimblett St
GOL/RIS/CUL WA3 * 70 B2
Pimbo La SKEL WN8 ..... 30 C5
Pimbo Rd RNFD/HAY WA11 44 B3
SKEL WN8 .... 29 H5
Pine Cl SKEL WN8 ...... 17 C4
Pine Dr RNFD/HAY WA11 68 B3
Pine Gv GOL/RIS/CUL WA3 70 D1
WHTN BL5 .... 37 H1
Pine Rd WGNW/BIL/OR WN5 57 F2
The Pines LEIGH WN7 ... 65 E3
Pine St TYLD M29 .... 53 H2
Pinevale WGNNW/ST WN6 10 D3
Pine Vw WGNS/IIMK WN3 46 C2
Pinewood AIMK WN4 .... 60 D4
SKEL WN8 .... 18 A2
Pinewood Cl WGNE/HIN WN2 49 C4
Pinewood Crs WGNE/HIN WN2 35 E2
Pinfold Cl WHTN BL5 .... 37 G2
Pinfold Pl SKEL WN8 .... 30 A4
Pinfold Rd WALK M28 ... 55 H2
Pinfold St WGNE/HIN WN2 35 F1
Pingot Rd WGNW/BIL/OR WN5 58 D5
The Pingot LEIGH WN7 .. 64 C1
The Pingots GOL/RIS/CUL WA3 71 C1
Pit Hey Pl SKEL WN8 .... 29 H5
Pitt St WGNS/IIMK WN3 . 2 B6
Plane Av WGNW/BIL/OR WN5 33 F1

Plane Tree Gv
  RNFD/HAY WA11 *................68 D2
Plank La LEIGH WN7................63 H2
Plantation Av WALK M28.........44 B4
Plantation Gates WGN WN1......22 D3
Platt Ct LEIGH WN7................65 H2
Platt Fold Rd LEIGH WN7.........52 B5
Platt Fold St LEIGH WN7..........65 F1
Platt Hill Av BOLS/LL BL3.........27 H1
Platt La WGN WN1..................3 G4
  WGN WN1............................6 A4
  WGNE/HIN WN2...................36 A3
  WHTN BL5............................38 C2
Platt St LEIGH WN7.................52 A5
Pleasance Wy NEWLW WA12....69 F5
Plodder La WHTN BL5.............27 H5
Ploughfields WHTN BL5...........25 H2
Plover Wy GOL/RIS/CUL WA3....71 F1
Plymouth Gv
  WGNNW/ST WN6................10 D3
Pocket Nook La
  GOL/RIS/CUL WA3................72 A2
Pocket Nook Rd HOR/BR BL6...26 C2
Poet's Nook LEIGH WN7...........64 D2
Poke St WGNE/HIN WN3..........34 C3
Polding St WGNS/IIMK WN3.....36 C2
Polegate Dr LEIGH WN7............51 G1
Pole St WGNNW/ST WN6..........10 B1
Pond St GOL/RIS/CUL WA3.......71 H1
Pondwater Cl WALK M28...........41 E5
Poolstock La WGNS/IIMK WN3...34 A2
Poolstock La WGNS/IIMK WN3...33 H4
Pool St WGNE/HIN WN2............36 A4
  WGNS/IIMK WN3..................34 A2
Poplar Av AIMK WN4................60 A1
  HOR/BR BL6..........................14 D1
  WGNE/HIN WN2....................36 A3
Poplar Dr SKEL WN8................17 E4
Poplar Gv WGNE/HIN WN2........51 F1
  WHTN BL5............................25 H5
The Poplars CHLY/EC PR7.........7 E1
  LEIGH WN7............................72 B1
Poplar St GOL/RIS/CUL WA3.....62 C5
  LEIGH WN7............................65 E5
  TYLD M29.............................53 H2
Porlock Cl WGNE/HIN WN2.......49 F2
Porter Av NEWLW WA12............69 F4
Porterfield Dr TYLD M29...........53 H3
Porters Wood Cl
  WGNNW/BIL/OR WN5...........32 C1
Porthleven Crs TYLD M29..........54 B3
Portland Cl WGNS/IIMK WN3....49 F2
Portland Rd WALK M28.............41 H3
Portland St NEWLW WA12.........68 C5
  WGNE/HIN WN2....................33 F2
Potter Pl SKEL WN8.................30 A3
Pottery Rd WGNS/IIMK WN3.....32 D2
Pottery Ter WGNS/IIMK WN3.....2 A7
Poulton Dr AIMK WN4..............60 C2
Powell Dr WGNW/BIL/OR WN5...58 C3
Powell St WGN WN1................2 D5
  WGNE/HIN WN2....................49 G2
Pownall St LEIGH WN7.............65 F1
Powys St ATH M46..................53 F2
Praeton Cl ATH M46................52 B2
Prefect Pl WGNW/BIL/OR WN5...24 D5
Presbyterian Fold
  WGNE/HIN WN2....................36 A2
Prescot Av ATH M46................39 F3
  TYLD M29.............................54 B2
Prescott Cl GOL/RIS/CUL WA3...62 A4
Prescott La
  WGNW/BIL/OR WN5.............20 C5
Prescott Rd SKEL WN8.............30 B4
Prescott St GOL/RIS/CUL WA3...62 B5
  WALK M28............................41 G5
  WGN WN1.............................3 H4
  WGNS/IIMK WN3..................21 H5
Prestbury Av WGNS/IIMK WN3...33 F5
Prestt Gv WGNS/IIMK WN3.......35 H1
Prestwich Av LEIGH WN7..........65 G1
Prestwich St ATH M46..............38 C4
Pretoria Rd AIMK WN4.............60 D1
Priestfields LEIGH WN7............60 C1
Priestners Wy LEIGH WN7.........51 H5
Primrose Av WALK M28.............55 C1
Primrose Bank WALK M28.........55 C1
Primrose Gv RNFD/HAY WA11...68 B2
  WGNW/BIL/OR WN5 * 5 F5
Primrose La LEIGH WN7............64 C1
Primrose St North TYLD M29.....53 H2
Primrose Vw AIMK WN4............61 E4
Primula Dr GOL/RIS/CUL WA3...71 F1
Prince's Av TYLD M29...............53 H5
Princes Gdns LEIGH WN7..........65 H1
Prince's Pk WGNNW/ST WN6....20 A1
Princess Av AIMK WN4.............61 F3
  ATH M46..............................38 D5
  RNFD/HAY WA11..................68 D2
Princess Rd AIMK WN4.............61 E3
  HOR/BR BL6..........................16 D1
  WGNE/HIN WN2....................20 D1
Princess St LEIGH WN7 *..........65 H1
  WGN WN1.............................35 • I5
  WGNS/IIMK WN3..................2 C7
Prince St AIMK WN4................60 D1
Printshop La ATH M46..............53 F5
Priorswood Pl SKEL WN8..........30 A2
Priory Cl WGNW/BIL/OR WN5...51 C2
Priory Ct WGNW/BIL/OR WN5...32 C5
Priory Nook SKEL WN8.............31 F1
Priory Rd AIMK WN4................60 C1
  SKEL WN8.............................31 F1
Proctor Cl WGNW/BIL/OR WN5..21 F4
Prodesse Ct WGNE/HIN WN2.....36 A2
Progress St WGNE/HIN WN2......36 A3
Prospect Pl FWTH BL4..............41 H1
  SKEL WN8.............................30 C3
Prospect Rd WGNNW/ST WN6...59 E5
Prospect St TYLD M29..............53 G2
  WGNE/HIN WN2....................36 A3
Prosser Av ATH M46................52 B1
Pryce Av WGNE/HIN WN2..........3 J6
Pump St WGNE/HIN WN2..........36 A4
Punch La WHTN BL5................27 E4
The Pungle WHTN BL5.............50 B5
Purbeck Dr HOR/BR BL6...........15 E2
Purbeck Wy TYLD M29.............53 H4

Pye Cl RNFD/HAY WA11............69 E1
Pyke St WGN WN1..................3 F2

Q

Quakerfields WHTN BL5...........37 G1
Quakers' Pl WGNNW/ST WN6....10 B1
Quantock Cl WGNS/IIMK WN3...46 D1
Quarry Pl WGN WN1................1 G1
Quarry Pond Rd WALK M28......41 F5
Quarry St WGNE/HIN WN2........54 D2
Quayside LEIGH WN7...............64 D2
Queen Ann Dr WALK M28.........55 G4
Queen's Av AIMK WN4.............61 E2
  ATH M46..............................38 D3
  GOL/RIS/CUL WA3................73 H2
Queens Cl WALK M28..............55 G4
Queens Dr GOL/RIS/CUL WA3...70 D1
  NEWLW WA12.......................69 F4
Queens Gdns LEIGH WN7..........65 H1
Queens Hall Pas WGN WN1 *....2 C5
Queen's Rd AIMK WN4.............61 E3
Queens Rd RNFD/HAY WA11.....68 D2
  WGN WN1.............................31 F5
Queen St GOL/RIS/CUL WA3 *...70 C1
  LEIGH WN7............................41 G5
  LHULT M38...........................41 G5
  WGNE/HIN WN2....................49 F1
  WGNS/IIMK WN3..................2 C6
  WGNW/BIL/OR WN5.............32 C2
  WHTN BL5............................25 H2
Queensway LEIGH WN7............66 A1
  RNFD/HAY WA11..................56 B1
  WALK M28............................55 C3
  WGN WN1.............................22 A3
  WGNE/HIN WN2....................23 F5
  WGNNW/ST WN6................20 A1

R

Radbourne Gv BOLS/LL BL3.....27 G1
Radcliffe Gv LEIGH WN7...........52 A4
Radnor Gv WGNE/HIN WN2......36 D5
Radnor Dr LEIGH WN7.............64 B1
Radway TYLD M29..................54 B2
Rail Cl RNFD/HAY WA11...........43 E1
Railway Rd
  GOL/RIS/CUL WA3................70 C1
  LEIGH WN7............................64 D1
  SKEL WN8.............................16 C5
Railway St ATH M46................38 C4
  WGNE/HIN WN2....................36 B1
  WGNW/BIL/OR WN5.............21 H4
Rainbow Dr ATH M46..............39 E4
Rainford By-Pass
  RNFD/HAY WA11..................41 C4
Rainford Rd ORM L39..............28 B4
  WGNW/BIL/OR WN5.............58 A1
Raithby Dr WGNS/IIMK WN3....36 C5
Rampit Cl RNFD/HAY WA11......68 C2
Ramsay Av FWTH BL4..............41 G1
Ramsden Cl WGNS/IIMK WN3...33 H3
Ramsey Cl AIMK WN4..............61 E4
  ATH M46..............................53 F1
Ramsey St LEIGH WN7 *...........51 G1
Ram St LHULT M38..................41 E4
Randall Av WGNNW/ST WN6.....9 F5
Randle Av RNFD/HAY WA11......42 D3
Randle Brook Ct
  RNFD/HAY WA11..................42 D3
Rands Clough Dr WALK M28.....55 G5
Ranicar Steet WGNE/HIN WN2...37 F5
Ranmore Av AIMK WN4............60 A2
Ranworth Dr
  GOL/RIS/CUL WA3................71 F2
Rassey Cl WGNNW/ST WN6......10 D3
Ratcliffe Rd WGNE/HIN WN2.....12 D4
Ratcliffe St LEIGH WN7.............52 A5
  TYLD M29.............................54 A2
Rathen Av WGNE/HIN WN2.......23 F4
Ravenhead Dr SKEL WN8..........30 D1
Ravenhead Wy SKEL WN8.........30 C2
Raven Rd BOLS/LL BL3 *..........27 H1
Ravenscraig Rd LHULT M38.......41 G2
Ravenswood Av
  WGNS/IIMK WN3..................33 G5
Ravenswood Dr
  WGNE/HIN WN2....................36 B2
Rawsthorne St TYLD M29.........54 D3
Rawtrey Pl WGNE/HIN WN2......49 E1
Raydale Cl GOL/RIS/CUL WA3...63 F5
Rayden Crs WHTN BL5.............37 H2
Recreation Av AIMK WN4..........61 G2
Recreation Dr
  WGNW/BIL/OR WN5 * 58 D1
Rectory Av GOL/RIS/CUL WA3...70 D1
Rectory Gdns WHTN BL5..........37 H4
Rectory La WGNE/HIN WN2......10 C1
Rectory Rd AIMK WN4.............60 A1
Red Barn Rd
  WGNW/BIL/OR WN5.............45 F5
Redbrook Rd WGNS/IIMK WN3..34 D2
Redburn Rd WGNS/IIMK WN3...34 A2
Red Cat La RNFD/HAY WA11.....57 F1
Red Delph La RNFD/HAY WA11..42 C2
Redfield Cft LEIGH WN7............65 E5
Redford Cl LEIGH WN7.............65 F1
Redgate Rd AIMK WN4.............48 A5
Redgrave Ri WGNS/IIMK WN3...33 E5
Red Hill Wy WGNE/HIN WN2.....49 E1
Redland Ct WGNE/HIN WN2......48 D4
Redmain Gv GOL/RIS/CUL WA3..71 F1
Redmayne Cl NEWLW WA12.....69 E5
Rednal Wk WGNS/IIMK WN3.....34 A2
Redpol Av LEIGH WN7.............64 D2
Redpoll Cl WALK M28..............55 C4
Redshank Gv LEIGH WN7..........64 D2
Redshank Gv LEIGH WN7..........52 B5
Redstart Cl GOL/RIS/CUL WA3...71 F1
Redstock Cl WHTN BL5.............36 B4
Redwater Cl WALK M28............55 F5
Red Waters LEIGH WN7............52 B5

Redwood WGNNW/ST WN6.......9 G4
  WHTN BL5............................37 G2
Redwood Av WGNS/IIMK WN3...21 G2
  WGNW/BIL/OR WN5.............32 B2
Reed Crs WGNS/IIMK WN3.......33 H4
Reedley Dr WALK M28..............55 H5
Reeds Brow RNFD/HAY WA11...43 G3
Reed's La RNFD/HAY WA11.......56 A3
Reedsmere Cl
  WGNNW/BIL/OR WN5...........33 G2
Reedymoor WHTN BL5.............37 H4
Reepham Cl WGNS/IIMK WN3...32 D5
Reeves St LEIGH WN7..............52 A5
Reeve St GOL/RIS/CUL WA3.....72 A1
Regaby Gv WGNE/HIN WN2......36 D5
Regency Ct WGN WN1..............2 E4
Regent Av AIMK WN4..............60 C1
  LHULT M38...........................41 H4
Regent Dr HOR/BR BL6............15 C3
Regent Rd GOL/RIS/CUL WA3...53 E4
  LEIGH WN7............................65 E4
  WGNE/HIN WN2....................36 A4
Regents Hi HOR/BR BL6...........15 H4
Regent St ATH M46.................53 F1
  WGNS/IIMK WN3..................35 H3
Regina Crs LEIGH WN7.............53 F5
Reginald St BOLS/LL BL3 *.......27 H5
Renfrew Cl WGNS/IIMK WN3....33 H5
Renfrew Dr BOLS/LL BL3..........27 G2
Renfrew Rd WGNE/HIN WN2.....13 E5
Renwick Sq AIMK WN4............60 C3
Repton Av WGNS/IIMK WN3.....35 H4
Reservoir St WGNE/HIN WN2....23 F5
Reynolds Cl WHTN BL5............39 G2
Reynolds Dr WHTN BL5............39 G1
Rhyl Fold LEIGH WN7 *............65 F1
Ribbesford Rd
  WGNS/IIMK WN3..................32 D5
Ribble Crs WGNW/BIL/OR WN5..58 B3
Ribble Dr WALK M28................55 E5
  WGNW/BIL/OR WN5.............32 B2
Ribble Gv LEIGH WN7..............64 B1
Ribble Rd WGNE/HIN WN2.......49 F1
Rose Hill Av
  WGNW/BIL/OR WN5.............4 C5
Richard Gwyn Cl WHTN BL5.....37 G3
Richards Rd WGNNW/ST WN6...4 C4
Richard St WGNS/IIMK WN3.....34 C2
Richmond Cl GOL/RIS/CUL WA3..71 E5
  WGN WN1.............................11 E5
Richmond Dr LEIGH WN7..........53 F4
Richmond Gv LEIGH WN7.........54 B3
Richmond Hl
  WGNW/BIL/OR WN5.............32 D2
Richmond Rd AIMK WN4..........60 C1
  WALK M28............................54 D4
  WGNE/HIN WN2....................36 D5
Richmond St WGN WN1...........2 B4
  WGNS/IIMK WN3..................33 H3
Ridge Av WGN WN1.................11 E3
Ridgeway GOL/RIS/CUL WA3....71 F2
Ridgewell Av
  GOL/RIS/CUL WA3................71 E1
Ridgmont Dr WALK M28...........55 E5
Ridgway HOR/BR BL6..............7 H5
Riding Cl TYLD M29.................54 C4
Riding La AIMK WN4................61 H1
The Ridings RNFD/HAY WA11...68 A3
Ridyard St LHULT M38..............41 H4
  WGNE/HIN WN2....................36 A5
Rigby Av WGN WN1.................3 H3
  WGNW/BIL/OR WN5.............33 F1
Rigby Gv LHULT M38...............40 D4
Rigby St AIMK WN4.................60 D3
  WGNE/HIN WN2....................36 B2
Rigbys Houses CHLY/EC PR7 *...6 D1
Riley La WGNE/HIN WN2..........12 C3
Riley Sq WGN WN1..................3 F4
Riley St ATH M46....................52 B2
Rimington Av
  GOL/RIS/CUL WA3................62 D5
Ringley Av GOL/RIS/CUL WA3...62 A5
Ringway Av LEIGH WN7............52 A5
Ripley Dr LEIGH WN7..............53 F5
  WGNS/IIMK WN3..................32 D4
Ripon Av GOL/RIS/CUL WA3.....71 E1
Ripon Cl NEWLW WA12............69 F5
Ripon Dr AIMK WN4................61 G4
The Rise WGNNW/ST WN6........20 D2
Riverdale Cl WGNNW/ST WN6...21 E2
Riverside WGN WN1.................3 F2
Riversmeade LEIGH WN7..........52 B5
Rivers St WGNW/BIL/OR WN5...31 H2
River Wy WGN WN1.................1 H5
Rivington Av
  GOL/RIS/CUL WA3................62 D5
  WGN WN1.............................22 A3
  WGNE/HIN WN2....................35 C5
Rivington Dr SKEL WN8............31 F1
Rivington St ATH M46..............52 B1
Rivington Wy WGNNW/ST WN6..10 C2
Rixton Dr TYLD M29................54 B2
Roach Gv WGN WN1................3 H5
Roadside Ct GOL/RIS/CUL WA3..70 D1
Robertshaw St LEIGH WN7.......51 H4
Robert St ATH M46.................53 F2
  WGNS/IIMK WN3..................35 F5
Robin Hill Dr WGNNW/ST WN6..4 C5
Robin Hill La WGNNW/ST WN6..4 C5
Robin Park Rd
  WGNW/BIL/OR WN5.............21 F5
Robin's La RNFD/HAY WA11.....44 C3
Rob La NEWLW WA12..............68 C5
Robson Wy GOL/RIS/CUL WA3..71 G1
Roby Mi SKEL WN8..................19 E2
Roby Well Wy
  WGNW/BIL/OR WN5.............58 C1
Rochester Av WALK M28...........55 F5
Rochester Cl GOL/RIS/CUL WA3..70 B1
Roch Pl WGNE/HIN WN2..........49 E1
Rockbourne Cl
  WGNE/HIN WN2....................36 A4
Rockingham Dr
  WGNE/HIN WN2....................35 H4
Rock St GOL/RIS/CUL WA3.......62 B4
Rocky Bank Ter
  WGNS/IIMK WN3 *................34 D3

Rodgers Cl WHTN BL5..............37 H2
Rodgers Wy WHTN BL5............37 H2
Rodney St ATH M46 *..............52 D1
  WGN WN1.............................2 D6
Roebuck St WGNE/HIN WN2.....37 F5
Roecliffe Cl WGNS/IIMK WN3...52 C5
Rogerton Cl LEIGH WN7...........65 G2
Rokeby Av GOL/RIS/CUL WA3...63 E5
Rokeden NEWLW WA12............68 C5
Roman Rd AIMK WN4..............60 D1
Romford Av LEIGH WN7...........52 A5
Romford Pl WGNE/HIN WN2.....36 D5
Romford St WGNE/HIN WN2.....36 D5
Romiley Dr SKEL WN8..............17 E3
Romiley Sq WGNNW/ST WN6....10 B1
Romney Wy WGN WN1.............22 A2
Romsey Cv WGNS/IIMK WN3....32 C5
Roocroft Sq HOR/BR BL6.........7 H5
Rookery Av AIMK WN4.............61 E4
  WGNNW/ST WN6................8 D2
Rookery Dr RNFD/HAY WA11....56 B1
Rookery La RNFD/HAY WA11....56 B1
The Rookery NEWLW WA12......68 C5
Roscoe Ct WHTN BL5...............58 A1
Roscoe St WGN WN1................3 C6
Rose Acre WALK M28...............55 G4
Rose Av RNFD/HAY WA11.........68 B3
  WGNE/HIN WN2....................49 G4
Rosebank HOR/BR BL6.............15 H4
Rose Bank Cl WGN WN1...........22 A1
Roseberry Rd AIMK WN4..........60 D1
Rosebery St WHTN BL5.............26 A5
Rosebridge Ct WGN WN1 *.......3 J6
Rosebridge Wy WGN WN1.........3 J6
Rosebury Av LEIGH WN7..........65 F1
Rosebury Cv LEIGH WN7..........52 C5
Rose Crs SKEL WN8.................16 D4
Rosedale Av ATH M46..............38 D5
  GOL/RIS/CUL WA3................70 D2
Rosedale Dr LEIGH WN7...........65 H1
Rose Dr RNFD/HAY WA11.........56 B1
Rose Hill Av
  WGNW/BIL/OR WN5.............32 D2
Rose Hill Vw AIMK WN4............47 C4
Rosemary Crs WGN WN1..........22 C3
Rosemary La WHTN BL5...........40 A2
Rose Pl RNFD/HAY WA11.........56 B1
Rose St WGN WN1...................36 A5
  WGNE/HIN WN2....................36 A3
Rosewood WHTN BL5..............37 F2
Rosewood Cl WGNE/HIN WN2...49 C4
Rosley Rd WGNS/IIMK WN3.....34 A5
Rossall Crs LEIGH WN7............65 F3
Ross Cl WGNE/HIN WN2...........3 J1
  WGNW/BIL/OR WN5.............58 D1
Rossdale Gv WGNNW/ST WN6...10 D3
Rossett Cl WGNS/IIMK WN3.....47 E1
Rostherne Av
  GOL/RIS/CUL WA3................71 E1
Rosthwaite Cl
  WGNS/IIMK WN3..................47 H1
Rosthwaite Gv
  RNFD/HAY WA11..................58 A5
Rothay St WGNE/HIN WN2.......36 A5
Rothesay Rd WGNE/HIN WN2...36 A5
Rothwell Crs LHULT M38...........40 D2
Rothwell La LHULT M38............40 D3
Rothwell Rd GOL/RIS/CUL WA3..72 C5
Roughlea Av GOL/RIS/CUL WA3..72 C5
Round House Av WGN WN1......3 H2
Roundmoor Rd
  WGNE/HIN WN2....................36 A5
Roundthorn La WHTN BL5........37 H1
Rowan Av GOL/RIS/CUL WA3....71 G2
  HOR/BR BL6..........................15 F4
  WGNNW/ST WN6................21 G2
Rowanhill Wk WGN WN1..........3 F2
Rowan St WGNW/BIL/OR WN5...17 C1
Rowbottom Sq WGN WN1.........2 C5
Rowe St TYLD M29 *................54 A5
Rowland St ATH M46................53 E1
Rowton Ri WGN WN1...............11 E2
Roxby Cl WALK M28.................41 G5
Royal Av WGN WN1.................2 D4
Royal Dr LEIGH WN7................53 E5
Royden Av WGNS/IIMK WN3....47 C1
Royden Crs
  WGNW/BIL/OR WN5.............58 D1
Royden Rd
  WGNW/BIL/OR WN5.............10 D3
Royston Cl GOL/RIS/CUL WA3...71 F1
Ruabon Crs WGNE/HIN WN2.....36 C4
Ruby Gv LEIGH WN7................64 D2
Rudd St WGNE/HIN WN2.........36 D5
Ruecroft Cl WGNNW/ST WN6...8 C2
Rufford Pl TYLD M29................29 G5
Rufford Rd RNFD/HAY WA11....43 E4
Rugby Dr WGNW/BIL/OR WN5...20 A5
Rumworth Rd HOR/BR BL6.......15 H4
Runshaw Av WGNNW/ST WN6...8 D2
Rupert St WGN WN1................3 J3
Rushdene WGNS/IIMK WN3.....33 H4
Rushmoor Av AIMK WN4..........61 H2
Rushton Av LEIGH WN7............51 C3
  NEWLW WA12.......................68 C5
Rushy Vw NEWLW WA12..........68 D5
Ruskin Av ATH M46.................53 F1
Ruskin Crs WGNE/HIN WN2......49 C2
Russeldene Rd
  WGNS/IIMK WN3..................33 H4
Russell Ct LHULT M38..............41 H5
Russell St ATH M46.................38 C4
  LHULT M38...........................41 H5
  WGN WN1.............................3 G5
Rutherford Dr WHTN BL5.........39 G1
Rutland Av ATH M46................39 F5
  GOL/RIS/CUL WA3................71 E2
Rutland Dr AIMK WN4..............61 G2
Rutland Gv FWTH BL4 *...........41 H1
Rutland Rd TYLD M29..............53 G1
  WALK M28............................55 H2
Rutland St LEIGH WN7............66 B2
Rydal Av WGNE/HIN WN2........36 D5
  WGNW/BIL/OR WN5.............32 A1
Rydal Cl AIMK WN4.................61 F2

  HOR/BR BL6..........................7 H5
  TYLD M29.............................
Rydal Gv FWTH BL4................
Rydal Pl WGNE/HIN WN2.........
  WGNE/HIN WN2
Rydal St LEIGH WN7................
Ryder Gv LEIGH WN7...............
Ryde St BOLS/LL BL3 *............
Ryecroft Av WGNS/IIMK WN3...
Ryecroft Dr WHTN BL5.............
Ryeford Ct WGNS/IIMK WN3....
Rye Hi WHTN BL5 *.................
Ryelands WHTN BL5................
Ryelands Ct WHTN BL5 *.........
Rylands St WGNNW/ST WN6....
Ryton Cl WGNS/IIMK WN3.......

S

Sabden Brook Dr
  WGNE/HIN WN2
Saddleback Cl WALK M28..........
  WGNE/HIN WN2
Saddleback Rd
  WGNW/BIL/OR WN5
Saffron Cl GOL/RIS/CUL WA3....
St Aidan's Cl
St Albans Cl RNFD/HAY WA11...
St Ambrose Rd TYLD M29.........
St Andrew's Crs
  WGNE/HIN WN2
St Andrews Dr LEIGH WN7........
St Andrew's Dr
  WGNNW/ST WN6
St Andrews Rd HOR/BR BL6.....
St Anne's Ct WGNE/HIN WN2....
St Anne's St WGNNW/ST WN6...
St Anne's Dr WGNNW/ST WN6...
St Aubyn's Rd WGN WN1 *.......
St Austell Av TYLD M29............
St Christopher Ct
St Clare Ter HOR/BR BL6 *.......
St Clement's Rd WGN WN1........
St Clement's St
  WGNS/IIMK WN3
St David's Crs WGNE/HIN WN2...
St Elizabeth's Rd
  WGNE/HIN WN2
St George's Av WHTN BL5..........
St Georges Ct TYLD M29..........
St George's Pl ATH M46............
St George's St TYLD M29..........
St Gregorys Cl FWTH BL4.........
St Helens Rd GOL/RIS/CUL WA3..
  LEIGH WN7
  RNFD/HAY WA11
St James Crs WGNE/HIN WN2...
St James Gv WGNS/IIMK WN3...
St James' Rd
  WGNW/BIL/OR WN5
St James St FWTH BL4.............
  WHTN BL5
St John's Av WHTN BL5............
St John's Ct HOR/BR BL6..........
  WGNE/HIN WN2
St John's Rd HOR/BR BL6.........
  WALK M28
  WGNE/HIN WN2
St John's St WGNE/HIN WN2.....
St John St ATH M46.................
  WALK M28
  WGNW/BIL/OR WN5
St Johns Wd HOR/BR BL6.........
St Katherines Dr HOR/BR BL6...
St Leonard's Av HOR/BR BL6....
St Luke's Av GOL/RIS/CUL WA3..
St Luke's Dr
  WGNW/BIL/OR WN5
St Malo Rd WGN WN1..............
St Mark's Av
  WGNW/BIL/OR WN5
St Mary's Av
  WGNW/BIL/OR WN5
St Mary's Cl ATH M46...............
St Mary's Cv GOL/RIS/CUL WA3..
St Mary's Rd WGNE/HIN WN2...
  WGNE/HIN WN2
St Mary's Wy LEIGH WN7 *.......
St Matthew's Cl
  WGNE/HIN WN2
St Michaels Av ATH M46...........
St Michael's Ct WGN WN1.........
St Nicholas Rd
  GOL/RIS/CUL WA3
St Oswalds Rd AIMK WN4.........
St Patrick St WGN WN1............
St Patricks Wy WGN WN1..........
St Paul's Av WGNS/IIMK WN3...
St Richards Cl ATH M46............
St Stephen's Av WGN WN1........
St Stephens Ct TYLD M29.........
St Stephen's Rd
  WGNW/BIL/OR WN5
St Thomas Ct SKEL WN8...........
St Thomas St WGNS/IIMK WN3...
St Wilfrid's Rd
  WGNW/BIL/OR WN5
Salcombe Cl WGN WN1............
Sale La TYLD M29...................
Salesbury Wy WGNS/IIMK WN3...
Salford Rd WHTN BL5..............
Salisbury Av WGNE/HIN WN2....
Salisbury Rd AIMK WN4 *..........
  HOR/BR BL6
  RNFD/HAY WA11
Salisbury St GOL/RIS/CUL WA3..
Salisbury Wy TYLD M29............
Salkeld Av AIMK WN4..............
Sallowfields
  WGNW/BIL/OR WN5

St WCN WN1 * 3 C2
ate BOLS/LL BL3 .... 27 C1
on Dr BOLS/LL BL3 .... 27 G3
1 Rd WGNS/IIMK WN3 .... 32 D4
WHTN BL5 .... 61 C3
CI WGNW/BIL/OR WN5 ...... 33 F4
St ATH M46 .... 53 G2
ld CI WGNW/BIL/OR WN5 ... 37 G2
wood Dr
   WGNW/ST WN6 .... 21 G2
ook Gdns
WN/BIL/OR WN5 .... 31 G3
ook Rd
ling CI WHTN BL5 .... 37 G2
ling Dr LEIGH WN7 .... 65 F1
ing Rd NEWLW WA12 .... 69 F5
son's Cft LEIGH WN7 .... 65 H2
son St LEIGH WN7 .... 64 D1
ld CI GOL/RIS/CUL WA3 ..... 71 F1
ld Crs
RIS/CUL WA3 .... 73 H2
ld Dr HOR/BR BL6 .... 15 H4
ate CI LEIGH WN7 .... 52 A5
cre WGNW/BIL/OR WN5 ..... 10 B2
ay CI WHTN BL5 .... 33 F3
g Dr COL/RIS/CUL WA3 ..... 62 B4
n Gv RNFD/HAY WA11 .... 43 F5
vn CI
t WCN WN1 * 73 E5
n Rd WGNNW/ST WN6 .... 21 F2
per CI FWTH BL4 .... 4 C1
cre WGNW/BIL/OR WN5 ..... 32 C4
rcroft Av WGN WN1 .... 3 C3
a CHLY/EC PR7 .... 7 E1
St LEIGH WN7 .... 63 H4
ld CI GOL/RIS/CUL WA3 ..... 30 A1
/HAY WA11 .... 57 G5
WN8 .... 16 C4
1 M29 .... 66 D2
E/HIN WN2 .... 36 C4
/IIMK WN3 .... 31 C4
Pk WGNE/HIN WN2 .... 36 D2
NW WGNE/HIN WN2 .... 36 C2
St GOL/RIS/CUL WA3 .... 71 F1
Dr GOL/RIS/CUL WA3 .... 71 F1
St WGNE/HIN WN2 .... 51 E1
ld Av GOL/RIS/CUL WA3 .... 71 E1
wood CI AIMK WN4 .... 60 C4
Av GOL/RIS/CUL WA3 .... 71 F1
WN8 .... 21 C2
n Dr WGNE/HIN WN2 .... 61 C3
rpe CI WGNS/IIMK WN3 ..... 33 E5
WGNW/BIL/OR WN5 .... 32 C2
Gv WGNW/BIL/OR WN5 .... 49 C1
Rd BOLS/LL BL3 .... 27 H1
rick Rd
/HAY WA11 .... 43 E4
rick St WCN WN1 .... 2 D2
Pk SKEL WN8 .... 29 F2
ld Gdns LEIGH WN7 .... 64 D5
ld La ATH M46 .... 38 A5
ld St LEIGH WN7 .... 64 D5
Field La WGN WN1 .... 3 F4
s WGN WN1 .... 3 F4
WN1 .... 3 G2
Brow
WGNW/BIL/OR WN5 .... 58 D1
Dr WGNW/BIL/OR WN5 ..... 58 D1
Houses SKEL WN8 * 17 G5
La AIMK WN4 .... 60 D4
WN8 .... 16 C4
WN8 .... 31 F1
/HIN WN2 .... 11 H2
NW/ST WN6 .... 10 A1
St AIMK WN4 .... 61 C1
M46 .... 52 C1
WGNS/IIMK WN3 .... 50 B1
H WN7 .... 51 H3
Gv WN7 .... 55 C5
WN7 .... 3 K6
Ter GOL/RIS/CUL WA3 * ... 70 B1
WGNE/HIN WN2 .... 13 E4
WGNW/BIL/OR WN5 .... 33 C1
v WGNE/HIN WN2 .... 36 B2
ld GOL/RIS/CUL WA3 .... 63 E5
ld LEIGH WN7 .... 65 F2
M29 .... 67 F2
NW/ST WN6 .... 2 A3
St AIMK WN4 .... 61 C1
M46 .... 52 C1
n Wy WGNE/HIN WN2 .... 53 H4
s Crs WGN WN1 .... 22 B2
aite CI TYLD M29 .... 53 H4
aite Rd FWTH BL4 .... 41 E1
r PI
W/BIL/OR WN5 .... 32 C1
ld SKEL WN8 .... 16 D2
Av ATH M46 .... 39 E4
M29 .... 67 E2
NW/ST WN6 .... 21 H5
St ATH M46 .... 38 D5
House Dr
WNW/ST WN6 .... 10 D3
PI SKEL WN8 .... 16 D2
St LHULT M38 .... 41 E5
WN8 .... 25 H3
eld Dr
WNW/ST WN6 .... 10 D3
Dr WHTN BL5 .... 37 H3

Sedgwick CI ATH M46 .... 39 F5
WHTN BL5 .... 38 A2
Sedwyn St WCN WN1 .... 2 C1
Seedley Av LHULT M38 .... 41 G4
Sefton Av AIMK WN4 .... 38 D5
WGNE/HIN WN2 .... 61 C3
Sefton CI WGNW/BIL/OR WN5 31 C3
Sefton Fold Dr
WGNW/BIL/OR WN5 .... 58 C1
Sefton La HOR/BR BL6 .... 14 D1
Sefton Rd AIMK WN4 .... 33 C4
WGNS/IIMK WN3 .... 33 C4
WGNW/BIL/OR WN5 .... 58 C1
Sefton St LEIGH WN7 .... 65 E1
Sefton Vw WGNW/BIL/OR WN5 31 C3
Selbourne CI WHTN BL5 ...... 26 B4
Selbourne St LEIGH WN7 ..... 52 A4
Selby Dr WGNS/IIMK WN3 ... 33 F5
Selby PI SKEL WN8 .... 16 C2
Selkirk Av AIMK WN4 .... 60 A2
Selkirk Cv WGNW/BIL/OR WN5 20 C5
Selside WGNW/BIL/OR WN5 . 48 A1
Selwyn CI NEWLW WA12 ...... 69 E4
Selwyn St LEIGH WN7 .... 52 A5
Senecar CI WGNE/HIN WN2 . 23 C3
Sennicar La WGN WN1 .... 11 F5
Sephton St WGNS/IIMK WN3 35 E2
Seven Oaks LEIGH WN7 .... 52 B5
Seven Stars Rd
WGN WN1 .... 33 H1
Severn CI WGNW/BIL/OR WN5 58 C2
Severn Dr WGNE/HIN WN2 ... 37 F5
WGNE/HIN WN2 .... 37 F5
Severn Rd AIMK WN4 .... 61 H1
Severn St LEIGH WN7 .... 65 C2
Sewell Wy LHULT M38 .... 41 E5
Shadwell Gv LEIGH WN7 ...... 51 F3
Shaftesbury Av HOR/BR BL6 . 15 E2
Shaftesbury Rd
WGNW/BIL/OR WN5 .... 20 B5
Shaftsbury St
WGNW/BIL/OR WN5 .... 58 C1
Shaftway CI RNFD/HAY WA11 68 C2
Shakerley La ATH M46 .... 39 C4
Shakerley Rd TYLD M29 .... 53 C2
Shakespeare Cv
WGNS/IIMK WN3 .... 33 H4
Shalbourne Rd WALK M28 .... 41 H5
Shalebrook CI ATH M46 .... 52 B1
Shalemere Ct ATH M46 .... 52 B1
Shalewood Ct ATH M46 .... 52 B1
Shap Ga WGNW/BIL/OR WN5 32 C1
Shared St WCN WN1 .... 3 F7
Sharon Sq WGNE/HIN WN2 .. 49 E3
Sharp St WGNE/HIN WN2 ..... 34 D2
Shawbrook Av WALK M28 ..... 55 C3
Shawbury Ct HOR/BR BL6 .... 13 E1
Shaw St AIMK WN4 .... 61 E1
RNFD/HAY WA11 .... 68 B3
WGN WN1 .... 2 D2
Shearwater Av TYLD M29 ..... 53 H3
Shearwater Dr WALK M28 ..... 41 H5
WHTN BL5 .... 37 C2
Shefford Crs WGNS/IIMK WN3 46 D1
The Sheilings
GOL/RIS/CUL WA3 .... 71 C1
Shelburne Dr WGNE/HIN WN2 35 H4
Sheldon Av WGNNW/ST WN6 5 F5
Sheldwich CI LEIGH WN7 ...... 65 E5
Shelley CI LEIGH WN7 .... 49 C2
WGNE/HIN WN2 .... 32 B2
Shelley Rd LHULT M38 * 41 F3
Shelley St LEIGH WN7 .... 51 F4
Shellingford CI
WGNNW/ST WN6 .... 8 C3
Shepherds CI HOR/BR BL6 ... 7 H4
Shepton Av WGNE/HIN WN2 . 49 F2
Sheraton CI
WGNW/BIL/OR WN5 .... 20 C4
Sherborne Av WGNE/HIN WN2 36 D5
Sherborne Rd
WGNW/BIL/OR WN5 .... 20 B5
Sherbourne St
WGNS/IIMK WN3 .... 33 H5
Sheridan Av GOL/RIS/CUL WA3 71 E2
Sheriffs Dr TYLD M29 .... 54 C2
Sherlock Av RNFD/HAY WA11 68 B2
Sherrat St SKEL WN8 .... 17 C2
Sherwood Av AIMK WN4 * 61 F2
TYLD M29 .... 53 H5
Sherwood Crs WGNE/HIN WN2 49 F1
WGNE/HIN WN2 .... 33 E1
Sherwood Dr SKEL WN8 .... 18 A2
WGNW/BIL/OR WN5 .... 33 E1
Sherwood Gv LEIGH WN7 ..... 65 C2
WGNW/BIL/OR WN5 .... 33 E1
Shevington La
WGNNW/ST WN6 .... 9 F4
Shevington Moor
WGNNW/ST WN6 .... 4 B5
Shildon CI WALK M28 .... 3 K1
Shillington CI WALK M28 .... 41 E5
Shipham CI LEIGH WN7 .... 51 C5
Shires CI WGNE/HIN WN2 ..... 36 B4
Shirewell Rd
WGNW/BIL/OR WN5 .... 31 H3
Shortland PI WGNE/HIN WN2 50 D3
Short St GOL/RIS/CUL WA3 * 62 C5
RNFD/HAY WA11 .... 68 B3
WGNS/IIMK WN3 .... 33 F5
Sidney St LEIGH WN7 .... 51 C4
Silcock St GOL/RIS/CUL WA3 62 B5
Silk St LEIGH WN7 .... 65 E1
WHTN BL5 * 25 H4

Sillitoe Dr WGNNW/ST WN6 . 21 H4
Silsbury Cv WGNNW/ST WN6 10 D2
Silsden Av GOL/RIS/CUL WA3 72 A1
Silver Birch Gv AIMK WN4 ..... 60 D1
Silverdale WGN WN1 .... 2 C1
Silverdale Av WGNE/HIN WN2 23 F5
Silverdale CI WHTN BL5 * 5 E3
Silverdale Rd NEWLW WA12 .. 69 E5
WGNE/HIN WN2 .... 36 C3
WGNS/IIMK WN3 .... 20 C5
Silver St WGNE/HIN WN2 ...... 49 C1
Silver Ter WGN WN1 .... 49 C2
Silvington Wy WGNE/HIN WN2 23 F3
Simfield CI WGNNW/ST WN6 . 10 A1
Simpkin St WGNE/HIN WN2 .. 49 C2
Simpson Gv WALK M28 .... 55 F5
Simpson Rd WALK M28 .... 55 C5
Sinclair PI WGNW/BIL/OR WN5 58 C1
Singleton Gv WHTN BL5 .... 26 C5
Siskin CI WGNE/HIN WN2 ...... 65 C1
Sittingbourne Rd WGN WN1 .. 22 B1
Sixpools Gv WALK M28 .... 55 F2
Size House PI LEIGH WN7 * ... 65 F2
Skelton St AIMK WN4 .... 47 C5
Skiddaw PI
WGNW/BIL/OR WN5 .... 32 D2
Skipton Av WGNE/HIN WN2 .. 36 D4
Skull House La
WGNNW/ST WN6 .... 8 C2
Skull House Ms
WGNNW/ST WN6 .... 8 B1
Slackey Fold WGNE/HIN WN2 51 E2
Slack La WHTN BL5 .... 26 A3
Slag La GOL/RIS/CUL WA3 ... 63 C4
Slaidburn Cr WGNS/IIMK WN3 33 H5
Slaidburn Crs
GOL/RIS/CUL WA3 .... 62 A4
Slate La SKEL WN8 .... 16 B3
Slater's Nook WHTN BL5 ...... 25 H4
Slater St North LEIGH WN7 ... 64 C1
Sledbrook St
WGNS/IIMK WN3 * 32 D3
Smallbridge CI WALK M28 ..... 55 H5
Smallbrook La LEIGH WN7 .... 37 H5
Smalley St WGNS/IIMK WN3 . 10 B1
Smallshaw CI AIMK WN4 .... 60 D4
Smethurst La
WGNS/IIMK WN3 .... 32 D3
Smethurst Park Hall
WGNW/BIL/OR WN5 .... 45 F1
Smethurst Rd
WGNW/BIL/OR WN5 .... 45 F1
WGNS/IIMK WN3 .... 32 D3
Smith Av WGNW/BIL/OR WN5 20 C5
Smith Brow HOR/BR BL6 ...... 1 F4
Smithfold La WALK M28 .... 41 H5
Smith's La WGNE/HIN WN2 ... 50 D3
Smith St ATH M46 * 52 C1
LEIGH WN7 .... 65 F1
SKEL WN8 .... 16 C4
WGNE/HIN WN2 .... 12 D5
Smithwood Av
WGNE/HIN WN2 .... 36 C2
Smithy Glen Dr
WGNS/IIMK WN3 .... 31 H4
Smithy Hl BOLS/LL BL3 .... 27 H1
Smithy St LEIGH WN7 .... 65 E2
Smock La AIMK WN4 .... 59 H2
Snowden Av WGNS/IIMK WN3 33 H4
Snowshill Dr WGNS/IIMK WN3 32 D4
Snydale CI WHTN BL5 .... 26 B3
Snydale Wy BOLS/LL BL3 ...... 27 E3
Soane CI AIMK WN4 .... 61 E1
Soham CI WGNE/HIN WN2 .... 36 B4
Soho St WGNS/IIMK WN3 ..... 33 C1
Solness St WGN WN1 .... 3 H2
Solway St AIMK WN4 .... 60 D2
Somerset Av TYLD M29 .... 39 C5
Somerset Rd ATH M46 .... 38 C4
WGNE/HIN WN2 .... 35 C2
Somerville Rd WGNNW/ST WN6 10 A1
Sommerville Rd WGN WN1 .... 22 B2
Sonning Dr BOLS/LL BL3 ...... 27 C3
Sougher's La AIMK WN4 .... 47 C5
South Av LEIGH WN7 .... 65 H3
Southcourt LEIGH WN7 .... 52 C5
Southdown Dr WALK M28 ...... 55 E5
Southern's Fold
WGNE/HIN WN2 .... 51 C3
Southern's La RNFD/HAY WA11 43 F5
Southern St
WGNS/IIMK WN3 .... 33 E3
Southern Av WGNS/IIMK WN3 33 E3
Southfield WGNE/HIN WN2 ... 49 C1
Southfield Dr WHTN BL5 .... 37 H1
South Gdns TYLD M29 * 66 D1
South Hey LEIGH WN7 .... 64 B1
Southlands Av
WGNNW/ST WN6 .... 10 B2
South La TYLD M29 .... 66 D1
Southover WHTN BL5 .... 37 H2
South St ATH M46 .... 53 F2
WGNE/HIN WN2 .... 38 D5
Southward Rd
RNFD/HAY WA11 .... 68 D2
Southway SKEL WN8 .... 17 C5
Southwell CI
GOL/RIS/CUL WA3 .... 70 A5
Southworth Rd NEWLW WA12 70 D1
Sovereign CI GOL/RIS/CUL WA3 71 F2
Sovereign Fold Rd LEIGH WN7 51 H3
Sovereign Rd WGN WN1 .... 2 E7
Spa Crs LHULT M38 .... 41 F2
Spa Cv LHULT M38 .... 41 F2
Spa La BRSC L40 .... 38 A5
LHULT M38 .... 41 F2
Sparta Av WALK M28 .... 55 H1
Spawell CI GOL/RIS/CUL WA3 63 F5
Speakman Dr
WGNNW/ST WN6 .... 8 B4
Speakman Av LEIGH WN7 ..... 65 G1
Speedwell CI
WGNNW/ST WN6 .... 69 F4
Spelding Dr WGNNW/ST WN6 21 E2
Spencer Rd WGN WN1 .... 22 A2

Spencer Rd West
WGNNW/ST WN6 .... 21 H2
Spencers La SKEL WN8 .... 17 C5
Spencer's La
WGNW/BIL/OR WN5 .... 31 C1
Spenlow LEIGH WN7 .... 65 H3
Spey CI WGNW/BIL/OR WN5 . 10 A1
Spilsby Sq WGNS/IIMK WN3 . 47 H1
Spindle Hillock AIMK WN4 ..... 60 A2
Spindlepoint Dr WALK M28 .... 55 H5
Spindle Wk WHTN BL5 .... 26 A3
Spindlewood Rd
WGNS/IIMK WN3 .... 34 D2
Spingdale LHULT M38 .... 40 C2
Spinnerette CI LEIGH WN7 .... 65 F1
The Spinney RNFD/HAY WA11 43 E4
Spinning Jenny Wy LEIGH WN7 65 F2
Spion Kop AIMK WN4 .... 61 C3
Spiredale Brow
WGNNW/ST WN6 .... 10 C1
Spires Cft LEIGH WN7 .... 65 F1
Sportsman St LEIGH WN7 ..... 64 C1
Springbourne
WGNNW/ST WN6 .... 21 C3
Springburn CI HOR/BR BL6 .. 14 C1
WGNNW/ST WN6 .... 55 F5
Spring Fld RNFD/HAY WA11 .. 42 D2
Springfield Av
GOL/RIS/CUL WA3 .... 70 A1
Springfield Rd ATH M46 .... 39 F4
HOR/BR BL6 .... 14 C2
WGNE/HIN WN2 .... 35 C2
WGNNW/ST WN6 .... 21 C3
Springfield St WGN WN1 .... 2 D1
Spring Gdns WGN WN1 .... 2 B5
Spring Gv WGN WN1 .... 3 F6
Springmount
GOL/RIS/CUL WA3 .... 71 F2
Springpool WGNS/IIMK WN3 . 46 C1
Spring Rd WGNW/BIL/OR WN5 20 A5
Spring St WGN WN1 .... 3 F6
WGNS/IIMK WN3 .... 33 C1
Spruce CI GOL/RIS/CUL WA3 71 C2
Spruce Rd WGNNW/ST WN6 . 21 F2
Squires La TYLD M29 .... 53 F5
Stadium Wy
WGNW/BIL/OR WN5 .... 21 F4
Stafford Rd WALK M28 .... 55 H2
Stafford St LEIGH WN7 .... 66 A2
SKEL WN8 .... 16 C3
WGNE/HIN WN2 .... 35 H5
Stainburn CI WGNNW/ST WN6 8 C2
Stainer CI NEWLW WA12 .... 69 E4
Stainforth CI
GOL/RIS/CUL WA3 .... 72 C5
Stamford St ATH M46 .... 39 F4
Stancliffe Gv WGNE/HIN WN2 12 D4
Standfield Dr WALK M28 .... 55 F5
Standish Av
WGNS/IIMK WN3 .... 58 D1
Standish Dr RNFD/HAY WA11 43 F4
Standishgate WGN WN1 .... 2 D3
Standish St TYLD M29 .... 53 H5
Standish Wood La
WGNNW/ST WN6 .... 10 B3
Standside Pk SKEL WN8 .... 16 C5
Stanedge Gv WGNS/IIMK WN3 48 A1
Stanhope St LEIGH WN7 .... 51 E5
Stanley Av RNFD/HAY WA11 . 42 D4
Stanley CI WHTN BL5 .... 38 B1
Stanley Dr LEIGH WN7 .... 51 C3
Stanley Gv WGNE/HIN WN2 .. 14 C1
Stanley PI LEIGH WN7 .... 51 F5
Stanley PI WGN WN1 .... 3 C4
Stanley Rd SKEL WN8 .... 30 D1
WGNE/HIN WN2 .... 12 D4
WGNS/IIMK WN3 .... 35 F5
Stanley St ATH M46 .... 52 C1
WGNW/BIL/OR WN5 .... 33 C2
Stanley Wy SKEL WN8 .... 16 D2
Stanmoor Dr WGNE/HIN WN2 12 D5
Stannanought Rd SKEL WN8 . 18 A2
Stansfield CI LEIGH WN7 * 64 B1
Stanton CI WGNS/IIMK WN3 . 23 E3
Stanton St WGNS/IIMK WN3 . 34 A5
Stapleford CI LEIGH WN7 ...... 64 B1
Staplehurst CI LEIGH WN7 .... 51 F5
Stapleton St WGNE/HIN WN2 49 F1
Starling Dr FWTH BL4 .... 41 C1
Startham Av
WGNW/BIL/OR WN5 .... 58 C3
Statham Rd BRSC L40 .... 16 C2
Station Av WGNNW/ST WN6 . 50 A2
Station CI WGNE/HIN WN2 .... 50 A4
Station Ms AIMK WN4 .... 60 A3
Station Rd AIMK WN4 .... 59 H3
CHLY/EC PR7 .... 7 E1
HOR/BR BL6 .... 13 F1
Staveley Rd SKEL WN8 .... 16 D2
Stavesacre LEIGH WN7 .... 65 E3
Stein Av GOL/RIS/CUL WA3 .. 62 B5
Stephenson St
WGNE/HIN WN2 .... 49 C3
Stephen St WGNE/HIN WN2 . 49 F1
Stephens Wy WGNS/IIMK WN3 33 C3
Sterndale Av WGNNW/ST WN6 5 F5
Sterndale Rd WALK M28 .... 55 C4
Stetchworth Dr WALK M28 .... 34 A5
Stevenson CI WGNS/IIMK WN3 34 A5
Stevenson St WALK M28 .... 41 C1
Stewart Av FWTH BL4 .... 41 C1
Stewart Rd WGNS/IIMK WN3 34 A5
Stewerton CI
GOL/RIS/CUL WA3 .... 62 A4
Stirling Av GOL/RIS/CUL WA3 62 B4
Stirling CI LEIGH WN7 .... 66 A1
Stirling Dr AIMK WN4 .... 60 A2
Stirling Rd WGNE/HIN WN2 ... 36 C4
Stirling St WGN WN1 .... 22 A3
Stockley Dr WGNNW/ST WN6 10 D2
Stocksfield CI LHULT M38 ...... 41 E3
Stockwell CI WGNS/IIMK WN3 33 E5
The Stokes Ct
GOL/RIS/CUL WA3 .... 71 F1
Stonacre HOR/BR BL6 .... 15 E2
Stonebridge CI HOR/BR BL6 . 15 H4
Stonechat CI
GOL/RIS/CUL WA3 .... 71 F1
WALK M28 .... 55 C3

Stonecrop WGNNW/ST WN6 . 8 C1
Stone Cross La North
GOL/RIS/CUL WA3 .... 70 D2
Stone Cross La South
GOL/RIS/CUL WA3 .... 70 D3
Stonefield TYLD M29 .... 54 B2
Stonehaven BOLS/LL BL3 ..... 27 C2
Stone Hvn WGN WN1 .... 2 D1
Stonehouse Rd
WGNW/BIL/OR WN5 .... 21 E5
Stone Lea Wy ATH M46 .... 52 B1
Stone Pit CI GOL/RIS/CUL WA3 63 C5
Stoney Brow SKEL WN8 .... 19 E5
Stoney La CHLY/EC PR7 .... 6 B1
Stonyhurst Av
WGNS/IIMK WN3 .... 34 C2
Stonyhurst Crs
GOL/RIS/CUL WA3 .... 72 C4
Stopford St WGNNW/ST WN6 21 H4
Storwood CI
WGNW/BIL/OR WN5 .... 31 H3
Stourbridge Av LHULT M38 ... 41 F2
Stour Rd TYLD M29 .... 54 B2
Stout St LEIGH WN7 .... 64 B3
Stowe Gdns LEIGH WN7 .... 65 E1
Stradbroke CI
GOL/RIS/CUL WA3 .... 71 F2
The Straits TYLD M29 .... 54 B5
Strand Av AIMK WN4 .... 61 C2
The Strand AIMK WN4 .... 61 C2
Strange St LEIGH WN7 .... 60 A3
Strange St LEIGH WN7 .... 64 A2
Stranraer Rd
WGNW/BIL/OR WN5 .... 20 D4
Stratford St WGNE/HIN WN2 . 21 H4
Strathmore Av AIMK WN4 ..... 60 D1
Stratton Dr WGNE/HIN WN2 . 35 C3
Streetgate LHULT M38 .... 41 F3
Stretton Av
GOL/RIS/CUL WA3 .... 71 E2
WGNS/IIMK WN3 .... 58 D1
Stretton CI WGNNW/ST WN6 10 B2
Strines CI WGNE/HIN WN2 ... 35 H4
Stringer St LEIGH WN7 .... 65 E1
Stroud CI WGNE/HIN WN2 ... 23 E5
Stuart Av WGNE/HIN WN2 ... 37 E5
Stuart CI WGNE/HIN WN2 .... 49 E1
Stuart Crs WGNW/BIL/OR WN5 58 B1
Studley Ct TYLD M29 .... 53 F5
Sturton Av WGNS/IIMK WN3 . 33 F5
Sudbrook CI
GOL/RIS/CUL WA3 .... 71 F1
Sudbury CI WGNS/IIMK WN3 48 H4
Sudbury Dr HOR/BR BL6 ...... 15 H4
Suffolk CI WGN WN1 .... 11 E2
Suffolk Gv LEIGH WN7 .... 64 C1
Sullivan Wy WGN WN1 .... 2 C3
Summercroft CI
GOL/RIS/CUL WA3 .... 70 B2
Summerfield Dr TYLD M29 .... 54 A3
Summer St SKEL WN8 .... 17 E1
Sumner St ATH M46 .... 38 D5
WGNE/HIN WN2 .... 13 E5
Sunderland PI
WGNW/BIL/OR WN5 .... 21 E4
Sundridge CI BOLS/LL BL3 ... 27 H2
Sunleigh Rd WGNE/HIN WN2 36 B2
Sunningdale Gv LEIGH WN7 . 53 E4
Sunnybank CI NEWLW WA12 69 F5
Sunnybank Rd TYLD M29 ..... 54 A5
Sunny Dr WGNW/BIL/OR WN5 58 C3
Sunnyfields WGNS/IIMK WN3 46 D1
Sunny Garth WHTN BL5 .... 25 H5
Sunnyside Rd AIMK WN4 ...... 47 C5
Surrey Av LEIGH WN7 .... 66 B3
Sussex CI WGN WN1 .... 11 E1
WGNE/HIN WN2 .... 36 D3
Sussex St LEIGH WN7 .... 66 B2
Sutherland Rd
WGNS/IIMK WN3 .... 33 H5
Sutherland St WGNE/HIN WN2 35 H3
Sutton Rd BOLS/LL BL3 .... 27 C1
Swallowfield LEIGH WN7 .... 65 F1
Swanfield Wk
GOL/RIS/CUL WA3 .... 62 A4
Swan La WGNE/HIN WN2 ..... 37 E4
Swan Meadow Rd
WGNS/IIMK WN3 .... 2 B7
Swann St WGNS/IIMK WN3 ... 2 A6
Swan Rd NEWLW WA12 .... 68 B5
Swift St WGNW/BIL/OR WN5 33 H1
Swinburn Gv
WGNW/BIL/OR WN5 .... 45 C2
Swinley La WGN WN1 .... 22 B3
Swinley Rd WGN WN1 .... 2 C1
Swinley St WGN WN1 .... 2 D1
Swinside WGN WN1 .... 3 K3
Sycamore Av
GOL/RIS/CUL WA3 .... 62 B5
TYLD M29 .... 54 C2
WGNE/HIN WN2 .... 36 C5
WGNNW/ST WN6 .... 21 F2
Sycamore Dr SKEL WN8 .... 16 D3
WGNS/IIMK WN3 .... 46 C2
Syderstone CI WGNE/HIN WN2 36 B2
Sydney Av WGNE/HIN WN2 ... 64 C4
Sydney St WGNE/HIN WN2 ... 35 F5
Sykes Crs WGNS/IIMK WN3 . 46 D2
Syresham St WGNE/HIN WN2 2 D1

T

Taberner CI WGNNW/ST WN6 10 C1
Taberner St WGNE/HIN WN2 . 49 C1
Tadcaster CI LHULT M38 .... 41 E4
Talbot At AIMK WN4 * 61 C2
GOL/RIS/CUL WA3 .... 70 B1
Talman Cv AIMK WN4 .... 61 C1
Tamer Cv LEIGH WN7 .... 51 F5
The Tamneys SKEL WN8 .... 17 E4
Tamworth Dr WGNE/HIN WN2 23 E3
Tanfields SKEL WN8 .... 17 E4

Tanhouse Av *TYLD* M29 ....54 C4
Tan House Dr
 WGNS/IIMK WN3............47 E2
Tan House La
 WGNS/IIMK WN3............46 D1
Tanhouse Rd *SKEL* WN8............17 H5
Tanner's La *GOL/RIS/CUL* WA3 ...70 C1
Tansley Sq
 WCNW/BIL/OR WN5............33 E3
Tarleswood Av *SKEL* WN8............17 E4
Tarleton Av *AIMK* WN4............17 E4
Tarleton Pl *BOLS/LL* BL3............27 H2
Tarlswood *SKEL* WN8............17 E4
Tarnrigg Cl *WGNS/IIMK* WN3 ...33 F5
Tarn Cl *AIMK* WN4............61 E1
Tarnside Rd
 WCNW/BIL/OR WN5............31 H2
Tarnway *GOL/RIS/CUL* WA3 ...71 G2
Tarrant Cl *WGNS/IIMK* WN3............47 E1
Tarvin Cl *GOL/RIS/CUL* WA3 ...71 F2
Tatham Gv *WGNS/IIMK* WN3............59 F1
Tattock Cl *WCNW/BIL/OR* WN5...58 D1
Tatton Dr *AIMK* WN4............60 C2
Taunton Av *LEIGH* WN7............51 C1
Tavistock Rd *WGNE/HIN* WN2 ...36 B4
Tavistock St *ATH* M46............38 C5
Tawd Rd *SKEL* WN8............17 F5
Taylor Gv *WGNE/HIN* WN2............49 E1
Taylor Rd *RNFD/HAY* WA11............68 C3
Taylor St *WGNS/IIMK* WN3............37 F5
Taylor's La *WGNS/IIMK* WN3............37 E5
Taylor St *LEIGH* WN7............51 G3
 SKEL WN8............16 B4
 WGNS/IIMK WN3............2 A6
Tayton Cl *TYLD* M29............54 B2
Taywood Rd *BOLS/LL* BL3............27 E3
Teal Cl *WGNS/IIMK* WN3............32 C4
Tebworth Dr *WGNE/HIN* WN2 ...36 B4
Teesdale Dr *LEIGH* WN7............65 H1
Telford Crs *LEIGH* WN7............51 C5
Telford St *ATH* M46............52 B1
Tellers Cl *ATH* M46............39 E5
Tempest Cha *HOR/BR* BL6............26 C1
Tempest Ct *HOR/BR* BL6............26 D1
Tempest Rd *HOR/BR* BL6............26 D1
Templegate Cl
 WCNW/BIL/OR WN5............5 G5
Templeton Cl *WHTN* BL5............25 H5
Templeton Rd
 WGNE/HIN WN2............49 G2
Tenbury Dr *AIMK* WN4............60 C2
Tenement St *WGNE/HIN* WN2 ...49 G2
Tennyson Av *LEIGH* WN7............51 F5
 WCNW/BIL/OR WN5............45 G2
Tennyson Dr *WGN* WN1............22 B2
Tennyson Rd *FWTH* BL4............41 G1
Tensing Av *ATH* M46............38 D3
Tenter Dr *WGNNW/ST* WN6............11 E3
Tetbury Cl
 WCNW/BIL/OR WN5............21 E4
Teversham *SKEL* WN8............17 E3
Tewkesbury Av *WGNE/HIN* WN2 ...48 C3
Tewkesbury Rd
 GOL/RIS/CUL WA3............70 C1
Thackeray Pl
 WGNS/IIMK WN3............33 H3
Thames Av *LEIGH* WN7............65 E5
Thames Dr
 WCNW/BIL/OR WN5............32 A1
Thanet Cl *LEIGH* WN7............65 F1
Thanet Gv *LEIGH* WN7............65 F1
Thealby Cl *SKEL* WN8............16 D3
Thelwall Cl *LEIGH* WN7............64 A2
Thetford Cl *WGNE/HIN* WN2 ...36 B4
Thicknesse Av
 WGNNW/ST WN6............21 G2
Thickwood Moss La
 RNFD/HAY WA11............56 B1
Third Av *TYLD* M29............67 E2
 WGNE/HIN WN2............21 H3
Thirlmere Av *AIMK* WN4............61 F2
 SKEL WN8............31 E1
 TYLD M29............53 H4
 WGNE/HIN WN2............35 G1
 WGNNW/ST WN6............49 G3
 WGNW WN1............10 D5
Thirlmere Dr *LHULT* M38............41 F3
Thirlmere Rd
 GOL/RIS/CUL WA3............62 D5
 HOR/BR BL6............7 H4
 WGNE/HIN WN2............36 B3
 WGNW WN1............32 D1
 WHTN BL5............9 H4
Thirlmere St *LEIGH* WN7............64 D1
Thirsk *SKEL* WN8............16 D3
Thistledown Cl
 WGNNW/ST WN6............21 H5
Thistleton Rd *BOLS/LL* BL3............27 G2
Thomas St *ATH* M46............39 E5
 GOL/RIS/CUL WA3............70 B1
 WGNE/HIN WN2............35 F1
 WHTN BL5............25 H2
Thompson St *AIMK* WN4............60 C2
 LEIGH WN7............64 A1
 WGN WN1............3 G2
 WGNS/IIMK WN3............33 H3
Thorburn Rd
 WCNW/BIL/OR WN5............32 D2
Thoresby Cl *WGNS/IIMK* WN3 ...33 F5
Thornbury *SKEL* WN8............17 E3
Thornbury Av
 GOL/RIS/CUL WA3............71 G2
Thornbush Cl
 GOL/RIS/CUL WA3............71 F1
Thorneycroft *LEIGH* WN7............65 H1
Thorneyholme Cl
 HOR/BR BL6............15 H4
Thornfield Cl
 WGNS/IIMK WN3............70 D1
Thornfield Crs *LHULT* M38............41 E3
Thornfield Gv *LHULT* M38............41 E3
Thornhill Rd *AIMK* WN4............59 H2
Thorn Lea *ATH* M46............51 H3
Thorn St *WGNE/HIN* WN2............36 A4
Thornton Cl *AIMK* WN4............60 C2
 FWTH BL4............41 H3
 LEIGH WN7............65 E5
 WALK M28............54 D4

Thornton Rd *WALK* M28............54 D4
Thornvale *WGNE/HIN* WN2............49 H4
Thornway *WALK* M28............55 F4
Thorn Well *WHTN* BL5............37 H1
Thornwood *SKEL* WN8............17 E3
Thorpe *SKEL* WN8............17 E3
Three Sisters Rd *AIMK* WN4 ...48 B4
Throstle Nest Av
 WGNE/HIN WN2............21 H4
Thurcroft Dr *SKEL* WN8............16 D3
Thurlby Cl *AIMK* WN4............61 G2
Thurlow *GOL/RIS/CUL* WA3 ...71 F2
Thurlwood Cft *WHTN* BL5............25 H4
Thursford Gv *HOR/BR* BL6............13 H1
Thurstan St *WGNS/IIMK* WN3 ...34 D4
Thurston *SKEL* WN8............16 D3
Thurston Av *WGNS/IIMK* WN3...34 A5
Tideswell Av
 WCNW/BIL/OR WN5............20 B4
Tilbury Gv *WCNNW/ST* WN6............8 C3
Tilcroft *SKEL* WN8............16 D3
Tilside Gv *HOR/BR* BL6............15 G4
Timperley La *LEIGH* WN7............51 G4
Tinkersfield *LEIGH* WN7............51 G4
Tintagel *SKEL* WN8............16 C3
Tintagel Rd *WGNE/HIN* WN2 ...36 D4
Tintern Av *AIMK* WN4............61 E1
 TYLD M29............54 B4
Tinwald Pl *WGN* WN1............3 J3
Tipping St *WGNS/IIMK* WN3 ...34 A2
Tithebarn Rd *AIMK* WN4............59 H4
Tithebarn St *SKEL* WN8............31 E1
The Barn St *WHTN* BL5............25 H4
Tiverton Av *LEIGH* WN7............51 C1
 SKEL WN8............16 D3
Tiverton Ct *TYLD* M29............54 B4
Toddington La
 WGNE/HIN WN2............12 C2
Tollgreen Cl *WGNE/HIN* WN2 ...36 A1
Toll St *WGNE/HIN* WN2............49 F2
Tongbarn *SKEL* WN8............16 D3
Tontine Rd *SKEL* WN8............31 F2
Toothill Cl *AIMK* WN4............61 E1
Top Acre Rd *SKEL* WN8............29 H1
Torquay Dr
 WCNW/BIL/OR WN5............45 H3
Torridon Cl *WGNNW/ST* WN6 ...10 D3
Torside Cl *WGNE/HIN* WN2............36 A2
Torver Cl *WGNS/IIMK* WN3 ...46 D1
Toulston Rd *WCNNW/ST* WN6...21 G3
Tower Gv *LEIGH* WN7............53 E5
Tower Hill Rd *SKEL* WN8............30 D5
Tower Nook *SKEL* WN8............30 D5
Towers Av *BOLS/LL* BL3............27 H1
Townfield Av *AIMK* WN4............61 E4
Townfields *AIMK* WN4............60 D3
Townsfield Rd *WHTN* BL5............37 H1
Townson Dr *LEIGH* WN7............65 E5
Tracks La *WCNW/BIL/OR* WN5...31 G5
Trafalgar Rd *WGN* WN1............2 C2
 WGNE/HIN WN2............36 A3
Trafford Dr *LHULT* M38............41 G3
Trafford Rd *WGNE/HIN* WN2 ...35 G1
Tram St *WGNE/HIN* WN2............49 F2
Trecastell Ct *WGN* WN1............3 J3
Treen Rd *TYLD* M29............54 B3
Tregaron Gv *WGNE/HIN* WN2 ...36 D5
Trencherfield Mi
 WGNS/IIMK WN3 *............2 B7
Trent Dr *WALK* M28............55 G1
 WGNE/HIN WN2............37 F5
Trent Gv *LEIGH* WN7............64 B2
Trent Rd *AIMK* WN4............61 H1
 WCNW/BIL/OR WN5............20 C5
 WGNE/HIN WN2............58 B2
Trescott Ms *WCNNW/ST* WN6 ...10 B2
Treswell Cl *WGNE/HIN* WN2 ...50 B1
Trevelyan Dr
 WCNW/BIL/OR WN5............45 G2
Trevore Dr *WGN* WN1............11 F1
Trinity Gdns *AIMK* WN4............60 C2
Troon Cl *BOLS/LL* BL3............27 G2
Troutbeck Av *NEWLW* WA12 ...68 B5
Troutbeck Dr *TYLD* M29............53 H4
Troutbeck Gv
 RNFD/HAY WA11............58 A4
Troutbeck Ri
 WCNW/BIL/OR WN5............32 C2
Troutbeck Rd *AIMK* WN4............61 F1
Truro Rd *TYLD* M29............54 B3
Tucker's Hill Brow
 HOR/BR BL6............12 C1
Tudor Av *FWTH* BL4............41 G1
Tudor Cl *RNFD/HAY* WA11............42 D5
Tudor Gv *WGNS/IIMK* WN3............47 F1
Tulip Dr *WGNE/HIN* WN2............21 G2
Tulip Rd *RNFD/HAY* WA11............68 C3
Tunstall La
 WCNW/BIL/OR WN5............33 E5
Turnberry *BOLS/LL* BL3............27 G2
 SKEL WN8............16 C3
Tumberry Cl *TYLD* M29............54 B3
Turncroft Wy *WALK* M28............55 E4
Turnditch Cl *WCNNW/ST* WN6...21 H1
Turner Av *WGNE/HIN* WN2............50 B2
Turner St *LEIGH* WN7............65 F2
 WGN WN1............3 F4
 WHTN BL5............37 H3
Turners Yd
 WCNW/BIL/OR WN5 *............31 H2
Turnill Dr *AIMK* WN4............61 E3
Turnstone Av *NEWLW* WA12 ...69 F5
Turnstone Cl *LEIGH* WN7............52 B5
Turret Hall Dr
 GOL/RIS/CUL WA3............71 F1
Turriff Gv *WGNE/HIN* WN2............48 D3
Turton St *GOL/RIS/CUL* WA3 ...70 B1
Tweed St *LEIGH* WN7............65 G2
Twiss Green Dr
 GOL/RIS/CUL WA3............72 D5
Twiss Green La
 GOL/RIS/CUL WA3............72 C5
Twist Av *GOL/RIS/CUL* WA3 ...70 D1
Twist La *LEIGH* WN7............64 C1
Tybyrne Cl *WALK* M28............55 E4
Tyldesley Old Rd *ATH* M46 ...53 F1
Tyldesley Pas *TYLD* M29............53 F1
Tyldesley Rd *ATH* M46............53 E1
Tyne Ct *WALK* M28............41 H5
Tynesbank *WALK* M28............55 H1

Tynesbank Cots *WALK* M28 * ...41 H5
Tyrer Av *WGNS/IIMK* WN3............33 G3

U

Ullswater Av
 WGNE/HIN WN2............32 A1
Ullswater Dr *FWTH* BL4............40 D1
 WGNE/HIN WN2............35 G1
Ullswater Rd
 GOL/RIS/CUL WA3............62 D5
 TYLD M29............53 H4
Ulverston Rd *WGNS/IIMK* WN3...33 G5
Umberton Rd *WHTN* BL5............39 G1
Union St *LEIGH* WN7............65 E1
 TYLD M29............53 G2
 WGNE/HIN WN2............23 F5
Unsworth Av
 GOL/RIS/CUL WA3............71 E1
 TYLD M29............53 H4
Unsworth St *LEIGH* WN7............51 H4
Upholland Rd
 WCNW/BIL/OR WN5............31 C5
 WGNS/IIMK WN3............58 B2
 LHULT M38............41 E2
Upper Dicconson St
 WGN WN1............2 D3
Upper George St *TYLD* M29 ...53 H3
Upper Lees Dr *WHTN* BL5............26 B4
Upper St Stephen St
 WGN WN6............2 A4
Uppingham *SKEL* WN8............16 C4
Upton Cl *GOL/RIS/CUL* WA3............71 E1
Upton La *TYLD* M29............54 B3
Upton Rd *ATH* M46............39 F4
Upwood Rd *GOL/RIS/CUL* WA3...71 E2
Urmston Av *NEWLW* WA12 ...69 E4
Urmston St *LEIGH* WN7............64 C1

V

Vale Cl *WGNNW/ST* WN6............8 D2
Vale Cft *SKEL* WN8............30 D2
Valentines Rd *ATH* M46............52 B2
The Vale *WGNNW/ST* WN6............8 C2
Valiant Rd *WCNW/BIL/OR* WN5...21 E5
Valley Rd *WCNW/BIL/OR* WN5...33 E3
Vanbrugh Gv
 WCNW/BIL/OR WN5............20 C4
Varley Rd *BOLS/LL* BL3............27 H1
Vauxhall Rd *WGN* WN5............3 F5
Vauze Av *HOR/BR* BL6............13 E1
Verda St *WGNE/HIN* WN2............49 F3
Vernon St *LEIGH* WN7............65 E1
Vicarage Av *WGNE/HIN* WN2 ...49 F1
Vicarage La *WGNNW/ST* WN6............9 F5
Vicarage Rd *AIMK* WN4............61 E4
 WALK M28............41 H4
 WGNE/HIN WN2............49 G2
 WCNW/BIL/OR WN5............31 G4
Vicarage Rd West *HOR/BR* BL6 ...7 G1
Vicarage Sq *LEIGH* WN7............65 E1
Vicars Hall Gdns *WALK* M28 ...55 E5
Vicars Hall La *WALK* M28............67 H5
Victor St *WCNW/BIL/OR* WN5...21 E5
Victoria Av *WGNE/HIN* WN2 ...50 B2
 WGNNW/ST WN6............9 E5
Victoria Cl *WALK* M28 *............55 F5
Victoria Crs *WGNNW/ST* WN6...10 B2
Victoria Pk *SKEL* WN8............16 B4
Victoria Rd *AIMK* WN4............60 D3
 GOL/RIS/CUL WA3............69 F5
 WGNE/HIN WN2............49 F2
Victoria St *LEIGH* WN7............51 H5
 RNFD/HAY WA11............43 E4
 SKEL WN8............16 B5
 WGNE/HIN WN2............35 G1
 WGNS/IIMK WN3............33 F2
 WHTN BL5............26 A5
Victoria Ter *WGNE/HIN* WN2 ...50 C3
Victoria Vw *LEIGH* WN7............51 H4
Vigo St *WGNE/HIN* WN2............23 E3
Villa Av *WGNE/HIN* WN2............21 H1
Village Cl *SKEL* WN8............16 C5
Village Vw *WCNW/BIL/OR* WN5...58 D1
Village Wy *SKEL* WN8............16 C5
Vincent Wy
 WCNW/BIL/OR WN5............21 E5
Vine Gv *WGNS/IIMK* WN3............2 C6
Vine St *WGN* WN1............3 F2
 WGNE/HIN WN2............36 A2
Viola Cl *WCNW/BIL/OR* WN5...21 E5
Violet St *AIMK* WN4............61 E4
 WGNS/IIMK WN3............34 D2
Virginia Wy
 WCNW/BIL/OR WN5............20 D5
Viscount Rd
 WCNW/BIL/OR WN5............21 E5
Vista Av *NEWLW* WA12............68 D5
Vista Rd *NEWLW* WA12............68 D5
Vista Wy *NEWLW* WA12............68 D5
Vulcan Dr *WGN* WN1............3 F6
Vulcan Rd *WCNW/BIL/OR* WN5...21 E5

W

Waddington Cl
 GOL/RIS/CUL WA3 *............71 G1
Wade Bank *WHTN* BL5............26 A5
Wadsworth Dr
 WGNNW/ST WN6............21 G3
Wainfleet Cl *WGNS/IIMK* WN3...33 F5
Wainscot Cl *TYLD* M29............54 A4
Wakefield Crs
 WGNNW/ST WN6............10 D5
Wakefield St *GOL/RIS/CUL* WA3...70 B2
Walcot Pl *WGNS/IIMK* WN3 ...47 H1
Waldon Cl *WGNE/HIN* WN2............36 C4
Waldorf St *WGNS/IIMK* WN3...47 E1

Walford Rd *AIMK* WN4............61 F3
Walkden Av *WGN* WN1............22 A3
Walkden Av East *WGN* WN1 ...2 C1
Walkdene Dr *WALK* M28............41 F5
Walkdens Av *ATH* M46............52 B1
Walker La *LEIGH* WN7............65 G4
Walkers Dr *AIMK* WN4............60 C3
Walkers St *WHTN* BL5............25 H5
The Walk *ATH* M46............39 E5
Wallace La *WGN* WN1............2 A1
Wallbrook Av
 WCNW/BIL/OR WN5............45 G2
Wallbrook Crs *LHULT* M38............41 G3
Wallcroft St *SKEL* WN8............16 D5
Wallgarth Cl *WGNS/IIMK* WN3...47 E1
Wallgate *WGNS/IIMK* WN3............2 B6
Walls St *WGNNW/ST* WN6............51 F1
Wall St *WGNNW/ST* WN6............21 C4
Wallwork Rd *TYLD* M29............54 C5
Walmer Rd *WGNE/HIN* WN2 ...36 D3
Walmesley Dr *RNFD/HAY* WA11...56 B1
Walmesley Rd *LEIGH* WN7............64 D1
Walmesley St *WGN* WN1............2 E6
Walmsley St *WGNE/HIN* WN2 ...36 A4
Walney Rd *WGNS/IIMK* WN3 ...47 E1
Walnut Av *WGN* WN1............22 B3
Walnut Gv *LEIGH* WN7............52 A3
Walpole Av *WGNS/IIMK* WN3...33 G5
Walsh Cl *NEWLW* WA12............68 D5
Walter Scott Av *WGN* WN1 ...11 E5
Walters Green Crs
 GOL/RIS/CUL WA3............62 A5
Walter St *AIMK* WN4 *............61 G2
 LEIGH WN7............65 E1
 WCNW/BIL/OR WN5............33 E2
Waltham Av *GOL/RIS/CUL* WA3...73 H2
 WGNS/IIMK WN3............71 E1
Waltham Gdns *LEIGH* WN7............21 G2
Walthew House La
 WCNW/BIL/OR WN5............20 C4
Walthew La *WGNE/HIN* WN2 ...49 F1
Walton St *ATH* M46............39 F4
 CHLY/EC PR7............7 F1
Wanborough Cl *LEIGH* WN7 ...52 A4
Warbeck Cl *LEIGH* WN7............36 B5
Warburton Pl *ATH* M46............39 G5
Wardend Cl *LHULT* M38............41 F2
Wardens Bank *WHTN* BL5............37 H3
Wardley Av *WALK* M28............55 G1
Wardley Rd *TYLD* M29............54 C5
Wardley Sq *TYLD* M29............54 C5
Wardley St
 WCNW/BIL/OR WN5............32 C3
Wardlow Av
 WCNW/BIL/OR WN5............20 B5
Wardour St *ATH* M46............52 D1
Ward St *WGNE/HIN* WN2............36 A1
Ware Cl *AIMK* WN4............61 G3
Wareing St *TYLD* M29............53 G3
Warlow Dr *LEIGH* WN7............51 G5
Warminster Gv
 WGNS/IIMK WN3............47 E1
Warncliffe St
 WCNW/BIL/OR WN5............33 E3
Warnford St *WGN* WN1............22 B3
Warren Cl *ATH* M46............52 A1
Warren Dr *NEWLW* WA12............70 A5
 WGNE/HIN WN2............2 E5
Warrington Rd *AIMK* WN4............61 E4
 GOL/RIS/CUL WA3............73 H4
 LEIGH WN7............70 B3
 NEWLW WA12............70 B5
 WGNE/HIN WN2............49 F1
 WGNS/IIMK WN3............47 C1
Warwick Av *AIMK* WN4............61 G4
Warwick Dr *WGNE/HIN* WN2 ...36 D3
Warwick Rd *ATH* M46............38 D5
 TYLD M29............55 H2
 WGNE/HIN WN2 *............12 D5
Warwick St *CHLY/EC* PR7............7 E1
 LEIGH WN7............66 A3
Wasdale Rd *AIMK* WN4............35 H4
Washacre *WHTN* BL5............38 A1
Washacre Cl *WHTN* BL5............38 A1
Washbrook Av *WALK* M28............55 G3
Washburn Cl *WHTN* BL5............25 G3
Wash La *LEIGH* WN7............65 G1
Washwood Cl *LHULT* M38 *............41 G2
Waterbeck Cl *WGN* WN1............3 J3
Water Dr *WGNNW/ST* WN6............11 E3
Wateredge Cl *LEIGH* WN7............64 D1
Watergate Dr *WHTN* BL5............38 B1
Watergate La *WHTN* BL5............40 B1
Waterhouse Knock
 HOR/BR BL6............7 F2
Waterloo St *WGNNW/ST* WN6...21 H4
Watermede
 WCNW/BIL/OR WN5............31 H5
Waters Av *WGNS/IIMK* WN3 ...34 D4
Water's Nook Rd *WHTN* BL5 ...26 D5
Waters Reach *WGN* WN1............3 J5
Water St *ATH* M46............39 E5
 CHLY/EC PR7............7 G2
 RNFD/HAY WA11............69 F5
 WGN WN1............2 D4
Waterview Pk *LEIGH* WN7............64 D2
Waterworks Dr *NEWLW* WA12...70 A5
Watson Av *AIMK* WN4............61 F3
Waverley Cl *WGN* WN3............62 A5
Waverley *SKEL* WN8............16 C4
Waverley St *WGNS/IIMK* WN3...33 E5
Waverley Cv *WGNS/IIMK* WN3...33 E5
Waverley Rd *GOL/RIS/CUL* WA3...63 G5
 WGNE/HIN WN2............35 H3
 WGNW WN1............33 E5
Wavertree Av *ATH* M46............38 C4
Wayfarer Dr *TYLD* M29............53 H3
Wayfaring *WHTN* BL5............26 A3
Wearhead Cl *WGNS/IIMK* WN3...70 B2
Wearish La *WHTN* BL5............25 F5
Weaste Av *LHULT* M38............41 G4
Weaver Av *WALK* M28............55 F1
Weaver Gv *LEIGH* WN7............65 H3
Webster's St *WGNE/HIN* WN2...36 A1
Wedgewood Dr
 WGNNW/ST WN6............21 E2
Weedon Av *NEWLW* WA12............69 E4
Welbeck Rd *AIMK* WN4............61 E3
 WGNS/IIMK WN3............33 G5

Welbourne *SKEL* WN8
Welch Hill St *LEIGH* WN7
Weldon Av *BOLS/LL* BL3
Weldon Gv *WGN* WN1
Welford Gv *GOL/RIS/CUL* WA3
Welland Rd *AIMK* WN4
Wellbrooke Cl *AIMK* WN4
Wellcross Rd *SKEL* WN8
Wellesley Cl *NEWLW* WA12
Wellfield Rd *RNFD/HAY* WA11
Wellfield Rd *GOL/RIS/CUL* WA3
 WGNE/HIN WN2
 WGNNW/ST WN6
Wellington Rd *ATH* M46
Wellington Cl *SKEL* WN8
Wellington Dr *TYLD* M29
Wellington Gv
 WGNE/HIN WN2
Wellington Rd *ATH* M46
Wellington St *GOL/RIS/CUL* WA3
 WHTN BL5
Well Rd *LEIGH* WN7
Wells Av *GOL/RIS/CUL* WA3
Wells Dr *WGNE/HIN* WN2
Wells Pl *WGN* WN1
Wellstock La *LHULT* M38
Well St *TYLD* M29
Welton Cl *LEIGH* WN7
Wendlebury Cl *WGNE/HIN* WN2
Wenlock Gv *WGNE/HIN* WN2
Wenlock Rd *LEIGH* WN7
 WGNE/HIN WN2
Wenlock St *WGNE/HIN* WN2 *
Wensleydale Rd *GOL/RIS/CUL* WA3
Wentworth Av *FWTH* BL4
Wentworth Rd *AIMK* WN4
Wescoe Cl *WCNW/BIL/OR* WN5
Wesley Av *RNFD/HAY* WA11
Wesley Cl *WHTN* BL5
Wesley St *ATH* M46 *
 WGNW/BIL/OR WN5
 WHTN BL5
Wessex Ct *WGN* WN1
Wessex Rd
West Av *GOL/RIS/CUL* WA3
 LEIGH WN7
 WALK M28
West Bank St *ATH* M46
Westbourne Av *LEIGH* WN7
Westbridge Ms *WGN* WN1
West Bridgewater St
 LEIGH WN7
Westbury Av *WGNS/IIMK* WN3
Westbury Ct *WHTN* BL5
West Cl *ATH* M46
Westcott Dr *WGNS/IIMK* WN3
Westcroft *WGNE/HIN* WN2
Westerdale Cl *TYLD* M29
Westfield Av *AIMK* WN4
Westfield Gv *WGNE/HIN* WN2
Westgate Dr *TYLD* M29
Westhead Av
 GOL/RIS/CUL WA3
Westinghouse Cl
Westlake Gv *WGNE/HIN* WN2
Westland Av *FWTH* BL4
Westleigh La *LEIGH* WN7
Westmead *WGNS/IIMK* WN3
Westmeade Rd *WALK* M28
Westminster Dr *LEIGH* WN7
 RNFD/HAY WA11
Westminster St
 WGNW/BIL/OR WN5 *
Westmoorland St *LEIGH* WN7
Westmorland Rd *TYLD* M29
West Mt *WGN* WN1
Weston Av *AIMK* WN4
Weston Pk *WGNNW/ST* WN6
Weston St *ATH* M46
West Park Cl *SKEL* WN8
Westrees *LEIGH* WN7
West St *WGNE/HIN* WN2
 WGNNW/ST WN6
West Wy *LHULT* M38
Westwell Gv *LEIGH* WN7
Westwell St *LEIGH* WN7
Westwood Av *WALK* M28
Westwood La
 WGNS/IIMK WN3
Westwood Pk
Westwood Ter
 WGNNW/ST WN6
Wetheral Cl *WGNE/HIN* WN2
Wetherby St *NEWLW* WA12
Wexham Gdns *WGNE/HIN* WN2
Weybourne Dr
 WGNNW/ST WN6
Weymouth Dr *WGNE/HIN* WN2
Whalley Av *GOL/RIS/CUL* WA3
 RNFD/HAY WA11
Whalley Cl *WGNS/IIMK* WN3
Whalley Gv *LEIGH* WN7
Whalleys Rd *SKEL* WN8
Wharfedale *WHTN* BL5
Wharmby Rd *RNFD/HAY* WA11
Wharncliffe St
Wharton Hall Cl *TYLD* M29
Wharton La *LHULT* M38
Wheatacre *SKEL* WN8
Wheatlea Rd *WGNS/IIMK* WN3
Wheatley Av *NEWLW* WA12
Wheatsheaf Wk
 WGNNW/ST WN6

Corpus Christi Catholic
Primary School
RNFD/HAY WA11 .... 43 E4
Crawford Village
Primary School
SKEL WN8 .... 30 B5
The Cricketer Sports Club
WGNS/IIMK WN3 .... 34 A3
Cricket Street
Business Centre
WGNNW/ST WN6 .... 21 H5
Crow Orchard
Primary School
SKEL WN8 .... 17 E3
Deane Leisure Centre
BOLS/LL BL3 .... 27 G1
Deanery CE High School
WGN WN1 .... 2 B4
Dean Wood Golf Club
SKEL WN8 .... 19 F5
Delph Side Primary School
SKEL WN8 .... 17 G5
De Vere Whites Hotel
HOR/BR BL6 .... 14 C3
Diamond Business Park
RNFD/HAY WA11 .... 56 C2
Dobson Park
Industrial Estate
WGNE/HIN WN2 .... 35 F2
Dodd Lane
Industrial Estate
WHTN BL5 .... 25 E1
Douglas Valley
Business Park
WGN WN1 .... 11 F5
Dukesgate Primary School
LHULT M38 .... 41 F3
East Gillbrands
Industrial Estate
SKEL WN8 .... 29 F1
Ellenbrook Primary School
WALK M28 .... 55 G4
Ellesmere Retail Park
WALK M28 .... 41 H5
Ellesmere Shopping Centre
LHULT M38 .... 41 H5
Empress Industrial Estate
WGNE/HIN WN2 .... 3 J6
Fairfield Hospital
RNFD/HAY WA11 .... 57 F4
Fairlie CP School
SKEL WN8 .... 17 G2
Fall Birch Hospital Lodge
HOR/BR BL6 .... 15 F1
Farnworth Social Circle CC
FWTH BL4 .... 41 H1
Firsdale Industrial Estate
LEIGH WN7 .... 51 F5
Fishwicks Industrial Estate
RNFD/HAY WA11 .... 68 C1
Foyer & Coops
Business Centre
WGN WN1 .... 2 B5
Fred Longworth High School
TYLD M29 .... 53 F2
The Galleries Shopping
Centre
WGN WN1 .... 2 C4
Garrett Hall Primary School
TYLD M29 .... 54 C4
Garswood Primary School
AIMK WN4 .... 59 H2
Garswood United FC
AIMK WN4 .... 59 G1
The Gates Primary School
WHTN BL5 .... 26 A3
Gathurst Golf Club
WGNNW/ST WN6 .... 9 E5
Gidlow Cemetery
WGNNW/ST WN6 .... 10 D5
Gilded Hollins
Primary School
LEIGH WN7 .... 64 B5
Glazebury CE Primary School
GOL/RIS/CUL WA3 .... 73 H2
Glenburn Sports College
SKEL WN8 .... 17 F5
Golborne Clinic
GOL/RIS/CUL WA3 .... 62 C5
Golborne CP School
GOL/RIS/CUL WA3 .... 70 B1
Golborne High School
GOL/RIS/CUL WA3 .... 62 D5
Grand Arcade Shopping
Centre
WGN WN1 .... 2 D4
Grange Valley
Primary School
RNFD/HAY WA11 .... 68 A4
Grasmere Street
Health Centre
LEIGH WN7 .... 51 H5
Greenbank Industrial Estate
WGNE/HIN WN2 .... 36 C5
Green Hall Primary School
ATH M46 .... 39 G4
Haigh Hall Country Park
WGNE/HIN WN2 .... 12 A4
Haigh Hall Golf Complex
WGNE/HIN WN2 .... 12 A4
Haligate Bus Station
WGN WN1 .... 2 C4
Hall Green Clinic
SKEL WN8 .... 31 E1
Harrop Fold School
WALK M28 .... 41 G5
Hart Common Golf Club
WHTN BL5 .... 37 E1
Haslemere Industrial Estate
AIMK WN4 .... 47 H3
Hawkley Brook
Trading Estate
WGNS/IIMK WN3 .... 47 F1
Hawkley Hall High School
WGNS/IIMK WN3 .... 34 A5
Haydock CC
RNFD/HAY WA11 .... 68 A2
Haydock English Martyrs
Catholic Primary School
RNFD/HAY WA11 .... 68 A2

Haydock Lane
Industrial Estate
RNFD/HAY WA11 .... 68 B1
Haydock Medical Centre
RNFD/HAY WA11 .... 68 A3
Haydock Park Golf Club
NEWLW WA12 .... 70 A4
Haydock Park Racecourse
AIMK WN4 .... 61 F5
Hazel Business Park
RNFD/HAY WA11 .... 56 D2
Heathfield Primary School
BOLS/LL BL3 .... 27 H3
Hesketh Fletcher CE
High School
ATH M46 .... 52 D1
Hewitt Business Park
WGNW/BIL/OR WN5 .... 31 H4
Higher Folds Primary School
LEIGH WN7 .... 53 E4
Highfield CC
WGNS/IIMK WN3 .... 32 D4
Highfield St Matthews CE
Primary School
WGNS/IIMK WN3 .... 32 D4
Highlea Secondary School
WALK M28 .... 55 E4
Hillside Community
Primary School
SKEL WN8 .... 18 A5
Hillside Health Centre
SKEL WN8 .... 17 H4
Hindley All Saints CE
Primary School
WGNE/HIN WN2 .... 36 B3
Hindley Business Centre
WGNE/HIN WN2 .... 36 A3
Hindley Green
Primary School
WGNE/HIN WN2 .... 51 E1
Hindley Hall Golf Club
WGNE/HIN WN2 .... 24 A5
Hindley High School
Arts College
WGNE/HIN WN2 .... 36 C3
Hindley Leisure Centre
WGNE/HIN WN2 .... 36 C5
Hindley Primary School
WGNE/HIN WN2 .... 36 A3
Hindsford CE Primary School
ATH M46 .... 53 F2
HM Prison
WGNE/HIN WN2 .... 50 A1
Holden Road Trading Estate
LEIGH WN7 .... 65 F1
Holland Business Park
BRSC L40 .... 16 B1
Holland Moor
Primary School
SKEL WN8 .... 30 B1
Hollywood Bowl
HOR/BR BL6 .... 14 C2
Holy Family RC
Primary School
WGNE/HIN WN2 .... 49 F2
Holy Family RC School
WALK M28 .... 54 D4
Hope Special School
WGNS/IIMK WN3 .... 47 G1
Houghwood Golf Club
RNFD/HAY WA11 .... 45 E4
Howe Bridge Crematorium
ATH M46 .... 52 A2
Howe Bridge Sports Centre
ATH M46 .... 52 C2
Hulton Hospital
BOLS/LL BL3 .... 27 H2
Ince CE Primary School
WGNE/HIN WN2 .... 35 F1
Ince Clinic & Community
Centre
WGNE/HIN WN2 .... 35 F1
Innkeeper's Lodge
GOL/RIS/CUL WA3 .... 71 F3
International Swimming Pool
WGN WN1 .... 2 D6
James Brindley
Primary School
WALK M28 .... 55 H2
John Street Medical Centre
GOL/RIS/CUL WA3 .... 70 B1
Kilhey Court Hotel
WGN WN1 .... 6 B5
Kingsdown High School
WGNW/BIL/OR WN5 .... 32 D1
Kingshill School
TYLD M29 .... 53 G3
Kirkfield Hotel
NEWLW WA12 .... 69 H5
Kirklees Industrial Estate
WGNE/HIN WN2 .... 23 F3
Ladybridge High School
BOLS/LL BL3 .... 27 G1
Lamberhead Green
Community Primary School
WGNW/BIL/OR WN5 .... 32 B1
Lamberhead Industrial Estate
WGNW/BIL/OR WN5 .... 32 C3
Landgate Industrial Estate
AIMK WN4 .... 47 H3
The Landgate School
AIMK WN4 .... 47 H4
Lathom High School
SKEL WN8 .... 17 E2
Leigh Business Park
LEIGH WN7 .... 65 G3
Leigh CC
LEIGH WN7 .... 64 D4
Leigh CE Infant School
LEIGH WN7 .... 65 E1
Leigh CE Junior School
LEIGH WN7 .... 65 E1
Leigh Central Primary School
LEIGH WN7 .... 65 E1
Leigh Centurions RLFC
LEIGH WN7 .... 51 H5
Leigh FC
LEIGH WN7 .... 51 H5

Leigh Golf Club
GOL/RIS/CUL WA3 .... 72 C5
Leigh Infirmary
LEIGH WN7 .... 52 B4
Leigh Rangers ARLFC
LEIGH WN7 .... 66 A2
Leigh RUFC
LEIGH WN7 .... 64 D5
Little Digmoor
Primary School
SKEL WN8 .... 29 G2
Little Hulton Skills Centre
WALK M28 .... 41 F4
Little Theatre
TYLD M29 .... 53 G3
Lockett Business Park
AIMK WN4 .... 61 F1
Longshoot Health Centre
WGN WN1 .... 3 F3
Lostock Industrial Estate
HOR/BR BL6 .... 14 D3
Lostock Primary School
HOR/BR BL6 .... 15 H4
Low Hall Community
Primary School
WGNE/HIN WN2 .... 35 F5
Lowton Business Park
GOL/RIS/CUL WA3 .... 71 H1
Lowton Community
Sports College
GOL/RIS/CUL WA3 .... 72 A1
Lowton J & I School
GOL/RIS/CUL WA3 .... 71 H2
Lowton St Marys CE
Primary School
GOL/RIS/CUL WA3 .... 72 A1
Lowton West Primary School
GOL/RIS/CUL WA3 .... 70 D1
Lyme Community
Primary School
NEWLW WA12 .... 68 C5
Mabs Cross Primary School
WGN WN1 .... 2 E2
Marketgate Shopping Centre
WGN WN1 .... 2 C4
Market Street Medical Centre
WGNE/HIN WN2 .... 36 A2
Marsh Green CP School
WGNW/BIL/OR WN5 .... 21 E5
Marsh Green Health Centre
WGNW/BIL/OR WN5 .... 21 E4
Marston Bentley
Industrial Estate
WGNW/BIL/OR WN5 .... 23 G3
Martland Mill Business Park
WGNW/BIL/OR WN5 .... 21 E3
Martland Mill
Industrial Estate
WGNW/BIL/OR WN5 .... 20 D5
Marus Bridge Health Centre
WGNS/IIMK WN3 .... 47 G1
Marus Bridge Primary School
WGNS/IIMK WN3 .... 47 F1
Mason Street
Industrial Estate
WGNS/IIMK WN3 .... 2 A6
Maternity & Child
Welfare Clinic
WGNE/HIN WN2 .... 35 H3
Mayflower Brewery
WGN WN1 .... 2 D3
Maypole Industrial Estate
WGNE/HIN WN2 .... 49 H4
Meadowbank
Primary School
ATH M46 .... 38 D4
Mere Oaks School
WGN WN1 .... 11 E5
Middlebrook Retail &
Leisure Park
HOR/BR BL6 .... 14 C2
Millbrook Business Centre
RNFD/HAY WA11 .... 56 D3
Millbrook Primary School
WGNW/BIL/OR WN5 .... 9 G4
Millingford Industrial Estate
GOL/RIS/CUL WA3 .... 70 C1
Montrose School
WGNW/BIL/OR WN5 .... 33 E1
Moorside Primary School
SKEL WN8 .... 30 B1
Mornington High School
WGNE/HIN WN2 .... 36 C3
Moss Industrial Estate
AIMK WN4 .... 64 A5
New Springs Holy Family RC
Primary School
WGN WN1 .... 23 F3
Newton Bank
Preparatory School
NEWLW WA12 .... 69 H5
Newton Health Clinic
NEWLW WA12 .... 69 G5
Newton-le-Willows
Community High School
NEWLW WA12 .... 69 G4
Newton-le-Willows
High School
NEWLW WA12 .... 69 G4
Newton-le-Willows
Sports Club
NEWLW WA12 .... 69 F5
Newton Westpark
Primary School
LEIGH WN7 .... 51 F3
Nicol Mere School
AIMK WN4 .... 60 D1
Norley Hall CC
WGNW/BIL/OR WN5 .... 32 C3
North Quarry Business Park
WGNNW/ST WN6 .... 8 C1
North Walkden
Primary School
WALK M28 .... 41 H3
Nugent House School
WGNW/BIL/OR WN5 .... 58 C2
Nye Bevan Swimming Pool
SKEL WN8 .... 17 G4
Oakhill Trading Estate
WALK M28 .... 41 G3

Old Boston Trading Estate
RNFD/HAY WA11 .... 68 D1
Orrell Clinic
WGNW/BIL/OR WN5 .... 31 H1
Orrell Holgate
Primary School
WGNW/BIL/OR WN5 .... 31 H3
Orrell Newfold Community
Primary School
WGNW/BIL/OR WN5 .... 31 G4
Orrell RUFC
WGNW/BIL/OR WN5 .... 31 H3
Orrell Water Park
WGNW/BIL/OR WN5 .... 31 H4
Our Lady Immaculate
Catholic Primary School
AIMK WN4 .... 47 E5
Our Lady of the Rosary RC
Primary School
LEIGH WN7 .... 64 A1
Our Lady Queen of Peace
Catholic High School
BRSC L40 .... 17 E1
Our Lady RC Primary School
WGNE/HIN WN2 .... 12 D5
Our Lady & the Lancashire
Martyrs RC Primary School
WGNW/BIL/OR WN5 .... 41 F5
PageField Industrial Estate
WGNW/BIL/OR WN5 .... 21 G4
Paragon Business Park
HOR/BR BL6 .... 14 D2
Park Business Centre
AIMK WN4 .... 36 A4
Park Industrial Estate
AIMK WN4 .... 60 B3
Parklee Primary School
ATH M46 .... 52 D1
Parochial CE Primary School
WHTN BL5 .... 25 H5
Parsonage Retail Park
LEIGH WN7 .... 51 H5
Peel Hall CP School
LHULT M38 .... 41 E5
Pemberton Business Centre
WGNW/BIL/OR WN5 .... 32 D2
Pemberton Clinic
WGNW/BIL/OR WN5 .... 33 E2
Pennington Flash
Country Park
LEIGH WN7 .... 64 B4
Pennington Golf Club
LEIGH WN7 .... 64 B3
Pepper Mill Business Park
WGN WN1 .... 2 E6
Pioneer Industrial Estate
WGNW/BIL/OR WN5 .... 33 F2
Platt Bridge Clinic
WGNE/HIN WN2 .... 49 F1
Premier Inn
AIMK WN4 .... 61 E4
GOL/RIS/CUL WA3 .... 70 C2
HOR/BR BL6 .... 15 E2
WGNNW/ST WN6 .... 9 C1
WGNS/IIMK WN3 .... 47 C2
WGNW/BIL/OR WN5 .... 32 A1
Prestwich Industrial Estate
ATH M46 .... 38 C4
Prospect House
Medical Centre
WGNW/BIL/OR WN5 .... 32 B2
Prospect Industrial Estate
WGNE/HIN WN2 .... 36 A3
The Quadrangle
Business Centre
WGNE/HIN WN2 .... 37 E4
Quality Hotel
SKEL WN8 .... 30 C3
WGN WN1 .... 2 E4
Rainford CE Primary School
RNFD/HAY WA11 .... 43 E5
Rainford Health Centre
RNFD/HAY WA11 .... 43 F5
Rainford High
Technology College
RNFD/HAY WA11 .... 43 F3
Rainford Industrial Estate
RNFD/HAY WA11 .... 56 C2
Ramada Hotel
HOR/BR BL6 .... 13 H3
Rectory CE Primary School
AIMK WN4 .... 60 A1
Reebok Museum
HOR/BR BL6 .... 14 C2
Regent Park Golf Course
HOR/BR BL6 .... 15 G3
R L Hughes Primary School
AIMK WN4 .... 60 D3
Robin Park Arena
WGNW/BIL/OR WN5 .... 21 G5
Robin Park Sports Centre
WGNW/BIL/OR WN5 .... 21 G5
Roby Mill CE Primary School
SKEL WN8 .... 19 E2
Rose Bridge High School
WGN WN1 .... 3 J4
Ross Business Centre
WGNW/BIL/OR WN5 .... 33 E3
Royal Albert Edward
Infirmary
WGN WN1 .... 22 B3
Sacred Heart Catholic
Primary School
WGNE/HIN WN2 .... 37 G5
Sacred Heart RC
Primary School
ATH M46 .... 53 F2
LEIGH WN7 .... 64 D1
WGNNW/ST WN6 .... 21 G3
WGN WN1 .... 26 A4
St Aelreds RC
Technology College
NEWLW WA12 .... 69 G5
St Aidans CE Primary School
WGNW/BIL/OR WN5 .... 58 D1
St Aidans RC Primary School
WGNE/HIN WN2 .... 47 E1
St Ambrose Barlow RC
Primary School
TYLD M29 .... 66 D1

St Andrews CE
Primary School
WGNNW/ST WN6 ....
WHTN BL5 ....
St Andrews Methodist
WALK M28 ....
St Annes CE Primary School
WGNNW/ST WN6 ....
St Benedicts Catholic
Primary School
WGNE/HIN WN2 ....
St Bernadettes Catholic
Primary School
WGNNW/ST WN6 ....
St Catharines CE
Primary School
WGN WN1 ....
St Catherines RC
Primary School
GOL/RIS/CUL WA3 ....
St Cuthberts RC
Primary School
WGNW/BIL/OR WN5 ....
St Davids CE Primary School
WGNE/HIN WN2 ....
St Edmund Arrowsmith
Catholic High School
AIMK WN4 ....
St Edmunds Catholic
Primary School
SKEL WN8 ....
St Edmunds RC
Primary School
LHULT M38 ....
St Francis of Assisi Catholic
Primary School
SKEL WN8 ....
St Gabriels RC Primary School
LEIGH WN7 ....
St Georges Central CE
Primary School
TYLD M29 ....
St Georges CE
Primary School
ATH M46 ....
WHTN BL5 ....
St Georges RC High School
WALK M28 ....
St Helens Community College
NEWLW WA12 ....
St James Catholic
Primary School
WGNW/BIL/OR WN5 ....
St James CE Primary School
FWTH BL4 ....
WGNS/IIMK WN3 ....
St James (Daisy Hill) CE
Primary School
WHTN BL5 ....
St James Primary School
RNFD/HAY WA11 ....
St James RC Primary School
SKEL WN8 ....
St John Fisher Catholic
High School
WGNNW/ST WN6 ....
St John Rigby College
WGNNW/ST WN6 ....
St Johns CE Infant School
WGNE/HIN WN2 ....
St Johns CE Primary School
WGNE/HIN WN2 ....
WGNW/BIL/OR WN5 ....
St Johns Mosley Common CE
Primary School
WALK M28 ....
St Johns RC Primary School
SKEL WN8 ....
St Josephs Catholic
Primary School
WGNNW/ST WN6 ....
St Josephs RC
Primary School
LEIGH WN7 ....
LHULT M38 ....
St Josephs RC School
HOR/BR BL6 ....
St Judes Catholic
Primary School
WGNS/IIMK WN3 ....
St Lukes CE Primary School
GOL/RIS/CUL WA3 ....
St Maries RC Primary School
WGNNW/ST WN6 ....
St Marks CE Primary School
WGNW/BIL/OR WN5 ....
St Mary CE Primary School
BOLS/LL BL3 ....
St Marys Catholic
Junior School
NEWLW WA12 ....
St Marys Catholic
Primary School
NEWLW WA12 ....
St Marys CE J & I School
WGNS/IIMK WN3 ....
St Marys RC High School
TYLD M29 ....
St Marys RC
Primary School
WGN WN1 ....
St Michaels CE Primary
Howe Bridge School
ATH M46 ....
St Nathaniels CE
Primary School
WGNE/HIN WN2 ....
St Oswalds RC J & I School
AIMK WN4 ....
St Patricks RC Primary School
WGN WN1 ....
St Pauls CE Primary School
WGNS/IIMK WN3 ....
St Pauls Peel CE
Primary School
LHULT M38 ....
St Peters Catholic
High School
WGNW/BIL/OR WN5 ....
St Peters CE Infant School
LEIGH WN7 ....

's CE Junior School
 N WN7 .... 64 B1
's CE Primary School
 WN4 .... 47 G5
's CE Primary School
 LW WA12 .... 69 G5
's CE Primary School
 E/HIN WN2 .... 35 H3
's CE Primary School
 M46 .... 39 F5
ards Catholic
 ary School
 WN8 .... 16 B4
ens CE
 ary School
 M29 .... 54 A5
as Catholic
 ary School
 WN8 .... 19 E4
as CE Primary School
 WN4 .... 61 F3
 RIS/CUL WA3 .... 62 C5
 / WN7 .... 65 G2
 BL5 .... 26 C4
as More Catholic
 School
 W/BIL/OR WN5 .... 33 G1
as the Martyr CE
 ary School
 WN8 .... 31 E1
ds Catholic
 ary School
 WN4 .... 61 G2
ds CE Primary School
 VW/ST WN6 .... 10 C1
ms RC
 ary School
 E/HIN WN2 .... 3 K7
ane Health Centre
 WN8 .... 16 C4
 Shopping Precinct
 WN1 .... 3 F4
he End CE
 ary School
 BR BL6 .... 13 F2
e Industrial Estate
 BR BL6 .... 13 F4
rooks
cal Centre
 M46 .... 39 E5
ey CE Primary School
 M29 .... 53 H1

Shevington Community
 Primary School
 WCGNW/ST WN6 .... 9 E4
Shevington High School
 WCGNW/ST WN6 .... 9 G3
Shevington Vale
 Primary School
 WCGNW/ST WN6 .... 8 D2
Skelmersdale & Ormskirk
 College (Northway Centre)
 SKEL WN8 .... 17 F4
Skelmersdale & Ormskirk
 Colleges (Westbank Centre)
 SKEL WN8 .... 17 F5
Skelmersdale Sports Centre
 SKEL WN8 .... 29 H1
Skelmersdale United FC
 SKEL WN8 .... 16 B5
South Lancashire
 Industrial Estate
 AIMK M46 .... 48 A5
Southside Industrial Park
 ATH M46 .... 38 C4
Sovereign Business Park
 WGN WN1 .... 3 F7
Spinning Gate
 Shopping Centre
 LEIGH WN7 .... 65 E1
Springbank
 Industrial Estate
 WGNE/HIN WN2 .... 35 G5
Spring View CC
 WGNE/HIN WN2 .... 35 F5
Standish Clinic
 WGNNW/ST WN6 .... 10 B2
Standish Community
 High School
 WGNNW/ST WN6 .... 4 D5
Standish Court Golf Club
 WGNNW/ST WN6 .... 10 C1
Standish CC
 WGNNW/ST WN6 .... 10 B2
Stone Cross Business Park
 GOL/RIS/CUL WA3 .... 70 C2
Stone Hill Industrial Estate
 FWTH BL4 .... 41 H1
Summersales
 Industrial Estate
 WGNS/IIMK WN3 .... 32 C4
Swan Meadow
 Industrial Estate
 WGNS/IIMK WN3 .... 2 A7

Tanfield Special School
 WGNE/HIN WN2 .... 36 C3
Thistle Hotel
 RNFD/HAY WA11 .... 69 E1
Three Sisters Racing Circuit
 AIMK WN4 .... 48 B4
Towngate
 Business Centre
 LHULT M38 .... 40 D3
Travelodge
 RNFD/HAY WA11 .... 68 B2
Trinity Primary School
 SKEL WN8 .... 16 D4
Tweed Street
 Industrial Estate
 LEIGH WN7 .... 65 G2
Twelve Apostles RC
 Primary School
 LEIGH WN7 .... 51 G3
Twiss Green Primary School
 GOL/RIS/CUL WA3 .... 72 D5
Two Porches School
 ATH M46 .... 39 E5
Two Porches Special School
 ATH M46 .... 38 D4
Tyldesley Cemetery
 TYLD M29 .... 54 C3
Tyldesley Primary School
 TYLD M29 .... 54 A4
Tyldesley Swimming Pool
 ATH M46 .... 53 F2
Up Holland High School
 WGNW/BIL/OR WN5 .... 31 F4
Victoria Industrial Estate
 LEIGH WN7 .... 51 H5
Victoria Trading Estate
 WGNS/IIMK WN3 .... 2 A6
Vue Cinema
 HOR/BR BL6 .... 14 C2
Warrington Road
 Industrial Estate
 WGNS/IIMK WN3 .... 33 F3
Washacre Primary School
 WHTN BL5 .... 38 A1
Waterside Trading Estate
 LEIGH WN7 .... 65 G2
Westfield
 Community School
 WGNW/BIL/OR WN5 .... 32 D2
West Gillbrands
 Industrial Estate
 SKEL WN8 .... 28 D1

Westhoughton CC
 WHTN BL5 .... 25 H5
Westhoughton Clinic
 WHTN BL5 .... 25 H5
Westhoughton Golf Club
 WHTN BL5 .... 25 G4
Westhoughton High School
 & Specialist Technology
 College
 WHTN BL5 .... 26 A4
Westhoughton
 Industrial Estate
 WHTN BL5 .... 25 H3
Westhoughton
 Primary School
 WHTN BL5 .... 26 A4
Westleigh CC
 LEIGH WN7 .... 64 C1
West Leigh House School
 LEIGH WN7 .... 64 B1
Westleigh Methodist
 Primary School
 LEIGH WN7 .... 51 G2
Westleigh St Pauls CE
 Primary School
 LEIGH WN7 .... 51 H3
Westwood Cemetery
 WGNS/IIMK WN3 .... 34 C3
Wharton Primary School
 LHULT M38 .... 40 D2
Wheatlea Industrial Estate
 WGNS/IIMK WN3 .... 47 G1
Whelley Hospital
 WGN WN1 .... 3 G1
Whiteledge Centre
 SKEL WN8 .... 17 G5
The Wiend Centre
 WGN WN1 .... 2 D5
Wigan Athletic FC &
 Wigan Warriors RLFC
 (The JJB Stadium)
 WGNW/BIL/OR WN5 .... 21 F5
Wigan Borough Cemetery
 WGNS/IIMK WN3 .... 34 C3
Wigan Crematorium
 WGNS/IIMK WN3 .... 34 C4
Wigan Golf Club
 WGN WN1 .... 6 C5
Wigan & Leigh College
 LEIGH WN7 .... 64 D1
 LEIGH WN7 .... 65 F3
 WGN WN1 .... 2 B1

Wigan & Leigh College &
 Community Sixth Form
 College
 LEIGH WN7 .... 64 D3
Wigan Little Theatre
 WGN WN1 .... 2 E4
Wigan Pier
 WGNS/IIMK WN3 .... 2 A7
Wigan RUFC
 WGN WN1 .... 11 G5
Willow Grove School
 AIMK WN4 .... 61 H1
Wingates Industrial Estate
 WHTN BL5 .... 25 G2
Winstanley College
 WGNW/BIL/OR WN5 .... 31 H5
Winstanley Medical Centre
 WGNS/IIMK WN3 .... 33 E5
Winstanley Primary School
 WGNS/IIMK WN3 .... 46 D1
Woodfield Primary School
 WGN WN1 .... 22 B1
Wood Fold Primary School
 WGNNW/ST WN6 .... 10 A2
Woodland Primary School
 SKEL WN8 .... 17 H3
Woodlands Hospital
 WALK M28 .... 41 E4
Woodlands Industrial Estate
 NEWLW WA12 .... 69 F3
Worsley Business Park
 TYLD M29 .... 55 E3
Worsley Mesnes
 Primary School
 WGNS/IIMK WN3 .... 33 H4
Worsley Road
 Industrial Estate
 FWTH BL4 .... 41 H2
Worsley Trading Estate
 LHULT M38 .... 40 D3
Worthington Lakes
 Business Park
 WGN WN1 .... 11 F2
Wrightington Hospital
 WGNNW/ST WN6 .... 8 D1
Wrightington Hotel &
 Country Club
 WGNNW/ST WN6 .... 4 A4
Yew Tree Trading Estate
 RNFD/HAY WA11 .... 68 A1

Acknowledgements

Schools address data provided by Education Direct

Petrol station information supplied by Johnsons

Garden centre information provided by:

Garden Centre Association Britains best garden centres

Wyevale Garden Centres

The statement on the front cover of this atlas is sourced, selected and quoted
from a reader comment and feedback form received in 2004

AA **Street by Street** QUESTIONNAIRE

Dear Atlas User
Your comments, opinions and recommendations are very important to us. So please help us to improve our street atlases by taking a few minutes to complete this simple questionnaire.

You do not need a stamp (unless posted outside the UK). If you do not want to remove this page from your street atlas, then photocopy it or write your answers on a plain sheet of paper.

Send to: Marketing Assistant, AA Publishing, 14th Floor Fanum House, Freepost SCE 4598, Basingstoke RG21 4GY

ABOUT THE ATLAS...

Please state which city / town / county you bought:

_____

Where did you buy the atlas? (City, Town, County)

_____

For what purpose? (please tick all applicable)

To use in your local area ☐   To use on business or at work ☐

Visiting a strange place ☐   In the car ☐   On foot ☐

Other (please state)

_____

Have you ever used any street atlases other than AA Street by Street?

Yes ☐   No ☐

If so, which ones?

_____

Is there any aspect of our street atlases that could be improved?
(Please continue on a separate sheet if necessary)

_____
_____
_____

ML201y

continued overleaf

Please list the features you found most useful:

_____

_____

Please list the features you found least useful:

_____

_____

_____

_____

LOCAL KNOWLEDGE...

Local knowledge is invaluable. Whilst every attempt has been made to make the information contained in this atlas as accurate as possible, should you notice any inaccuracies, please detail them below (if necessary, use a blank piece of paper) or e-mail us at _streetbystreet@theAA.com_

_____

_____

_____

ABOUT YOU...

Name (Mr/Mrs/Ms) _____

Address _____

                                         Postcode _____

Daytime tel no _____

E-mail address _____

Which age group are you in?

Under 25 ☐ **25-34** ☐ **35-44** ☐ **45-54** ☐ **55-64** ☐ **65+** ☐

Are you an AA member? YES ☐ **NO** ☐

Do you have Internet access? YES ☐ **NO** ☐

Thank you for taking the time to complete this questionnaire. Please send it to us as soon as possible, and remember, you do not need a stamp (unless posted outside the UK).

We may use information we hold about you to telephone or email you about other products and services offered by the AA, we do NOT disclose this information to third parties.

Please tick here if you do not wish to hear about products and services from the AA. ☐